"Gerard Mannion is to be congratulated for this splendid collection on the papacy of John Paul II. Well-focused and insightful essays help us to understand his thoughts on philosophy, the papacy, women, the church, religious life, morality, collegiality, interreligious dialogue, and liberation theology. With authors representing a wide variety of perspectives, Mannion avoids the predictable ideological battles over the legacy of Pope John Paul; rather he captures the depth and complexity of this extraordinary figure by the balance, intelligence, and comprehensiveness of the volume. A well-planned and beautifully executed project!"

D1562751

—James F. Keenan, SJ
Founders Professor in Theology
Boston College
Chestnut Hill, Massachusetts

"Scenes of the charismatic John Paul II kissing the tarmac, praying with global religious leaders, addressing throngs of adoring young people, and finally dying linger in the world's imagination. This book turns to another side of this outsized religious leader and examines his vision of the church and his theological positions. Each of these finely tuned essays show the greatness of this man by replacing the mythological account with the historical record. The straightforward, honest, expert, and yet accessible analyses situate John Paul II in his context and show both the triumphs and the ambiguities of his intellectual legacy. This masterful collection is absolutely basic reading for critically appreciating the papacy of John Paul II."

—Roger Haight, SJ
Union Theological Seminary
New York

"The length of John Paul II's tenure of the papacy, the complexity of his personality, and the ambivalence of his legacy make him not only a compelling subject of study, but also a challenging one. This book, however, succeeds admirably in depicting both the light and shadow of John Paul. The authors have crafted a text that is comprehensive in its themes, nuanced in its approach, and always accessible in its expression. The book will serve as a valuable guide for all those wishing to engage further with John Paul II."

—Richard Lennan
Professor of Systematic Theology
School of Theology and Ministry
Boston College

"Pope John Paul II was a towering figure in contemporary Catholicism. His was the second longest pontificate in the history of the church and it may prove to be one of the most influential. He wrote more encyclicals, canonized more saints, and visited more countries than any other pope in history. John Paul II's ambitious papacy left a mark on the church sure to endure for decades to come. It is precisely the breadth of his contributions that has made any comprehensive assessment of this pontificate so difficult. Yet Gerard Mannion and a team of internationally renowned scholars have responded admirably to the need for a clear-headed guide into the thought and enduring influence of John Paul II. They offer us a volume of superb essays that avoid the extremes of hagiography and angry polemic in favor of penetrating analysis. This volume has set a very high standard for any future studies of the first Slav pope in modern history."

—Richard R. Gaillardetz, PhD
Thomas and Margaret Murray
    and James J. Bacik Professor of Catholic Studies
University of Toledo

The Vision
of
John Paul II

Assessing His Thought
and Influence

Gerard Mannion, Editor

A Michael Glazier Book

LITURGICAL PRESS
Collegeville, Minnesota

www.litpress.org

A Michael Glazier Book published by Liturgical Press

Cover design by David Manahan, OSB. Cover photo © *L'Osservatore Romano*, dated 1979, Chicago.

Unless otherwise noted, excerpts from documents of the Second Vatican Council are from *Vatican Council II: The Basic Sixteen Documents*, by Austin Flannery, OP © 1996 (Costello Publishing Company, Inc.). Used with permission.

1   2   3   4   5   6   7   8   9

Library of Congress Cataloging-in-Publication Data

The vision of John Paul II : assessing his thought and influence / Gerard Mannion, editor.
    p. cm.
    "A Michael Glazier Book."
    Includes bibliographical references and index.
    ISBN 978-0-8146-5309-8 (pbk.)
    1. John Paul II, Pope, 1920–2005.   I. Mannion, Gerard, 1970–
BX1378.5.V573 2008
282.092—dc22   2008021822

For Philomena Cullen
Grá Mo Chroí Thú

Contents

Acknowledgments

First, my heartfelt and very deep gratitude to all the contributors for believing in the project and for devoting their time, expertise, energies, and insights toward making the final product what I hope will prove an informative and readable collection and a useful and enjoyable resource. A very big thank-you, indeed, to Hans Christoffersen, Susan Sink, Stephanie Lancour, Colleen Stiller, and all at Liturgical Press for their excitement and enthusiasm for the project and their advice and support along the way. Many thanks, also, to Kate Brett, who first encouraged me to pursue this idea, and my very deep gratitude to Peter Phan, who went out of his way to support and further encourage the pursuit of the project toward fruition. The very final stages of this book were completed in the wonderful city of Leuven in Belgium. Hence especial thanks are due in particular to Peter De Mey, the Centre for Ecumenical Research, and also to Lieven Boeve and the Research Group in Systematic Theology of the Katholieke Universiteit Leuven, my hosts here in Belgium. My deep gratitude also to the faculty of theology as a whole, with particular thanks to the dean, Mathijs Lamberigts, for graciousness in awarding me a senior fellowship of their prestigious faculty. Finally, much appreciation is due to all the staff of the Maurits Sabbe Library for their wonderful custodianship of a true treasure trove.

Gerard Mannion
Groot Begijnhof, Leuven
Feast of the Chair of St. Peter the Apostle

Abbreviations

of works frequently referenced

General

AAS   Acta Apostolica Sedis
CDF   Congregation for the Doctrine of the Faith
CELAM   Consejo Episcopal Latinoamericano
CU   Secretariat for Promoting Christian Unity
ITC   International Theological Commission

Karol Wojtyla

AP   *The Acting Person*
LR   *Love and Responsibility*
SR   *Sources of Renewal:*
         the Implementation of the Second Vatican Council

Pope John Paul II

Encyclicals

RH   *Redemptor Hominis* (1979)
DM   *Dives in Misericordia* (1980)
LE   *Laborem Exercens* (1981)
DeV   *Dominum et Vivificantem* (1986)
RMA   *Redemptoris Mater* (1987)
SRS   *Sollicitudo Rei Socialis* (1987)

RM	*Redemptoris Missio* (1990)
CA	*Centesimus Annus* (1991)
VS	*Veritatis Splendor* (1993)
EV	*Evangelium Vitae* (1995)
UUS	*Ut Unum Sint* (1995)
FR	*Fides et Ratio* (1998)
EdE	*Ecclesia de Eucharistia* (2003)

Other Teachings

AS	*Apostolos Suos* (1998)
CL	*Christifideles Laici* (1988)
CT	*Catechesi Tradendi* (1979)
EAf	*Ecclesia in Africa* (1995)
EAm	*Ecclesia in America* (1998)
EAs	*Ecclesia in Asia* (1999)
FC	*Familiaris Consortio* (1981)
MD	*Mulieres Dignitatem* (1988)
NMI	*Novo Millennio Ineunte* (2001)
OS	*Ordinatio Sacerdotalis* (1994)
PDV	*Pastores Dabo Vobis* (1992)
RD	*Redemptionis Donum* (1984)
TMA	*Tertio Millennio Adveniente* (1994)
TA	*Tredecim Anni* (1982)
VC	*Vita Consecrata* (1995)

Books

| TB | *Theology of the Body* (1997) |

CDF Documents

DI	*Dominus Iesus* (2000)
DVer	*Donum Veritatis* (1990)
LC	*Libertatis Conscientia* (On Christian Freedom and Liberation) (1986)
LN	*Libertatis Nuntius* (Instruction on Certain Aspects of the Theology of Liberation) (1984)

Other Ecclesial Texts and Sources

EN	*Evangelii Nuntiandi* (1975)
ID	*Interreligious Dialogue:*
	The Official Teaching of the Catholic Church from
	the Second Vatican Council to John Paul II (1963–2005)
HV	*Humanae Vitae* (1968)
PP	*Populorum Progressio* (1967)
PT	*Pacem in Terris* (1963)

Vatican II

AA	*Apostolicam Actuositatem* (1965)
AG	*Ad Gentes* (1965)
DH	*Dignitatis Humanae* (1965)
DeV	*Dei Verbum* (1965)
GS	*Gaudium et Spes* (1965)
LG	*Lumen Gentium* (1964)
NA	*Nostra Aetate* (1965)
SC	*Sacrosanctum Concilium* (1963)
UR	*Unitatis Redintegratio* (1964)

Introduction

The Challenges of Discerning the Legacy of Pope John Paul II

Gerard Mannion

Task and Challenge

To attempt to offer some account, explication, interpretation, and evaluation of any major historical figure is obviously a demanding task. When that figure has been the spiritual leader for over a quarter century of a church that grew in numbers from 757 million to well over a billion people, the challenge is magnified several times over. Karol Wojtyla was a profound person in so many ways. Attempting to offer an assessment of any pope and any pontificate is to enter into an exercise in hermeneutics. When it is a recent pope, with his impact and influence still so fresh, with issues and debates remaining very live in the church, the hermeneutical task requires a sharper edge to it still. So to offer a range of perspectives concerning the most recent pontificate of all demands that the task of interpretation should seek to remain true to the fundamental principles of hermeneutics and shun the temptation to be swayed by accounts too formed by deference, misplaced loyalty, polemics, or ecclesial politics of any wing.

The pope who is the subject of this study was a fascinating, intriguing, and yet in ways elusive character to try to assess. The many levels on which the profundity and ambiguity of his character, his passions, his beliefs, and his hopes existed have eluded precise fathoming and may well continue to do so in perpetuity.

The last weeks of John Paul II's life bore testimony to the global significance of the first Slav pope. The evident sadness and also enormous excitement, interest, and debate generated in the lead-up and aftermath of his passing demonstrated that this pastor was one of the leading figures of the twentieth century. People traveled from far and wide to pay their respects and file past his body and say a prayer for him. Around the world, Catholic churches were kept open long into the night while countless others offered prayers from afar. Such interest mirrored that generated when he was elected to the chair of Peter back in 1978, the first non-Italian to occupy that chair for four centuries. Just fifty-eight years old at the time, Cardinal Karol Wojtyla (b. 1920) adopted the title "Universal Pastor of the Church" and followed the example of the two preceding popes, whose names he combined as his own, by declining to have a coronation ceremony. And yet this papacy would be the focus of renewed divisions within the Catholic Church and wider Christian church alike, and would see the figure of the pope himself become the object of a personality cult of hitherto unprecedented global adoration and adulation.

In 1979 one of our contributors, Ronald Modras, stated that "if comparing the ideas of John Paul II since he became pontiff with his earlier writings shows anything, it is that he is consistent."[1] In relation to the subject matter of that article (John Paul's understanding of magisterium and of the role and task of Catholic theologians), Modras is surely correct. Indeed, in a way resembling the constant determination to be steadfastly consistent of St. Augustine of Hippo (another "man from a far country" who went to Italy and left an incredibly deep impression upon the church forevermore), it is true that Pope John Paul sought to reiterate and reaffirm fundamental messages and teachings again and again. He certainly sought to be and indeed believed that he was utterly consistent. He sought to be the rock for the church in troubled and transitional times as befitting Jesus' commissioning of Peter. And yet that is only part of the story, as our chapters will illustrate and, indeed, as Modras indicated in that article composed so early in the papacy itself.

The Hermeneutics of a Papacy of Paradoxes

My own relationship with this pontificate mirrors that of so many late-twentieth-century Catholics in being neither monochrome nor uniform

1. Ronald Modras, "Solidarity and Opposition in a Pluralistic Church," *Commonweal* (September 14, 1979): 493–95, at 493.

in character. Thus for myself the many differing characteristics of John
Paul II and his pontificate have been enduring inspirations and challenges alike. Indeed no univocal and monochrome portrait of this servant of the servants of God could ever hope to suffice. At both the
outset and in the aftermath of John Paul's pontificate, obviously assessments were legion.[2] Many tensions, enigmas, and, above all else, paradoxes of the man, his thought, teachings, writings, addresses, and
actions remained to the end. So it is a daunting task to try to assess the
life, thought, and influence of a Supreme Pontiff who served the church
for so long a period. But, in the midst of the outpouring of judgments
since his death, perhaps enough time has now elapsed to attempt to
bring together a balanced range of perspectives. This was truly a person
who evaded simplistic bracketing, this in relation to each of the personal, intellectual, and doctrinal aspects of his life and pontificate. No
straightforward conclusions can be drawn in relation to much of his
legacy. In fact, to suggest that he was, in so many ways, a paradoxical
pope, is neither a pejorative nor a polemical statement, but rather reflects the intricacies that present themselves if anyone should neatly try
to compartmentalize or pigeonhole particular aspects of the life, work,
and ministry of Karol Wojtyla. As we will see, certainly there was much
consistency in relation to various aspects of his life and thought, but
numerous others demand a careful hermeneutical investigation that
leaves preconceptions aside but which nonetheless entails a balanced
ordering of both the principles of suspicion and retrieval alike. Numerous scholars and commentators have helped illustrate the dangers and
pitfalls involved in assessing this giant figure of ecclesiastical history,
whether in too positive or negative a light.

Many of these paradoxes were simply products of the cultural and
social world in which this pontificate was served out. John Paul II
bridged the transition of both church and world from the late modern
to the postmodern era, with the joy and hope, the grief and anguish
such entailed. Let us survey, albeit briefly, some of the complexities

2. Cf., for example, the telling remarks by, in the same issue, Edward Cuddy, "Unfortunately rebels have also been known to adopt the absolutism they once opposed. And the
Pope's roots in and East European Catholicism where religious survival was an endless
struggle may spell a rigorously conservative papacy" in his article, "The Rebel Function in
Catholicism," *Commonweal* (September 14, 1979): 495–97, at 497.

involved in an assessment of this pontificate, many of which go far beyond the personal character of John Paul.

Consider, for example, the ironic fact, as Paul Thibaud put it back in 1979, that "the conclave was able to regenerate Roman centrality only by choosing a pope from the outside."[3] Indeed, that same 1979 issue of *Commonweal* (in which Modras's essay also appeared) offered multiple articles that explored the tensions evident between the new pope's past role as a rebel and dissident against pseudo-communist and totalitarian Polish society, and the role he would now adopt as guardian of the faith and one who would demand unswerving obedience of theologians to the magisterium. As with so many Catholic periodicals, *Commonweal* mirrored this range of assessment with a series of articles following John Paul's death. And these equally illustrated the many paradoxes that one encounters in attempting to interpret the significance of this imposing figure.[4]

It is of great significance for the church and history alike the extent to which John Paul's papal teachings bear the hallmarks of his own challenging and complex background, and how, under the totalitarian regimes of first the Nazis and then the pseudo-communists, he developed a philosophical and theological outlook that has been described as Christian humanism or personalism. His calls for a new economic way between capitalism and Marxist communism would prove to be preemptive of later developments in world politics, at least in terms of political ideology if not practice. He encouraged much renewal in Catholic spirituality and devotional practices, and canonized more saints than all his predecessors combined. A relentless traveler, his social progressiveness and earlier philosophical dynamism became matched in intensity by a theological conservatism in relation to many issues. To name but a few controversial examples that attracted the attention of the media on frequent occasions, he vociferously upheld church opposition to artificial birth control and the ordination of women, and upheld the norm of priestly celibacy.

It is fair to say that the pontificate of John Paul was no stranger to controversy, and he had not only admirers and devotees aplenty but

3. Paul Thibaud, "The New Face of Spiritual Authority," *Commonweal* (September 14, 1979): 489–92, at 492.

4. "John Paul II: Assessing His Legacy," *Commonweal* (April 22, 2005): 13–20, including assessments by Nancy A. Dallaville, Stanley Hauerwas, Richard P. McBrien, Irving Greenberg, Terence W. Tilley, and Jim Forest.

also his critics both within and without the Catholic Church. Although he pledged to see the Second Vatican Council through to its full implementation, some accused him of undermining its legacy and of steering the church in a direction more resonant with the church of a bygone age.

Again, regardless of one's approval or otherwise of such, it is beyond question that under John Paul II the church became still more centralized in authority and governance, with dissent little tolerated and outspoken theologians, philosophers, and church people rebuked. During his pontificate the official church condemned many progressive movements (e.g., liberation theology, We Are Church) particularly with regard to aspects of their calls for societal and ecclesial reform.

And yet the paradoxes of this pontificate are brought into particularly sharp relief when one considers how conservative and right-wing ecclesial movements (e.g., Opus Dei, Communion and Liberation, Focolare) were actively encouraged. The founder of Opus Dei, Josemaría Escrivá, who is alleged to have frequently castigated the legacy of Pope John XXIII and even Vatican II itself, and at whose tomb in Rome Cardinal Karol Wojtyla often prayed, was canonized with rapidity, while Oscar Romero, although designated a "servant of God" by John Paul, still awaits beatification even to this day. While Pope John Paul II demanded unswerving obedience to the magisterium, particularly affirming the need for submissiveness to diocesan bishops, he removed Opus Dei from the jurisdiction of local bishops in 1982. Indeed, critics suggest that Rome regularly bypassed the College of Bishops on innumerable occasions during his pontificate, the prefect of the Congregation for the Doctrine of the Faith (CDF) going so far as to deny that national episcopal conferences have any teaching mandate at all.

This was the pope who gifted stoles and pectoral crosses to successive archbishops of Canterbury, who prayed with them and who joined with them in significant ceremonies in richly symbolic venues such as Canterbury Cathedral and St. Paul Outside the Walls in Rome. And yet during this pontificate, the prefect of the CDF would suggest that Leo XIII's pronouncement that Anglican orders were invalid was a teaching beyond question, indeed "definitive doctrine," and much of the work of the Joint Anglican-Roman Catholic International Commission would be rejected and downplayed in significance by Rome itself.

In the early years of his reign ecumenism flourished, but in later years it stalled in many ways, despite the pope inviting dialogue on the future nature of the papacy and on his papal primacy. Statements on numerous topics, such as theological inquiry, interfaith questions, and lay ministry similarly became more conservative and restrictive in outlook the longer this pontificate endured.

Many have attempted and yet struggled to unravel the further paradoxes that embraced both a radical commitment to social justice and an authoritarian rule of the church from Rome. This pope regarded the downfall of the old pseudo-communist Eastern European states as a major triumph for the church, yet elsewhere he forbade priests from actively engaging in politics. He vociferously defended human rights at the same time that his curial departments were accused of breaching the rights of church members accused of dissent and error. Yet, with a fervent energy even in the midst of failing health, he sought to prepare the church for a new millennium, calling all to renewal and forgiveness. He apologized for many of the past failings and wrongs of those in the church.

In previous assessments, some critics even pointed to a "betrayal" of Vatican II; others wondered how much John Paul was a "prisoner" of the Vatican and curial system. He was a great pastor and churchman in Poland and initially transferred this personal devotion of the faithful to the world stage. But in his later years many Catholics became increasingly ambiguous toward this long-serving pontiff, mirroring the paradoxical nature of both the era and many aspects of the pontificate itself.

Yet the outpouring of devotion, admiration, and sadness at his passing, along with the fervent praise for his achievements witnessed throughout the church and wider world alike, demonstrated that John Paul had at least as many devoted supporters as critics. Indeed, the instant clamor for his canonization, along with the immediate campaign to have him henceforth known as "John Paul the Great," further illustrate that history will record him as a giant figure not only in the long story of the church but also in the story of the wider world in the second half of the twentieth century.

The Purpose of this Volume

Thus the impact of John Paul II, one of the longest-serving popes in history, upon not just the Catholic Church but, indeed, upon the world at large, has been deemed to be immense by his most fervent supporters and sternest critics alike. There have been many, many books written about John Paul II and they greatly range in form, style, and quality. Some veer toward the hagiographical, while others are equally imbalanced in their one-sided negativity. Some study particular aspects of his life and thought, while some attempt to give a biographical picture or a general account of his ideas and achievements. This volume seeks to avoid merely concentrating upon the formulaic styles and topics of discussion that are frequently covered elsewhere and aims, instead, to broaden the range of the perspectives and debates on John Paul II, his life, his work, and his teachings.

Hence, the collection of essays is designed to provide a range of perspectives on the life, thought, and influence of John Paul II and to serve as a handbook and academic resource that can be used profitably by all engaged with and interested in not just John Paul II but also the recent story and future prospects for the Catholic Church. It is designed not to be a definitive judgment on this pope and his legacy, but rather to provide an ongoing resource and timely provision of overviews and assessments on a number of key topics of historical, ecclesial, and moral significance. In particular, the majority of chapters attend to themes that will remain pertinent to contemporary discussions and debates for some time to come.

A Balanced Range of Perspectives

Seeking to constitute a balanced collection of essays, we have collected an international group of contributors with perspectives included from scholars and specialists hailing from Africa, Asia, Europe, Latin America, and North America, including several scholars renowned in their respective fields, and encompassing specialists in systematic and moral theology, ecclesiology, social doctrine, ecumenism, interfaith dialogue, and philosophy. True to the overarching hermeneutical intention of the volume, the various essays attempt to explain, explore, analyze, assess, and evaluate the life, writings, work, ministry, and ecclesial vision of the person and pope; Karol Wojtyla and Pope John Paul II cannot and should not be divorced from one another. With the exception of a single essay that appeared previously (on John Paul II and Vatican II), each chapter has been commissioned for this volume. There is no hagiography in these pages, but neither is there polemic in the opposite direction. Instead there are genuine and honest attempts to assess various aspects of the significance of a very long papacy. The triumphs and controversies alike are covered. To do otherwise would present a misleading impression and would be unfair to not only our readers, but to the subject of the volume himself.

Our collection begins with a biographical chapter, followed by chapters exploring John Paul II's philosophical background and corpus and his relationship to Vatican II, before turning to consider his vision of and for the church itself, embracing a general analysis of ecclesiology during this pontificate as well. There follows a discussion of his "defense of the faith," particularly in relation to the changing understanding and exercise of magisterium during his pontificate and the impact this had upon Catholic theological inquiry and practice. Several chapters concern still further aspects of his work and influence, hence an assessment of John Paul's legacy in relation to justice followed by a wider consideration of the sources of moral theology in his thought and teachings. The topic of theologies of liberation is considered without balking at the difficulties involved in opening up such ecclesial wounds once more. Additional chapters discuss broader issues of ecclesiological significance, such as episcopal collegiality. So, too, are the experiences of women and those who opted for the consecrated life during this papacy explored. Final chapters cover the very important areas of ecumenism and interreligious dialogue. Hence, several chapters explore various debates in relation to John Paul's life and influence that remain "live issues." Although, of course, there is necessary cross-referencing between the chapters, we have taken every step to ensure complementarity as opposed to repetition.

This volume does not seek to be the final word but rather to encourage further discussions and reflection upon a papacy and a person of truly great and lasting significance for church and world alike. In a richly evocative paragraph that concludes one of his many illuminating journal articles, Richard Gaillardetz offers some wise words concerning the

attempt to discern John Paul's legacy that I hope readers will continue
to bear in mind as they read through this volume:

> It would be a mistake to underestimate [John Paul's] formidable intel-
> lectual gifts, his indomitable energy, even in his waning years, and his
> sweeping world vision. In many and important ways this pope has been
> a unifying force in the Church by sheer power of personality and by the
> common recognition of his unique role as a voice for truth and justice in
> our world. Yet in the end, this pontificate, as with all others, will have to
> await the judgment of history. Only the passing of time will confirm the
> ultimate success or failure of his ambitious program to provide one
> united voice to a world desperately in need of the saving message of Jesus
> Christ.[5]

Thus one hopes that the provisionality of the approach and ideas put
forward in this volume will be seen as a strength. "Final words" will not
be offered, and it is hoped that few will come seeking such. In reflecting
upon a pope who gave so much to the world and who generated such
great affection, debate, and even controversy, who stirred passions and
energies in so many quarters, yet in an age when for many the church
has also been forced to endure a starless night, perhaps it is fitting to
leave the last words here to Karol Wojtyla himself, as we recall his verse
of penetrating self-assessment, which, when all is said and done, calls us
to silent pondering of the legacy of this ofttimes enigmatic pontiff:

> I am a giver, I touch forces that expand the mind;
> sometimes the memory of a starless night
> is all that remains."[6]

5. Richard Gaillardetz, "*Ad tuendam fidem*: An Emerging Pattern in Current Papal Teaching," *New Theology Review* 12 (February 1999): 43–51, at 50–51.

6. Karol Wojtyla, "A Bishop's Thoughts on Giving the Sacrament of Confirmation
in a Mountain Village," in *Easter Vigil and Other Poems*, trans. Jerzy Peterkewiecz (London:
Hutchinson, 1979), 52.

From Karol Wojtyla to John Paul II: Life and Times

Michael Walsh

By whatever standard one chooses, the life of Karol Wojtyla was extraordinary. There are many accounts of his life and, full of incident as it was, perhaps no life of a recent pope has been so well known.[1] In part this is simply a result of the length of his reign. As Pope John Paul II, Wojtyla's pontificate was the second longest in the two millennia of the church's history, from October 16, 1978, "the year of the three popes"[2]—remarkable enough in itself—down to his death on April 2, 2005. Leaving aside the "papacy" of St. Peter, in length of time it was outdone only by the thirty-two-year reign of Pius IX who was fifty-two years old when elected, six years younger than Wojtyla.

Such longevity itself has consequences, not least the opportunity to model the church according to one's own conception of what it should be—which, one cannot help thinking, is why the cardinals in conclave after a long pontificate choose an older man to succeed to the throne.

---

1. John Paul II has attracted a large number of biographers. The most sympathetic, and the most detailed, is George Weigel's *Witness to Hope* (New York: Cliff Street Books, 1999). Both Tad Szulc's *Pope John Paul II: The Biography* (New York: Scribner, 1995) and Jonathan Kwitny's *Man of the Century* (New York: Henry Holt; London: Little, Brown, 1997) are useful. My own *John Paul II: A Biography* (London: HarperCollins, 1994) and John Cornwell's study of the pope's closing years, *The Pope in Winter* (London: Viking, 2004), are more critical of the pontificate.

2. Peter Hebblethwaite published a book with this title (London: Collins, 1978). Paul VI died August 6, 1978; John Paul I was elected August 26th and died September 28th.

Perhaps the cardinal electors recognize, maybe even subconsciously, that there is something not quite "catholic" about the church when one person, no matter how highly placed, can attempt with some success to mold the church according to his own particular vision. Be that as it may, no pope has issued more encyclicals than John Paul II, no pope has proclaimed more saints, and none has created more cardinals. But then only two, Pius IX and Leo XIII, had quite as much time to do so. Indeed, given the difference in the number of years each presided over the church, Pope Paul VI at least managed a proportionally comparable number of cardinals to the creations of John Paul II.

But undoubtedly no other pope traveled so widely. Until the time of Paul VI, of course, no Roman pontiff had a realistic opportunity of doing so. It is true Pope Paul traveled, but to eucharistic congresses, to the UN, or to the Holy Land: quite specific voyages of which much was made at the time. They were highlights of his pontificate but not part of its very essence, as the papal voyaging has appeared to be during the last quarter of the twentieth century. The figures are staggering. Quite apart from his many journeys around the Italian peninsula in his nearly twenty-seven years as pope, John Paul II left Italy nearly a hundred times.[3]

Above all, and despite the warning that comparisons are odious, it is doubtful that there has ever been so intellectually gifted a bishop of Rome, with two well-earned doctorates, one in theology, the second in philosophy. Previous popes have published books, though usually before, rather than during, their pontificates. Pope John Paul published three books while pope. His most significant writing, apart from his encyclicals, was a hefty, challenging, and philosophically sophisticated study, *The Acting Person*, which was first published in Polish in 1969 when he was Archbishop of Krakow.[4]

Early Career

There is no doubting his intellectual achievements in philosophy and theology, but by all accounts he was also no mean soccer player, his preferred

---

3. He touched down in 181 countries, some of them more than once, and Poland eight times. He visited two Muslim countries, Sudan and Morocco—three, if Turkey is included.

4. The English edition (Dordrecht: D. Reidel, 1979) was a much-revised version.

position being, somewhat predictably as it now seems, that of goalkeeper. He was also a canoeist, a skier, and something of a mountaineer. And not only was he an all-around sportsman, he acted, and considered taking up the stage as a career. He wrote plays, at least one of which was thought good enough to be performed in a major theater.[5] Even as an assistant bishop he still found time to publish theater criticism.[6] He also went on to compose and, what is more unusual, to publish poems, a collection of which appeared while he was pope.

He found scope for at least some of these talents at the Jagiellonian University in Krakow, which he attended after leaving school. There he studied the humanities, specializing in Polish literature. The choice of the Jagiellonian University was perhaps inevitable, given its proximity to his hometown, but it was also significant.

The university had been named after Jagiello, the grand duke of Lithuania whose marriage in 1386 to the eleven-year-old Polish queen Jadwiga brought about the union of Poland and Lithuania, a high point in the history of both nations. Krakow was then the capital, and re- mained so until the end of the sixteenth century. It was chiefly the Jagiel- lonian that supplied teachers to staff the universities elsewhere in the new Poland that emerged after World War I, for it was in Krakow in particular that the sense of Polish identity, language, culture, and religion was preserved through the long years of suppression after the country had been partitioned among Russia, Prussia, and Austria. For a time in the nineteenth century, Krakow was a Free City, in the governance of which the rectors of the Jagiellonian played a leading role. Even after the Free City had disappeared into the relatively benign rule of the Austro- Hungarian Empire in 1846,[7] it still served as a center of Polish national- ism. In this confused historical geography of the period, the future pope's father, also named Karol, had served in the army of the empire, rising through the ranks to become a noncommissioned officer.

5. *The Jeweller's Shop* was given its world premier in Hammersmith, London, in April 1979.

6. Karol Wojtyla, *Collected Plays and Writings on Theater*, trans. Boleslaw Taborski (Berkeley: University of California Press, 1987).

7. Relatively benign compared with Russia, which tried to impose Orthodoxy, and with Prussia, which did likewise for Protestantism. This region of the Austro-Hungarian Empire was known as Galicia.

Lolek, as the young Karol Wojtyla was nicknamed, was born on May 18, 1920, not two years after Poland had been reestablished as an independent state in the aftermath of World War I, and only a few months after its boundaries had been redrawn formally to include Krakow and Wojtyla's birthplace of Wadowice, a small town of—then—some fifteen thousand inhabitants, fifty kilometers to the southwest of Krakow. In 1980, addressing a UNESCO gathering in Paris, he said:

> I am the son of a nation that has lived through the greatest experiences in history, a nation which, though condemned to death by its neighbours, has survived and remained itself. It has conserved, regardless of foreign occupation, its national (as distinct from its political) sovereignty, not by depending on the resources of physical power, but uniquely by depending on its culture. As it happened, this culture revealed itself as being a greater power than all the other forces.[8]

In September 1938 Lolek began his studies in Polish language and literature at the Jagiellonian. He was not left free to study for long. On September 1, 1939, just a year after he had become an undergraduate, Germany invaded Poland. Soon afterward 184 professors of the university were arrested and deported to Sachsenhausen. Wojtyla was sent first to a quarry, where he worked for a year, and then to a chemical factory; when he wrote in his encyclicals about the hard toil of laborers he, perhaps alone of the popes (since in the early centuries of the church when some were sent as captives to the lead mines of Sardinia), knew firsthand the reality of which he was speaking.[9] And although the city of Krakow itself survived unscathed, at least outwardly, the pope likewise knew firsthand some of the terrors of war, the clandestine meetings, the fear of arrest, the disappearance of those judged hostile to the regime. And Krakow, of course, is not far from the horrors of Auschwitz.

While still at school, he had several times taken part in plays put on by a history teacher at a neighboring girls' school. In all he took part in ten such productions, always being allotted the leading role, which was usually a heroic, patriotic one. After the fall of Poland the friend who had directed plays in Wadowice came to Krakow, and Wojtyla once

---

8. *L'Osservatore Romano*, English weekly edition, June 23, 1980, 11.
9. He wrote a poem, "The Quarry," included in his *Collected Plays and Poetry* (Krakow: Znak, 1972).

more took up acting. Together they founded a new theater company, the Rhapsodic Theatre, which survived the war only to be closed down by the communist regime. Plays were performed in private houses. There was no scenery and few props; all had to depend on the power of the word, which Wojtyla regarded as an advantage.

Explicitly or implicitly, the plays performed by the theater company had a heroic and patriotic message. He wrote of the fall of Poland in November that year:

> No matter how this has come about and who is to blame for it, one thing becomes obvious: in Europe, Poland has been the greatest martyr, she whom He [God] had raised as Christ's bulwark for so many centuries . . . I think that our liberation ought to be a gate for Christ, I think of an Athenian Poland, but more perfect than Athens with all the magnitude of Christianity, such as our great poets imagined, those prophets of Babylonian captivity. The nation fell like Israel because it had not recognised the messianic ideal, already raised like a torch—but unrealised.[10]

In nineteenth-century Polish romantic literature, by which Wojtyla was much influenced, the dismembered country had been a figure of the suffering Christ.

Wojtyla explored these themes in two plays he wrote about this time. In the prologue to *Job* he explicitly draws a parallel between the time of Job and Poland in 1940. He develops a similar argument in *Jeremiah*, which he even subtitles "a national drama." The first two acts of the play take place on Palm Sunday 1596, at the outset of Poland's greatest period of power, its "golden age." Wojtyla saw its role as a buffer between infidel Turk and schismatic Russian. The setting of the play is a gathering for a sermon to be delivered by a Jesuit priest, Piotor Skarga, who was renowned for prophesying that Poland would fall if it did not put its house in order. Skarga is a historical character, as are the other dramatis personae, though in reality they were not all alive at the same time. One of the central characters is St. Andrew Bobola, another Jesuit and a Polish aristocrat, who was murdered by Cossacks in 1657 and canonized as a martyr in 1938. Wojtyla's play closes in 1620 with a Polish defeat in battle. In his sermons Skarga analyzed the ills of society

---

10. Quoted in Wojtyla, *Collected Plays and Writings on Theater*, 73.

and condemned in particular the oppression of the poor. As Wojtyla did in his play, Skarga equates Poland with Jerusalem. "Let the theatre be a church where the national spirit can flourish,"[11] wrote Wojtyla to his friend the theater director.

Lolek's mother had died when he was nine, and his elder brother—by more than a dozen years—died a couple of years later, leaving his father as his only close relative.[12] Father and son lived together in a flat in Krakow, and it was only after his father's death—and surviving being accidentally knocked down by a German truck—that Wojtyla decided to become a priest rather than an actor. He started his studies in secret while still working at the chemical plant. He later joined those preparing for the priesthood in the clandestine seminary hidden within the palace of Archbishop Adam Stefan Sapieha. The immediate occasion of his taking refuge in the archiepiscopal palace was a roundup by the Germans of all young men who might have taken up arms against them. The house where Wojtyla was living was searched, but he escaped unnoticed and took refuge in the archiepiscopal palace.

When the war was over he traveled to Rome for doctoral studies, leaving Krakow just a fortnight after his ordination on November 1, 1946. His supervisor in Rome for his thesis on the notion of faith in the Carmelite mystic St. John of the Cross[13] was Réginald Garrigou-Lagrange, perhaps the leading Dominican Thomist of his day. He became, though after Wojtyla had traveled back to Poland, the chief adversary of what was known as "the new theology," a theology characterized by a "return to the sources," to the Bible and the fathers of the church. Pope John Paul's Thomism owes far more to that of Garrigou-Lagrange than it does to the modern school, though it is the theology of Karl Rahner, Yves Congar, and Edward Schillebeeckx, all influenced by *la nouvelle théologie*, which had the most impact upon the documents of Vatican II.

11. Ibid., 5.

12. Much has been made of the impact on the life of Wojtyla by the early death of his mother. "Such speculations, frequently based on amateur psychoanalysis conducted from afar, are of no use to serious students of Wojtyla's life," says Weigel (*Witness to Hope*, 29). There had also been a sister, but she died, it seems, when only a few weeks old.

13. Wojtyla had been introduced to the writings of the Carmelite mystics by a devout layman in Krakow, Jan Tyranowski.

But in fact it was not neoscholasticism of any variety that became Karol Wojtyla's preferred style of philosophical or theological thought. After his return to Poland for a brief period in a country parish and then work in Krakow itself as a curate and university chaplain, he went to the university of Lublin to begin a doctorate in ethics, making a special study of the ethics of Max Scheler—a man whose own ethics, one should perhaps add, scarcely lived up to the ideals that moral philosophers put before their readers. Scheler and many others, including Edith Stein whom Wojtyla as John Paul II was, rather controversially,[14] to canonize, had been much influenced by the thought of the founding father of phenomenology, Edmund Husserl. Not that John Paul would ever forget the rather traditional Thomism of Garrigou-Lagrange. As the Fordham philosopher John Conley commented on reading the pope's writings, "I often have the impression of banging into scholastic steel as I wander through the phenomenological fog."[15] But in the end it was in philosophical phenomenology rather than in theological scholasticism that John Paul was to be most comfortable.[16]

As a theologian, John Paul did not greatly return to the "sources" in the manner of the practitioners of the *nouvelle théologie*. His use of the Bible, for instance, falls more into a meditative than a strictly scientific category and is sometimes the despair of Scripture scholars.[17] Nonetheless he has used it powerfully to put before the world that fundamental question which straddles the boundaries of philosophy and theology: what is it to be human? This is a topic he treats in a distinctly phenomenological fashion.[18]

14. To be more exact, the controversy was attached to her beatification in Berlin in 1987. Stein, known as a Carmelite nun under the name of Sister Teresa Benedicta of the Cross, was beatified as a martyr. A martyr, of course, is someone who dies for his or her faith. But Edith Stein was put to death because she was by birth a Jew, not because she had become a Christian.

15. John M. McDermott, ed., *The Thought of Pope John Paul II* (Rome: Editrice Pontificia Università Gregoriana, 1993), 28.

16. Cf. also, chapter 3 of the present volume.

17. See the article by Terrence Prendergast and the response to it by James Swetnam in McDermott, *The Thought of Pope John Paul II*, 69–97.

18. See my article "John Paul II" in *The Oxford Companion to Christian Thought*, ed. Adrian Hastings, 351–52 (Oxford University Press, 2000).

An example of this approach is to be found in his first book, *Love and Responsibility*.[19] It was published when he was already a bishop—he was named assistant bishop of Krakow in July 1958, learning of the appointment while on a canoeing and camping trip with students, and was consecrated on September 28th that year. The origins of the book lay somewhat earlier. He had been a popular student chaplain and an equally popular lecturer at the University of Lublin. Students willingly accompanied him on these camping and canoeing holidays. In their discussions, especially with a group he took to the Mazurian Lakes in 1957, lay the genesis of this book on sexual ethics. He reflected upon their experience, assisted by a close friend, an eminent woman psychiatrist in Krakow.

The book was a spirited, if radical, defense of Catholic sexual ethics in the face of a communist government's efforts to undermine the church by undermining traditional family values. It stays close to the traditional Catholic view that marriage, though it may have many purposes, is primarily for the procreation of children, a position which, less than a decade later, the Second Vatican Council carefully avoided endorsing. Although Wojtyla regularly puts the female before the male (i.e., "woman and man," rather than vice versa), there are limits to such feminism: trusting "surrender" of the wife to her husband is for him the distinctive trait of the woman in love, and "possession" is the characteristic modality of the devotion of the man to the woman he loves.[20] There is no mention of abortion, none of premarital sex or homosexuality. On the other hand, it is remarkably frank on the sexual pleasure enjoyed by both men and women. Too frank for some, it seems, and Wojtyla apparently considered dropping that particular section from his book, though in the end, and with the encouragement of the Jesuit Henri de Lubac, he retained it.[21] It was this book that encouraged Pope Paul VI to appoint the by-then Archbishop Wojtyla (he was named Archbishop of Krakow on December 30, 1963) to his commission on birth control. In the end he never attended, the Polish government making it difficult for him to obtain a visa to leave the country. Whether he

19. Karol Wojtyla, *Love and Responsibility*, trans. H.T. Willetts (London: Collins, 1981).
20. Op. cit., 98–99, 251.
21. Cf. Weigel, *Witness to Hope*, 143.

would in any case have been swayed by the arguments eventually contained in what became known as the "Majority Report" in favor of the church approving at least some methods of artificial contraception, one may well doubt. He was opposed to such means in *Love and Responsibility* and remained so throughout his life.

This was evident in his preaching as well as in his encyclicals, especially *Veritatis Splendor* of 1993 and the follow-up, *Evangelium Vitae,* two years later. That these issues of sexual morality loom so large in the papal teaching, however, is perhaps not simply because they were in themselves major issues. Although many if not most Catholics shared the pope's opposition to abortion, the same could not be said of their reaction to Pope Paul VI's *Humanae Vitae* of July 1968. It is generally acknowledged that very many Catholics simply ignored Pope Paul's endorsement of the Minority Report produced by his birth control commission. This appeared to John Paul as a significant act of disobedience to the papal magisterium. It was the desire to call Catholics back into line that determined one aspect of the trajectory of Wojtyla's papacy. It was that which took him from Rome to so many different Catholic communities around the globe.

Election

But first he had to be elected. He was chosen by his fellow cardinals on the eighth ballot, on October 16, 1978. Conclaves are intended to be secret and to remain so. George Weigel remarks that little is known about what happened beyond the fact that Wojtyla occupied cell 91, and that he took with him into the conclave, presumably as recreational reading, a journal of Marxist philosophy.[22] It is nonetheless generally accepted that the main contenders were the cardinal of Genoa, Giuseppe Siri, and the cardinal of Florence, Giovanni Benelli, representatives respectively of the conservative and liberal factions among the cardinals. When it became evident that neither stood a chance of defeating the other by the requisite two-thirds majority, the candidature of Wojtyla rapidly advanced. It is also widely agreed that his chief backer, the "great elector" in conclave parlance, was the cardinal of

22. Ibid., 252.

Vienna, Franz König, who knew him, liked him even if he thought him somewhat conservative, and in any event wanted a non-Italian.

Despite Weigel's remarks on conclave secrecy, a detailed account of the voting is provided by Francis Burkle-Young,[23] and his version sounds highly credible. He accepts that König was the main player in the choice of Wojtyla, but argues that the election came about as the conservative faction, realizing they could not move forward with Siri,[24] switched their votes to the cardinal of Krakow.[25] Thus if Burkle-Young is to be believed, Wojtyla was elected because he was conservative, not something that was evident to the church at large, who knew little of him before he appeared to acknowledge the applause of a rather stunned crowd in the piazza below. "Forgive me if I make mistakes in your—no, our, language," said Papa Wojtyla, addressing the crowd from the loggia of St. Peter's. The "your—no, our" was very theatrical—the former actor had not lost his old skills—but it had the desired effect: the Italians, deprived of an Italian pope for the first time since the death of the Utrecht-born Hadrian VI in 1523, loved him for it.

Among the Polish romantic poets of the late eighteenth and the nineteenth centuries whom Karol Wojtyla had once so assiduously studied, there was a strong sense of destiny. For an oppressed people without leaders they provided a different kind of leadership and elevated the national consciousness of the Polish people by portraying them as liberators not only of their own land, under Russian, Prussian, and Austrian domination, but of other countries as well. Some put this into practice, leaving Poland to fight in the American and Italian revolutions. They were therefore not enamored of popes such as Gregory XVI and Pius IX who, in 1830 and 1848 respectively, appeared to betray nationalist aspirations. One of the chief among the romantic poets, Juliusz Slowacki (1809–49) even wrote a poem on the flight of Pope Pius IX

---

23. Francis Burkle-Young, *Passing the Keys* (Lanham, MD: Madison Books, 2001), 265–86.

24. Siri had announced in a newspaper interview that, were he elected, he would reverse many of the changes brought about by Vatican II. He had intended that the interview would not appear before the conclave opened, and would therefore not be seen by the cardinal electors, *incommunicado* in the Sistine Chapel. Unfortunately for Siri, *Gazzetta del Popolo* published it a day early.

25. Wojtyla had become archbishop of Krakow on March 8, 1964, and was named cardinal on June 28, 1967.

from Rome in November 1848. In the poem he foretold the coming of a "Slavic pope," a "brother to all mankind."[26] This Slavic pope would be made of sterner stuff than Pius IX. John Paul II was the first Slavic pope, and he was conscious of his destiny.

The first of his many overseas journeys was to Puebla, Mexico, in January 1979. This visit to the meeting of the Latin American bishops (CELAM) was to have been undertaken by Paul VI. John Paul took over and set the tone for the remainder of his pontificate. He was vigorous in defense of human rights, but equally vigorous in criticizing what he regarded as the politicization of the church in the name of liberation theology. Though not itself Marxist, liberation theology undoubtedly drew some of its inspiration from a Marxist analysis of Latin American society. Though ready enough himself from time to time to use Marxist concepts (that of "alienation" in particular[27]), he had lived too closely with a communist regime to be prepared to tolerate what appeared to be so close an adhesion to Marxist philosophy.[28]

Naturally he had no such problems during his visit to Poland, his next foreign trip out of Rome. He spoke again of human rights, but his message to the episcopate was different. They had, he said, a special obligation to preserve, not Catholicism precisely, but Polish culture. "It is well known," he said, "it is precisely culture that is the first and fundamental proof of a nation's identity."[29] That took him on to the issue of European identity:

> Europe, despite its present long-lasting divisions of regimes, ideologies and economic and political systems, cannot cease to seek its fundamental unity, and must turn to Christianity. Christianity must commit itself anew to the formation of the spiritual unity of Europe. Economic and political reasons alone are not enough. We must go deeper to the ethical reasons. The Polish episcopate, all the episcopates and churches have a great task to perform.

26. Cited in Weigel, *Witness to Hope*, 35.

27. Cf., for example, *Centesimus Annus* 41.

28. In *Centesimus Annus* he provides his own critique of Marxism, cf. 22–24. This was, of course, after the collapse of communist regimes in Europe.

29. John Paul II, *Return to Poland* (London: Collins, 1979), 83–84. The collected translations in this volume are taken from the English edition of *L'Osservatore Romano*.

Despite its unhappy history, Poland had retained its identity through its culture, at the heart of which was Christianity; Europe, the pope seemed to be saying, ought to do likewise.

The papacy has always been Eurocentric. Despite his many travels, that remained true of John Paul II. At the opening of his pontificate, the pope from Poland was understandably preoccupied by the communist domination of so much of Eastern Europe. In April 1979 he addressed members of the European parliament. He told them very firmly that Western Europe was not Europe; Europe included also the states of the East. Soon afterward he addressed the European bishops. Europe, he said, is the cradle of creative thought. Toward the end of 1980 he declared Cyril and Methodius, the apostle of the Slavs to whom he afterward dedicated an encyclical, patron saints of Europe. On October 8, 1988, he visited various European institutions in Strasbourg, including once again the European parliament, where the Reverend Ian Paisley, later to be Northern Ireland's first minister in a power-sharing executive embracing Catholics and Protestants, had to be removed from the chamber for abusing the pope as Antichrist. On this occasion, John Paul II warned the members not to have too narrow a notion of what constituted Europe. "Other nations could certainly join those which are represented here today," he said. "My wish as supreme pastor of the universal church, someone who has come from Eastern Europe and who knows the aspirations of the Slav peoples, that other 'lung' of our common European motherland, my wish is that Europe . . . might one day extend to the dimensions it has been given by geography and still more by history."

A year and a half earlier he had spoken of Europe as embracing the continent "from the Atlantic to the Urals." By the time he used that phrase, during a homily at Spire in France in May 1987, the die, as far as the Soviet bloc was concerned, was already cast. Opinions will differ about the significance of the role played by the pope in the collapse of communism.[30] Nonetheless it is highly probable that if the pope had not

---

30. I do not accept the line taken by Carl Bernstein and Marco Politi in their biography of John Paul II that there was an unacknowledged agreement between the Vatican and the Reagan administration on how to bring down communism. One has only to recall that in December 1981 the Vatican took the unusual step of calling a press conference to deny Reagan's claim that the Holy See favored sanctions against Poland. Cf. *His Holiness* (New York: Doubleday, 1996), 358–61.

made his historic visit to his homeland in 1979, Solidarity, the Polish trade union and populist movement, would never have become the force that it did. The support given by the pope to Lech Walesa and the other leaders of Solidarity kept them, at least to a degree, safe from government persecution and prevented the complete suppression of their movement. And what happened in Poland proved a catalyst for the other nations of Eastern Europe.

John Paul II was appropriately modest about his own role. His encyclical *Centesimus Annus* of 1991 contains a very realistic assessment of the failure of communism, for economic as well as ideological reasons. Agostino Casaroli, Cardinal Secretary of State from 1979 to 1990, once remarked that the Holy See was surprised by the speed of the collapse, and it is highly unlikely that John Paul II himself was expecting quite so sudden a demise. He, like Cardinal Wysziński, had in 1981 been afraid of a Russian invasion of their country, though there were others in Poland who believed, probably correctly, that Russia, bemired in Afghanistan, was by that time no longer in a position militarily to suppress an uprising in its satellite countries.

But if the USSR could not suppress revolt, did it attempt to eliminate the pope himself? On May 13, 1981, at 5:17 in the afternoon Mehmet Ali Ağça, a member of the fascist Turkish group the Grey Wolves, shot the pope as he was being driven across the Piazza of St. Peter's in his open popemobile. At least three shots were fired and two in the crowd of pilgrims were injured, but not seriously. The gravely wounded pontiff was driven directly to the hospital, where he was to remain until June 3rd. He was, perhaps, released from care too soon: on June 20th he was back in the hospital, this time not returning to the Vatican until August 14th, though during that time he was able to conduct much of the routine business of the papacy, including nominating Jozef Glemp, his former secretary, to replace the Polish primate, Cardinal Wysziński, who died a fortnight after the assassination attempt.

A mystery surrounds Ali Ağça. He was already a convicted terrorist, having assassinated the editor of a respected Turkish newspaper in 1979. He had, rather remarkably, escaped from custody, and had written a letter to the newspaper whose editor he had murdered, saying he would kill the pope were he to visit Turkey, which the pope had done without incident. It is difficult to believe that Ağça mounted the assassination attempt entirely on his own, but there is no evidence from such material as has become available since the breakup of the USSR that the KGB was involved, as many suspected.[31] Some thought at the time that the KGB was acting by proxy through the Bulgarians (there was a series of suspicious events at the Bulgarian embassy in Rome just at that time), but that also has been largely discounted.[32] The affair remains without an adequate explanation. The pope, who immediately forgave his would-be assassin and visited him in prison, appeared to make a full recovery. Much later, however, Monsignor (now Cardinal) Stanislaw Dziwisz, John Paul's secretary who was with him in the popemobile, commented that the assassination attempt had in the long term damaged the pope's health.[33] The pope's own interpretation centered not on the attempt but on the fact that the professional assassin failed to kill him, which he clearly regarded as miraculous[34] and gave thanks to Our Lady of Fatima, whose feast day falls on May 13th. He later visited Fatima and gave the shrine the bullet that had struck him in the stomach. It is now in the crown on the head of the statue of the Virgin of Fatima.

If John Paul had suspicions that one of the communist satellite regimes, or the KGB itself, was behind the assassination attempt, he kept them to himself. It is perhaps one of the surprising aspects of John Paul II that, as already remarked, he was not wholly unsympathetic to Marxism. He has made a great deal of use, both as a philosopher and in his social encyclicals, of the concept of alienation, and he readily accepts that there are "grains of truth" in the socialist program.[35] And he was clearly no great admirer of the consumerism which seems to be inevitably associated with Western capitalism: one may recall the howls of protest which arose, especially in the United States, at the "moral equivalence" he once seemed to be suggesting between capitalism and communism.

31. See Felix Corley, "Soviet Reaction to the Election of Pope John Paul II," *Religion, State and Society* 22, no. 1 (1994): 37–64. Corley discusses the assassination attempt on pp. 58–59.

32. Cf. Edward Herman and Frank Brodhead, *The Rise and Fall of the Bulgarian Connection* (New York: Sheridan Square Publications, 1986).

33. John Paul II, *Memory and Identity: Personal Reflections* (London: Weidenfeld and Nicolson, 2005), 185–86.

34. Ibid., 179–85.

35. See also the speeches of "The Stranger" in *Our God's Brother* (Wojtyla, *Collected Plays and Writings on Theater*, 188–92).

Whereas previous popes in their social encyclicals had condemned the injustices suffered by workers, from his experience of living under a communist regime the late pope recognized that it is the dehumanizing processes which they suffer under oppressive systems of whatever kind that is the greater threat to their dignity. His solutions were therefore not solely economic but also cultural and religious.

Similarly, John Paul's vision of one Europe from the Atlantic to the Urals was not simply a political one. It was also cultural and religious. One has to remember that the Poland of today is a much more religiously homogeneous nation than the Poland into which Lolek Wojtyla was born. It is not just that the Jewish population has, tragically, been vastly reduced in number, but the Greek Rite Catholics with whom Lolek Wojtyla would have been familiar in his youth have disappeared back into the Ukraine. There of course, after World War II, their style of Catholicism was brutally suppressed and forced into the Orthodox Church.

In re-creating a unity across Europe the pope was, from the beginning, conscious of the need to improve relations with the Orthodox Churches, and especially, though not only, with the Russian patriarchate.[36] This proved to be one of the major failures of the pontificate, though it is something for which John Paul II himself can hardly be blamed. The revival of the Catholic Churches of the Byzantine Rite, particularly though not only in the Ukraine, has given rise to innumerable problems, not least problems concerning the ownership of property. The Byzantine Catholics have perhaps not always behaved in the most conciliatory manner, but the pope believed that right is on their side.

This does not alter the fact that the revival of the Catholic Byzantine Rite Churches has been resented by the Orthodox. And the Moscow patriarchate has also been angered by what it sees as Roman Catholic proselytism in the sacred territory of Holy Russia. It is perhaps difficult for those used to living in a religiously plural world to understand the depth of Orthodox feeling or to sympathize with it. But the Vatican under John Paul II was not always as sensitive as it might have

---

36. Here cf. also chapter 13 of the present volume which explores ecumenism in greater detail.

been to Orthodox susceptibilities: witness the appointment of a Polish-born archbishop[37] to preside over Catholics in Moscow.

What was at issue was the link between religion and national identity, a link important to the Russians but also to John Paul II. It has been remarked above that Krakow was the center of Polish national identity when Poland itself did not, politically, exist. Catholicism was central to that identity. The pope has constantly urged the many nations he has visited to take pride in their national culture and to recognize as the cement that holds that culture together the power of religion. This is one of the reasons for his creation of so many saints, and his desire whenever possible to beatify or to canonize them in their native or adopted lands. Saints are for the pope not only exemplars of Christian living, heroes, one might say, of the Catholic faith, they are markers in the Christian history of a people, reminders of the faith of one's ancestors which he believes ought to be celebrated as a central aspect of one's national history and cultural identity.[38]

But the identification of religion and national identity is a heady, and dangerous, doctrine: just how dangerous has been seen above all in the Balkans. The former communist regime had suppressed without—except perhaps in the case of Albania—extirpating religion, and kept warring Catholics, Orthodox Serbs, and Muslims in more or less peaceful coexistence. As his warning to the late President Franjo Tudjman of Croatia bore witness, the pope was aware that the revival of religious consciousness as part of a struggle for national identity had its dangers.

---

37. Transferred by John Paul's successor to a less-controversial see.

38. It is well known that John Paul II created a large number of new saints. From the first papal canonization in 996 down to the establishment in 1588 of the Congregation of Rites, which was originally charged with overseeing the process, the number of formal canonizations is 111; those canonized from 1588 down to 1963—i.e., down to the election of Pope Paul VI, is 350. Paul VI created 92 saints in 20 ceremonies. John Paul II conducted 52 ceremonies, an average of 2 ceremonies for each year of his pontificate in comparison with Paul's 1.3. In the course of the 52 ceremonies he canonized no fewer than 483 saints. Those doing the math will realize that, taking all formally canonized saints together, up to the pontificate of John Paul II, 551 persons had been raised to the altars. In other words, the late pope canonized more saints than all his predecessors of the past 450 years—from the establishment of the Congregation of Rites—put together, and practically as many as had been canonized from the time the popes started to take the process over. He canonized three times as many saints each year as did Paul VI.

It was as much a challenge for Christians as it is for Muslims—and indeed, though in a somewhat different context, for Jews.

The late pope's concern for ecumenical relations in the context of the reunification of Europe has been mentioned. He also tried to reach out across the faiths. As a boy in Wadowice one of his closest friends was Jewish, an unusual situation in Poland.[39] Karol Wojtyla shared little or none of the prejudices of many of his fellow countrymen. As pontiff, relations with Judaism meant an accord between the State of Israel and the Holy See, the first visit of a reigning pontiff to a synagogue, and the deeply emotional visit to the Holy Land in March 2000. He also visited Muslim countries, and was generally, though not everywhere,[40] welcomed, but relations between Catholicism and Islam have not greatly progressed. John Paul II was no supporter of peace at any price, as his attitude to conflict in Kosovo and Rwanda indicated. Nonetheless his unremitting opposition both to the Gulf War and the more recent war in Iraq reflected the very reasonable fear that these wars do serious damage to relations between Christians and Muslims.

So among what might be called Pope John Paul II's geopolitical aims were the overcoming of communism, the reunification of Europe, improved relations with other churches but especially with the Orthodox Churches of Eastern Europe, and the establishment of links with other faiths, Judaism in particular and to a lesser extent Islam. Some of these aims progressed but with varying success.

This essay has attempted to demonstrate some of the ways in which the early life of Karol Wojtyla helped to form the style of the pontificate of Pope John Paul II. As has been seen, one of the aspects of his youth was the impact, both through his acting and through his study of literature, of the vision of the Polish romantic poets of the nineteenth century, and in particular the poetry of Juliusz Slowacki with his "prophecy" of a Slavic pope. Wojtyla's apparently charmed life before his entry into the seminary and the fact that he so narrowly escaped death in the as-

---

39. His friend survived the war and eventually settled in Rome, where the friendship was reestablished.

40. During a visit to Nigeria early in his pontificate, a group of imams who had been scheduled to meet him failed to appear.

sassination attempt[41] reinforced his belief that he had a particular mission given him by God. "I am constantly aware," he said in an interview, "that in everything I say and do in fulfilment of my vocation, my ministry, what happens is not just my own initiative. It is not I alone who act in what I do as the Successor of Peter."[42] He carried this messianic sense with him to the end of his life.

Final Years

Even in the early 1990s it was clear that he was ill, an illness rapidly identified as Parkinson's disease, though the Vatican was unwilling, at least initially, publicly to acknowledge the fact. He continued with his punishing round of foreign visits but could no longer kneel to kiss the earth as he descended from his plane. At first it seemed admirable, but as time went by it was painful to watch. It is known from his testament that he considered resigning, and Cardinal Dziwisz has confirmed it. Clearly he was suffering, but he had a very positive view of suffering: "The passion of Christ on the cross," he wrote in *Memory and Identity*, "gave a radically new meaning to suffering, transforming it from within. It introduced into human history, which is the history of sin, a blameless suffering, accepted purely for love."[43] Christ, he said to a general audience, did not come down from the cross. The comparison is illuminating. Christ's suffering was redemptive. Did Pope John Paul, as an element in his almost messianic vision of his papacy, see his own suffering as in some way also redemptive? If so, it would explain why he struggled on to his death in the Vatican Palace on April 2, 2005. The presence of such hordes of world leaders at the funeral mass witnesses to the huge impact Karol Wojtyla had exercised in his years on the throne of St. Peter.[44]

Each papacy molds the church, and, as I remarked at the beginning, only one pope has had a longer time to do so than did Pope John Paul II. But he also molded the papacy itself. He altered the form of papal

41. "It was as if someone was guiding and deflecting that bullet," John Paul II, *Memory and Identity*, 179.

42. Ibid., 187.

43. Ibid., 190.

44. On his declining health, see Cornwell, *The Pope in Winter*, 262–70.

discourse, which no longer wholly depended upon the hitherto traditional language of natural law theory when talking about ethics. He
claimed for the papacy the role of moral arbiter in world affairs. He
changed the understanding of the manner in which a pope fulfills his
office. Nonetheless, one may question how long the late pope's model
of the church will survive. Forms of papal governance, it could be argued, have tended to mirror those contemporary forms of governance
found in society at large. So there have been popes who were medieval
barons, popes who were renaissance princes, popes who were enlight-
ened despots, popes who veered to the democratic, and there have even
been popes who were simply bishops of Rome (though that was rather
a long time ago). And now, it seems, as a legacy of Pope John Paul II we
have a presidential pope.

Karol Wojtyla the Philosopher

Ronald Modras

With the very first words of his 1998 encyclical, *Fides et Ratio*, Pope John Paul II declared his high personal esteem for philosophical inquiry: "Faith and reason are like two wings on which the human spirit rises to the contemplation of the truth."[1] With the metaphor of a soaring bird, the sometimes poet-playwright described how closely linked philosophy and theology are to one another in the Catholic tradition. (And, by implication, how crippled and defenseless is a Reformation theology of *sola Scriptura*.) For Karol Wojtyla, faith and reason together are indispensable for human beings to come to know "the truth about the human person," a phrase that arguably more than any other became the hallmark of his papal teaching.

The purpose of this brief essay is to present the main outlines of the pre-papal philosophical writings of Karol Wojtyla along with some indications of how they influenced his papal teaching. In itself this is no small enterprise, since his complete pre-papal bibliography exceeds 250 titles.[2] And as the opening words of *Fides et Ratio* indicate, his philosophical deliberations cannot be easily disengaged from his theological intentions. Father Karol Wojtyla never chose to become a philosopher. To understand what he attempted to argue philosophically, one must be

---

1. *Fides et Ratio*, in J. Michael Miller, CSR, ed., *The Encyclicals of John Paul II* (Huntington, IN: Our Sunday Visitor, 2001), 850.

2. For a select bibliography of the more significant writings, see John M. Grondelski, "Sources for the Study of Karol Wojtyla's Thought," in *At the Center of the Human Drama: the Philosophical Anthropology of Karol Wojtyla/Pope John Paul II*, ed. Kenneth Schmitz (Washington, DC: Catholic University of America Press, 1993), 147.

aware of his pastoral and theological intentions, and this requires knowing the context.

Education and Context

Wojtyla's first serious encounter with philosophy was in the autumn of 1942 under the brutal circumstances of Nazi occupation. Working by day at a chemical works factory, he began his priesthood studies underground in the residence of Archbishop Adam Sapieha of Krakow. There Wojtyla was given a book on metaphysics, Thomas Aquinas's development of Aristotle's philosophy of being. Up to that point, his university education had focused entirely on Polish language and literature. Metaphysics posed a whole new world of questions about potentiality and act, essence and existence. As he later recalled, his struggle with these new concepts was such that he "actually wept" over the book. Finally, after two months, it opened up to him a "new approach to reality" that would become the foundation for his own philosophical thinking. Particularly important would be the categories of potentiality and act.[3]

By the time Wojtyla was ordained a priest in November 1946, Poland had exchanged Nazi occupation for life under Soviet communist domination. Archbishop Sapieha obviously believed the young priest had a potential for intellectual leadership that would be necessary in the looming struggle with Marxist ideology. Two weeks after his ordination Wojtyla was sent to Rome. There he began doctoral studies under the Dominicans at the Angelicum, renamed in 1963 the Pontifical University of St. Thomas. Though his doctoral dissertation would treat the understanding of faith in the writings of Spanish mystic St. John of the Cross, the perspective on all aspects of theology was that of neoscholastic Thomism. Noteworthy, though not surprising, is Wojtyla's Thomistic intellectualist (not biblical) understanding of faith as an "assent to revealed truths" and his assumption of revelation as "conceptual propositions" that impart a "type of information."[4]

---

3. The book was titled *Ontologja czyli metafizyka* (*Ontology or Metaphysics*) by Rev. Kazmierz Wais. See George Huntston Williams, *The Mind of John Paul II: Origins of His Thought and Action* (New York: Seabury, 1981), 86–87.

4. John Paul II, *Faith According to Saint John of the Cross* (San Francisco: Ignatius Press, 1981), 246, 263.

Neoscholastic Thomism was the result of Pope Leo XIII's 1879 encyclical *Aeterni Patris*, which mandated the restoration of Thomism in Catholic seminaries and colleges as the sole philosophical authority within the Catholic Church. Despite their medieval provenance, Thomistic principles, derived from Aristotle but as interpreted by St. Thomas Aquinas, were deemed perennially valid and were to function as an antidote to the errors of modern philosophy. The Angelicum served as the flagship of the restoration, especially under the intellectual leadership of Réginald Garrigou-Lagrange, the foremost authority on Thomism and the mentor of Wojtyla's dissertation. For several centuries already the Catholic Church had formulated its doctrinal and moral teaching in the categories of Thomistic philosophy. It was within these categories that Wojtyla learned to do his thinking as a young doctor of theology.

Returning to Poland after two years in Rome, Wojtyla was assigned to pastoral work, first to a small country parish and then to a large church just minutes away from the Jagiellonian University in Krakow. There he sought out and met regularly with the university students, accompanying them on outings in the mountains, providing them with seminars and weekend retreats. His active engagement with young people, especially preparing them for marriage, had a profound effect on Wojtyla, not only on the World Youth Days that would mark his papacy but also on his theological and philosophical reflections. Looking back on those days working with young people, he wrote, "*As a young priest I learned to love human love*. This has been one of the fundamental themes of my priesthood—my ministry in the pulpit, in the confessional, and also in my writing."[5]

After only two years working with young people in Krakow, Wojtyla found himself reassigned again, this time to do a second doctoral thesis (the so-called habilitation) that would qualify him to teach philosophical ethics at the university level. He pleaded for permission to continue his pastoral work at least part time, but to no avail. He bowed to his archbishop's wishes and accepted the prospect of an academic life as a way

---

5. John Paul II, *Crossing the Threshold of Hope*, Vittorio Messori, ed. (New York: Alfred A. Knopf, 1994), 123. Emphasis in original. See also, John Paul II, *Gift and Mystery: On the Fiftieth Anniversary of My Priestly Ordination* (New York: Doubleday, 1997), 63.

to become "more fully" a priest.[6] In other words, studying and writing philosophy was not a vocation Wojtyla chose for itself. He saw it as part of his priestly ministry. Even the topic of his philosophical dissertation was not to be his own but one selected for him, Max Scheler's critique of Kantian ethics and his attempt to replace it with an ethical personalism based on values.[7]

The choice of topic was neither arbitrary nor fortuitous. As Wojtyla himself recalled the situation, Marxist philosophers were attempting an apologia for atheism by making the well-being of the human person part of their polemic against religion. Furthermore, empiricism was rampant in Polish academic circles like that of the Polish school of logic. Reducing all knowledge to what was empirically verifiable, to matters of fact and measurable data, inevitably led to skepticism and ethical relativism. Anthropology became a central issue of contention. What does it mean to be human? Before his seminary days Wojtyla had been interested in how human beings created language and were the subject of literature; as a priest he had found himself answering young people's questions about love, marriage, and how we are to live.[8] Philosophical anthropology as a basis for ethics was a topic Wojtyla found intriguing.

Scheler (1874–1928) had been a colleague with Edmund Husserl in the so-called phenomenological movement. Both of them struggled with the impact and implications of Immanuel Kant's critiques of pure reason and practical reason. In answering the question What can I know? Kant answered that we cannot know objective reality, things-in-themselves (so-called *noumena*) but only phenomena, things as they appear to us. In other words, there are limitations and an inherent subjectivity in all knowledge.

To the question, "What must I do?" Kant answered, not externally imposed moral laws (heteronomy) for the sake of some external purpose (like happiness) but one's "duty." One Kantian formulation of that duty was the moral imperative to treat human persons always as ends in themselves and never merely as means to one's own ends. Kant's answer

---

6. John Paul II, *Gift and Mystery*, 64.

7. The topic was selected for him by Father Ignacy Rózycki, a professor in the theological faculty of the Jagiellonian University. See Williams, *The Mind of John Paul II*, 115.

8. John Paul II, *Crossing the Threshold*, 109–10.

to the question, "What is knowledge?" left Husserl attempting to establish certitude in knowledge by careful descriptions of immediate experience (phenomena), bracketing off the question of their correspondence with reality-in-itself. Scheler employed Husserl's phenomenological description of experience to go beyond Kant's formal imperative and seek more content to ethics than simply Kant's version of the golden rule. Scheler found this content in the experience of values, which he insisted had objective referents and were not the result of purely emotional, subjective states.

This all-too-schematic description of Scheler and the phenomenological movement are sufficient to suggest why Wojtyla and his mentors found them attractive topics for philosophical investigation. They too wanted to find some way beyond what was to their minds Kant's hopelessly subjective idealism. But they also refused to allow realism to be identified with Marxist materialism. They insisted on metaphysics as being of more than mere historical interest. Research into the classical and medieval sources of objectivism was to offer an alternative to German idealism and Marxist materialism. This was the central conviction of a group of philosophers at the Catholic University of Lublin who would go on to create what came to be known as "Lublin Thomism."[9] They were given the responsibility by the Polish bishops to produce the textbooks that would provide the philosophical education for all of Poland's future priests. To no one's surprise then, the conclusions of Wojtyla's inquiries into Scheler's ethics comported with the anti-subjectivist concerns of the Polish bishops and the Lublin Thomists.

Wojtyla's dissertation on Scheler is a key to understanding the entire corpus of his later philosophical endeavors. The title of his published dissertation translates as *An Evaluation of the Possibility of Constructing a Christian Ethic on the Principles of the System of Max Scheler.*[10] He turned to Scheler, he tells us, because of Scheler's endeavor to create an ethics of

9. For an introduction to the Lublin Thomists, see Theresa Sandok, "Karol Wojtyla at the Catholic University of Lublin," in *Person and Community: Selected Essays* by Karol Wojtyla, trans. Theresa Sandok, OSM, xix–xxvi (New York: Peter Lang, 1993). See also Mieczyslaw A. Krapiec, *I–Man: An Outline of Philosophical Anthropology* (New Britain, CT: Mariel Pub, 1983), v–vi. Krapiec, a Dominican priest, was the leader of Lublin Thomists.

10. Karol Wojtyla, *Ocena mozliwosci zbudowania etyki chrzescijanskiej przy zalozeniach systemu Maksa Schelera* (Lublin: KUL, 1959).

rigid and absolute objectivism. After an exposition of Scheler and then a critique, Wojtyla concluded that, although Scheler's work contains some objective tendencies, its objectivity breaks down. Because of Scheler's phenomenological principles, good and evil only "appear" as phenomena of intentional feelings. Scheler's "emotional intuitionism," as Wojtyla described it, considers values in isolation from human action and so is unable to determine acts as good or evil in themselves. To ade-quately interpret the moral data of Christian revelation, a philosophical ethics must be able to determine acts as good or evil in themselves. For moral values to be real and objective, they must be based on principles that are "meta-phenomenological, or, frankly, meta-physical."[11]

Wojtyla concluded his dissertation with two theses. The first is negative: The phenomenological method describes the experience of what is, and therefore of an ethos that is culturally conditioned and therefore necessarily relative. Scheler's emotionalist principles do not suffice for a scientific interpretation of Christian ethics which flow from the sources of revelation. A Catholic theologian may not dispense with metaphysics and be a phenomenologist. The second thesis is positive: Scheler's way of doing philosophy can be "accidentally helpful" for Christian ethics insofar as it "facilitates the analysis of ethical facts on the plane of phenomena and experience." Phenomenology permits one to penetrate into the ethical experience of the believing Christian and observe discernible patterns there.[12]

In 1953 Wojtyla defended his dissertation on Scheler for the theological faculty at the Jagiellonian University, where he had already begun teaching. Shortly after, the communist government removed the theology faculty from the university. Wojtyla returned to pastoral work among young people in Krakow but also joined the Lublin Thomists part time, teaching philosophical anthropology and ethics as a docent at Lublin's Catholic University (KUL), the only Catholic university allowed to function in Poland. Four years later, in 1958, he was named an auxiliary bishop of Krakow, and in 1964, Krakow's archbishop. Throughout this time he continued to take the train from Krakow to Lublin to teach at

---

11. Wojtyla, *Ocena mozliwosci*, 60. For a more detailed analysis of Wojtyla's dissertation on Scheler, see Williams, *The Mind of John Paul II*, 131–40.

12. Wojtyla, *Ocena mozliwosci*, 122, 125.

KUL. Throughout this time too, teaching and reflecting on ethics and anthropology, he took his own counsel. He began using phenomenological description to penetrate his own ethical experience.

Early Writings

The problem with modern philosophy, as Wojtyla saw it, began with Rene Descartes and his shift away from metaphysics to epistemology, from the philosophy of being to that of knowledge. With this anthropocentric turn to the subject, subjective consciousness became the one absolute. In its wake came the Enlightenment rejection of "all that was fundamentally Christian in the tradition of European thought."[13] Wojtyla was not averse to the anthropocentric turn of modern philosophy but to its rejection of metaphysics. He believed that he could take the point of departure made by Descartes and developed by Kant but without necessarily accepting their conclusions.

In a 1959 article Wojtyla reflected on moral theology and its relationship to philosophical ethics.[14] Both deal with the question of norms, with what qualifies a person's actions as good or bad. Philosophers attempt to answer that question from reason alone; moral theology mines Scripture and tradition as the sources of revelation to discern "the mind of God." But moral theology also needs to go beyond collecting and cataloging revealed commands, counsels, and prohibitions. It needs to find language to translate these norms into the language of philosophy so as to make them "digestible" for contemporary culture. And it needs to substantiate these revealed norms, most of which are contained in natural law. Without this substantiation, we may know what the moral law (natural or revealed) commands us to do but not why we must do so.

Returning to the topic several years later, Wojtyla made the same point that theology needs to interpret the moral teaching found in Scripture and tradition with the help of a particular philosophical system.[15] This time he conceded that Thomas Aquinas was the "only example of

13. John Paul II, *Crossing the Threshold*, 51–52.
14. Karol Wojtyla, "*Czym powinna byc teologia moralna?*" *Atheneum Kaplanskie*, 56, no. 1 (January 1959): 97–104.
15. Karol Wojtyla, "*Etyka a teologia moralna*," *Znak* 19 (1967): 1077–82. An English translation of the essay can be found in *Person and Community*, 101–6.

this kind of theology."[16] He went on to describe Thomistic moral theology as a work of "monumental proportions not only for its own era but capable to this day of arousing the admiration of anyone who only takes the effort to understand and evaluate it."[17] But Thomistic moral theology is not perfect, he granted. By taking his definition of person from Boethius, *an individual substance of a rational nature*, Thomas reduced the person to nature. Wojtyla was sure that the method used by phenomenology to describe consciousness could enrich the concept of the human person and in turn enrich moral theology in its interpretation of revelation.

With Thomas Aquinas as his role model, Wojtyla set about substantiating the norms he found in Catholic moral tradition; like Thomas, he found their substantiation in human nature. In a 1959 article on human nature as a basis for moral formation, he stated that revelation "in a fundamental way confirms the law of nature."[18] We are human beings because of our rational nature, from which flows our freedom to do good or evil. Free will not only initiates human acts, it is also the faculty for self-formation. Every human action forms or deforms us, resulting in virtue or vice.

In 1961 Wojtyla authored an essay titled "Thomistic Personalism," in which he assembled and analyzed what he regarded as personalist elements in St. Thomas's writings, especially his ethics.[19] In it he describes personhood as the "highest perfection" in creation and morality as its foremost characteristic. In his analysis of the human person as a rational composite and a creator of culture, one is struck by his emphasis upon the will and the concept of domination. "Thanks to our will, we are masters of ourselves and our actions."[20] For Wojtyla love is truly human when "sensory energies and desires are subordinated to a basic understanding of the true worth of the one loved.[21] The concepts of

16. Ibid., 1078.

17. Ibid., 1079.

18. Karol Wojtyla, "*Natural ludska jako podstawa formacji etycznej*," *Znak* 9, no. 6 (June 1959): 693–97, at 694.

19. Karol Wojtyla, "*Personalizm Tomistyczny*," *Znak* 13, no. 5 (May 1961): 664–76. English translation: *Person and Community*, 165–75.

20. Ibid., 172.

21. Ibid., 173.

self-mastery and subordination would become central to Wojtyla's later anthropological writings.

Philosophy and Sexual Ethics

As pointed out above, Wojtyla enjoyed pastoral work with young people preparing for marriage. It is not surprising then that he gave considerable thought to questions of sexual ethics, in particular to the church's traditional prohibition against artificial birth control. The fruit of this thinking was his 1960 book *Love and Responsibility*, widely translated years later when he became pope, the fullest expression of his thought on sexual morality.[22] The book, he wrote, was a response to a "state of crisis" brought about by attempts to solve problems of overpopulation with artificial birth control and changes in traditional family life. Married women working outside the home appeared to him to be the "main symptom" of the crisis (LR 268). The population problem was an economic one, not to be resolved by contradicting what Wojtyla called the "personalist norm" (LR 65).

By the personalist norm Wojtyla meant the commandment to love, which he translates into the Kantian moral imperative: one must treat human persons always as ends in themselves and never *merely* as means to one's own ends (LR 40). Wojtyla uses the words *person* and *love* repeatedly in his book, saying at the outset that his treatment throughout will be of a personalist character (LR 18). He also regularly refers to the Kantian imperative, assuming that it makes his argument more compelling ("digestible"?) to his readers. Problematically, however, after citing it correctly the first time, he thereafter omits the crucial word *merely*.

The main point of Wojtyla's book on love and responsibility is that artificial contraception is a matter of two people using one another for "mutual, or rather, bilateral enjoyment" (LR 228), and that such using does violence to the essence of the other (LR 27). "Those who cut themselves off absolutely from the natural results of conjugal intercourse ruin the spontaneity and depth of their experiences, especially if artificial means are used to this end" (LR 69). One should note here the

---

22. Karol Wojtyla, *Love and Responsibility*, trans. H. T. Willets (New York: Farrar, Straus, Giroux, 1981), (hereafter, LR).

words *natural results* and the absence of any attempt to provide empirical evidence for the claim. For all his efforts to use personalist language, Wojtyla had to resort regularly to the Thomistic arguments of natural law.

Wojtyla rejects head-on the accusation that the prohibition against artificial birth control is a subordination of the human person to nature. He claims in so many words that we dominate nature by subordinating ourselves to it. "Nature cannot be conquered by violating its laws" (LR 229). He makes a direct connection between love and the subordination to natural law: "In the order of love a man can remain true to the person only insofar as he is true to nature. If he does violence to 'nature,' he also 'violates' the person by making it an object of enjoyment rather than an object of love" (LR 229).

Wojtyla has a very specific understanding of the word "love." True love, the kind commanded by the gospel, is not an emotion but the virtue of good will (*benevolentia*), whereby the rational will affirms the value of a person. Such affirmation requires "subordination" to the laws of nature and a constant struggle with the "burden" that is erotic desire or "concupiscence." There is a tension, if not inconsistency, in Wojtyla's thinking about the erotic, emotional aspects of sexuality. He says at first that genuine love or good will can "keep company" with the love that is sexual desire, so long as desire "does not overwhelm all else" (LR 84). Later in his book, however, he writes that the will "combats" the sexual urge and "atones for the desire to have the other person" (LR 137). Genuine love, he writes, is the antithesis of emotional desire. Couples "must free themselves from those erotic sensations which have no legitimacy in true love" (LR 146). To a distrust of the emotions, Wojtyla adds a Kantian appeal to duty. He describes sexual desire as the constant tendency merely to enjoy, whereas "man's duty is to love" (LR 160).

Assisting us in performing this duty is the virtue of chastity, which Wojtyla writes, "implies a liberation from everything that 'makes dirty.' Love must be so to speak pellucid." He does not explicitly describe sexual feelings as dirty but does state that "sensations and actions springing from sexual reactions and the emotions connected with them tend to deprive love of its crystal clarity" (LR 146). He identifies chastity with humility confronted with the greatness of personhood, and then identifies such humility with subordination to nature. Wojtyla did not regard sexual emo-

tions or enjoyment as evil in themselves but only if dissociated from procreation. With a homespun analogy he compares God's attitude toward
contraception to that of a father when his child, having been given bread
and jam, throws away the bread and eats only the jam (LR 309, n. 66).

Continuing in this vein Wojtyla wrote a 1965 essay, "The Problem of
Catholic Sexual Ethics," in which he reiterated his claim that the church's
natural law ethics governing sexuality are implicitly personalistic and
that a couple practicing artificial contraception "degrade themselves as
persons."[23] Particularly noteworthy in this essay is Wojtyla's insistence
that the prohibition is not only authentic Catholic teaching drawn from
philosophical reflection on the natural law but also "revealed knowledge,"[24]
contained, he contends, in the gospel command of love.[25]

In another short but telling essay Wojtyla wrote again on true love as
opposed to erotic, sexual desire (concupiscence).[26] True love is disinterested in itself and enriches the world. Sexual desire contradicts love, de-
stroys human dignity, and impoverishes the world. Even concepts like
salvation and Christ as "Savior of the world" are more fully intelligible in
the context of "overcoming concupiscence."[27] In other words sexual ethics were no secondary matter for Wojtyla. This he made clear in a 1978
article defending Pope Paul VI's 1968 encyclical, *Humanae Vitae*, with its
restatement of the church's prohibition against artificial contraception.[28]
Acknowledging that the encyclical explicitly appealed to the laws of nature and rarely used the word "person," Wojtyla still insisted that it was
personalistic throughout. Moreover, this was a matter with "such powerful
anthropological implications," that it can turn out to be the field for a
"struggle over the dignity and meaning of humanity itself."[29]

Wojtyla can be forgiven if his 1978 defense of *Humanae Vitae* appeared ten years after its appearance. When *Humanae Vitae* was issued,

23. Wojtyla, "The Problem of Catholic Sexual Ethics," in *Person and Community*, 293.
24. Ibid., 297.
25. Ibid., 289.
26. Karol Wojtyla, "*Notatki na margiesie konstytucji 'Gaudium et Spes,'*" *Atheneum Kaplanskie* 74, no. 1 (1970): 3–6.
27. Ibid., 6.
28. Karol Wojtyla, "*Antropologia encykliki 'Humanae Vitae,'*" *Analecta Cracoviensia* 10 (1978): 9–28.
29. Ibid., 13.

the Cardinal Archbishop of Krakow was in the midst of completing another kind of defense altogether of the encyclical, although it has not been generally recognized as such. As pointed out above, Wojtyla had long claimed that ethics, including sexual ethics, must be derived from anthropology, and that ethical norms needed to be substantiated philosophically if they were to be accepted. In 1969 Wojtyla's anthropological substantiation of Thomistic sexual ethics appeared in his most ambitious philosophical work, *Osoba i Czyn* (Person and Action), translated ten years later into English as *The Acting Person.*[30]

The Acting Person

Both with respect to the Polish original and its English translation, *The Acting Person* has been charitably described as "very difficult to read in any language." Even experts in the field puzzle over it and acknowledge their uncertainty as to its meaning.[31] The reason for the book's difficulty, I would suggest, is not only its subtle, sometimes unclear distinctions, elusive language, and high level of abstraction, but also its intent. Philosophers have read it as a work of purely philosophical anthropology. Phenomenologists have read it as a work of phenomenology. But as indicated above, Karol Wojtyla was intent on doing theology, in this case theological anthropology, using philosophy the way Thomas Aquinas did in his *Summa Theologiae.* And his intentions were to provide a philosophical, in this case personalist and phenomenological, substantiation for church teaching, specifically for its prohibition against artificial contraception.

The Acting Person has been interpreted as a work in dialogue with Marxism. But the social nature of the human person is treated only in the seventh and last chapter, where Wojtyla himself admits that his treatment is

---

30. Karol Wojtyla, *The Acting Person* (Dordrecht and Boston: D. Reidel, 1979), (hereafter, AP). The title page describes it as "translated and revised from the 1969 Polish edition, *Osoba i Czyn.* This definitive text of the work established in collaboration with the author; by Anna-Teresa Tymieniecka." For the background and a detailed analysis, see Williams, *The Mind of John Paul II*, 186–218.

31. Williams, *The Mind of John Paul II*, 186. On how Polish philosophers found the original unreadable and how Polish priests joked that reading it constituted purgatory, see Jonathan Kwitny, *Man of the Century: The Life and Times of Pope John Paul II* (New York: Henry Holt, 1997), 228.

"cursory."[32] In it Wojtyla discusses two "authentic attitudes" necessary to achieve the common good that is the foundation and goal of existence in community, namely, "solidarity" and "opposition." Solidarity refers to a constant readiness to accept and realize one's share in the community and to complement the action of other members. It works for the common good, even when this means assuming duties not one's own. Opposition consists of voicing disagreement with a community without thereby withdrawing from it but disagreeing precisely out of concern for the common good. Wojtyla goes on in this chapter to critique the contrary attitudes of "conformism" and "noninvolvement." He was clearly thinking of the situation of Poles under communism when he wrote that, though it puts a certain strain on community, opposition is "essentially constructive" (AP 286). He did not harbor the same opinion when it came to Catholic theologians dissenting from his conclusions regarding sexual ethics.[33] Surely there were reasons for the inconsistency. One must ask why.

Even in his last chapter on sociality, however, Wojtyla's accent, as in all the previous chapters, is on the individual. Actions are performed by individuals, not groups, and the common good of a community consists of the good of the individuals who comprise it. In a preface to the English translation, Wojtyla acknowledges that his approach here runs counter to that of philosophers who reflect on history (read here Hegel and Marx), as well as those philosophers who, since Descartes, have focused on the human person as thinking. His focus instead is on the human person as acting. He concedes too that his is "an attempt at reinterpreting certain formulations" found in St. Thomas (AP xiii), addressing the issue of "man in his struggle" by reflecting on "the struggles of the author himself" (AP vii). One is reminded here of the second thesis with which Wojtyla concluded his dissertation on Scheler. Phenomenology permits one to penetrate into the ethical experience of the believing Christian and observe the patterns discernible there. Wojtyla put himself in the place of that "believing Christian" and proceeded to observe the patterns he discerned within himself.

---

32. Avery Dulles, "John Paul II and Theology," in *A Celebration of the Thought of John Paul II*, ed. Gregory R. Beabout (St. Louis, MO: Saint Louis University Press, 1998), 4.

33. See Ronald Modras, "Solidarity and Opposition in a Pluralistic Church," *Commonweal* (September 14, 1979): 493–95.

First using phenomenological description of his experience and then making metaphysical arguments based on it, Wojtyla distinguishes between spirituality (the soul) and transcendence. He defines transcendence as self-determination or governance, which in turn depends upon self-possession. We experience ourselves governing and possessing ourselves, and at the same time being governed and possessed. Spirituality or immateriality is not experienced as such but inferred as a commensurate cause of our self-determination, as well as of our experience of freedom, responsibility, and obligation. It is our spiritual nature that allows us to experience ourselves as a unity amid this complexity of experiences. The soul is the principle of integrity whereby we possess and govern our bodies, employing them as a "compliant tool" (AP 206).

Wojtyla conceptualized the human person according to the classical hierarchical model of spheres, rising from the physical and psychic or emotive to the spiritual. Authentic spiritual power consists in the intellect and will subordinating the physical and emotive spheres, if need be in an "absolute" manner (AP 315, n. 72). Integrity consists of controlling that which is "lower" in us by that which is "higher." Such self-control allows for the fullest exercise of self-determination, which is "probably the most fundamental manifestation of the worth of the human person himself" (AP 264). Self-mastery is a fundamental category in Wojtyla's anthropology. Only those who possess themselves can give themselves freely as persons conscious of their dignity. For Wojtyla, there is no freedom, no human dignity, and no self-giving or self-fulfillment without self-control.

The Truth about the Human Person

Less than a year after his election, Pope John Paul began a series of addresses on sexuality and marriage drawing from his reflections on the first chapters of Genesis. The addresses, subsequently published with footnotes, bear all the features of a book he had been writing prior to his election.[34] Developing ideas found in his *Love and Responsibility*, he once again affirmed the importance of self-control. But now, instead of using

34. The addresses first appeared in English in the *L'Osservatore Romano*, English edition. They were subsequently compiled and reprinted in *Original Unity of Man and Woman: Catechesis on the Book of Genesis* (Boston: St. Paul, 1981).

Aquinas's word "good will," he described genuine love as a person's ability to make a "self-gift" to another. This he termed the "nuptial" or "spousal" meaning of the body. In those addresses he inferred from the Genesis story that human beings were created to enjoy "self-mastery" and "self-control,"[35] to be capable of totally disinterested self-giving. But because of human sinfulness (original sin), the human heart has become a "battlefield" between the "sincere giving" that is love and the lust that seeks to "appropriate" another as an object of enjoyment.[36]

There is no doubt that Pope John Paul II regarded his understanding of love and responsibility (the "nuptial" meaning of the body) to be part of "the truth about man," a phrase he used to describe his first encyclical.[37] He made reference in that encyclical to Vatican II's teaching that Christ, the New Adam, "fully reveals man to himself" (RH 8.2). Time and again in his encyclicals he refers to the "truth about the human person" and the need for human freedom to be governed by that truth.[38] In his encyclical *Veritatis Splendor* (Splendor of Truth), however, he made it his central focus and the basis for his understanding of morality.

This is not the place for a discussion of *Veritatis Splendor*, except to point out that in the very introduction the pope contrasted "the truth" with "relativism and skepticism" (VS 1.2). The very purpose of the encyclical is to address the "influence of currents of thought which end by detaching human freedom from its essential and constitutive relationship to truth" (VS 4.2). That truth is not only what Christ reveals, but as the pope states explicitly: "the traditional doctrine regarding the natural law, and the universality and the permanent validity of its precepts" (VS 4.2). Thus, we can see why Cardinal Wojtyla could write that "opposition" within a community for the sake of the common good was "essentially constructive" and why, as Pope John Paul II, he could not tolerate it from theologians who were dissenting from his understanding of natural law and sexual ethics. The church's teaching on natural law

35. Ibid., 51.

36. Ibid., 75–77.

37. The descriptive phrase is found in his second encyclical, *Dives in Misericordia* (1.2). See Miller, ed., *The Encyclicals of John Paul II*, 104.

38. For a detailed overview of Pope John Paul II's use of the phrase in his encyclicals, see Charles E. Curran, *The Moral Theology of Pope John Paul II* (Washington, DC: Georgetown University Press, 2005), 8–28.

and its prohibition against artificial birth control were essential components of the "truth about the human person."

The word "truth" has a variety of referents, giving it a variety of meanings. There is a difference between true friends and true statements, between Jesus as "the way, the truth, and the life" and truth of doctrinal formulas. There is a difference too between truths of faith regarding human existence and the specific conclusions that can be drawn from true but general moral principles. For philosopher, or rather, moral theologian, Karol Wojtyla, the truth was to be found in the church's official teachings (magisterium), including that involving sexual ethics. As indicated above, he saw the issue of birth control as a field for a "struggle over the dignity and meaning of humanity itself."

Karol Wojtyla had little sympathy for philosophers who took cognizance of the perspectival, sociologically biased nature of all knowledge. He tried to convince his readers that one could get behind Kant and attain pure objectivity. But it is generally recognized today that even in the natural and physical sciences total objectivity is an impossibility. All knowledge is personal and relational (which is not to say relative). Truth can no longer be naively regarded simply as a correspondence of the intellect to a reality "out there." There is no way to transcend the relationship between the knowing intellect and the reality known so as to objectively determine that correspondence. The "impartial observer" is unattainable in any science. Truth, rather, needs to be recognized as the result of a continuing process whereby we develop an ever more adequate and productive relationship with reality. In other words, truth is something we must continually seek to have more adequately; we cannot simply claim to have it already.

There is much to admire in the moral philosophy of Karol Wojtyla. It can be argued that his idea of true love as totally disinterested self-giving is psychologically beyond achievement, but it provides an ideal born out of his own asceticism. It may be pointed out too that his successor, Pope Benedict XVI, in *Deus Caritas Est*, his own first encyclical on love, implicitly corrected his quite negative view of erotic love. But my intention here is not a critique of Karol Wojtyla so much as a clarification. He tried to put a personalist face on the Catholic Church's natural law teaching on sexual ethics. In this he was not so much a philosopher as an evangelist.

4

John Paul II and Vatican II

Paul McPartlan

Pope John Paul II participated in the Second Vatican Council from start to finish. As its texts matured, so, by his own testimony, did his participation mature.[1] In 1962 he was a young auxiliary bishop; by 1965 he was Archbishop of Krakow and a major figure. To read the book *Sources of Renewal: The Implementation of the Second Vatican Council*,[2] which he wrote in 1972 to mark the tenth anniversary of the start of the council and to guide his own newly launched archdiocesan synod, is to appreciate the understanding that he had, first, of the council's teaching as a highly integrated whole, second, of its purpose as being to enhance *faith*, and third, of his responsibility as a bishop "to elicit that response of faith which should be the fruit of the council and the basis of its implementation" (SR 11). If such was his task as a bishop, we can safely assume that it was writ large in his understanding of his new role as pope in 1978.

The first conciliar passage quoted by him was from the Constitution on Divine Revelation, *Dei Verbum* (DV): "as the centuries go by, the church is always advancing towards the plenitude of divine truth" (DV 8). He commented: "The enrichment of faith is nothing else than increasingly full participation in divine truth. This is the fundamental viewpoint from which we must judge the reality of Vatican II and seek ways of putting it into practice" (SR 15). He quickly made it plain that, for him, the reality of Vatican II was what we might call doctrine in

1. John Paul II, *Crossing the Threshold of Hope* (London: Jonathan Cape, 1994), 158.
2. Karol Wojtyla, *Sources of Renewal: The Implementation of the Second Vatican Council*, trans. P. S. Falla (London: Collins, 1980), (hereafter, SR).

practice, or *lived* doctrine. So it is that when bishops perform the "essential task" of teaching about "faith and morals," these are not really two separate areas but one: "on the one hand doctrinal acts of the magisterium have a pastoral sense, while on the other pastoral acts have a doctrinal significance, deeply rooted as they are in faith and morals. These pastoral acts contain the doctrine that the church proclaims; they often make it clearer and more precise, striving incessantly to achieve the fulness of the divine truth (cf. John 16:13)" (SR 17).

It was in this deep sense of almost removing the easily presumed distinction between doctrine and practice that Cardinal Wojtyla understood Vatican II to have been "pre-eminently a pastoral Council," as Pope John XXIII many times emphasized that it should be (SR 16). As such, the council resonated with Wojtyla's own philosophical convictions expounded in his earlier book, *The Acting Person* (1969), in which he set himself firmly against the cognitive approach of Descartes by asking: "Does man reveal himself in *thinking* or, rather, in the actual *enacting* of his existence?" It is not by "speculating" or "reasoning" that man reveals himself, but "in the confrontation itself when he has to take an active stand upon issues requiring vital decisions and having vital consequences and repercussions."[3] Summarizing this view, we might say not *by their deeds shall you know them*, but rather *by their acts shall they know themselves.* So much is at stake, indeed our very identity, in our actions, and so much of John Paul's pontificate was foreshadowed in the words just quoted, not least the unshakable stand that he personally took on doctrinal and moral issues. There was a hint of the link between his own weighty philosophical background and his interpretation of the specific character of Vatican II when he said in 1972: "A 'purely' doctrinal council would have concentrated on defining the precise meaning of the truths of faith, whereas a pastoral council proclaims, recalls or clarifies truths for the primary purpose of giving Christians a life-style, a way of thinking and *acting*." His purpose as a bishop was expressly to foster the "attitudes" that Christians "should acquire." "These attitudes, springing from a well-formed Christian conscience, can in a sense be regarded as

---

3. Karol Wojtyla, *The Acting Person*, trans. Andrzej Potocki, definitive text established in collaboration with the author by Anna-Teresa Tymieniecka, Analecta Husserliana 10 (Dordrecht and Boston: D. Reidel, 1979), vii–viii (emphasis in original).

true proof of the realization of the Council" (SR 18, emphasis added), he said, and the fundamental attitude for him, to which we shall return below, was one of "self-abandonment to God" (SR 20).

The mold-breaking document that most epitomizes Vatican II as a pastoral council, in the radical Wojtyla sense, is, of course, *Gaudium et Spes*. It is no coincidence that this was the document upon which the future pope worked most. It is with this document that we must start.

Gaudium et Spes

The key to the pontificate of John Paul II lies in *Gaudium et Spes* (GS), the council's final document, which he himself wanted to be styled the *Pastoral Constitution* on the Church in the Modern World. In late November 1965, a quarter of the assembled bishops wanted this most unusual text, still being hastily completed, to be called simply a "Declaration" or a "Letter," but Archbishop Wojtyla, who had worked intensely on the draft since 1964 and was now a key member of the mixed commission finalizing it, spoke up in favor of the title which at once emphasized both the high status and the newness of the document. "The document is really a 'Constitution' but one that is 'pastoral.' This latter term should be carefully explained. It is much more concerned with life than with doctrine."[4]

Speaking of the document at the end of an international symposium on the implementation of Vatican II, held in Rome, February 25–27, 2000, Pope John Paul said:

> The Pastoral Constitution *Gaudium et Spes* which posed the fundamental questions to which each person is called to respond repeats to us still today words which have lost nothing of their relevance: "it is only in the mystery of the Word made flesh that the mystery of man truly becomes clear." These are words as dear to me as ever, that I have wanted to set forth repeatedly at fundamental points in my magisterium. Here is found the true synthesis to which the Church must always look when in dialogue with the people of this or of any other age: she is aware of possessing a message

---

4. Xavier Rynne, *Vatican Council II* (New York: Orbis, 1999), 550.

which is the vital synthesis of the expectation of every human being and the response that God addresses to each one.[5]

The extract from GS 22 quoted here is rendered in accordance with an early translation.[6] A more recent translation of the key passage (originally, "*nonnisi in mysterio Verbi incarnati mysterium hominis vere claresci*") goes as follows: "it is only in the mystery of the Word incarnate that light is shed on the mystery of humankind."[7] While it has the benefit of being inclusive, this translation loses something of the stark solitude conveyed by the singular "man," or "woman," a solitude that is itself an essential part of the human predicament that *Gaudium et Spes* analyzes. "*Quid est homo?*" it asks repeatedly (GS 10, 12), what is this solitary creature, man or woman? Each is a "mystery" (GS 10) and a riddle: "each individual remains to himself or herself an unsolved question . . . dimly perceived" (GS 21), "divided interiorly" (GS 13), "weak and sinful" (GS 10) yet "thirsting for a life which is full and free and worthy of human beings" (GS 9). The answer must fundamentally be an answer to solitude, because God made us not as solitaries but as social beings (GS 12). However, the council insists on the need for a true answer and its words seem even more apt in this internet age: "people's relationships are multiplying continually, and at the same time *socialisation* is introducing new relationships without necessarily promoting *personalisation*, or a maturing of the person and genuinely personal relations" (GS 6, emphasis in original; cf. GS 23).

The true answer lies in *communion*, and the Christian revelation has much to contribute to promoting what is truly a life of communion between persons (GS 23). "The outstanding feature of human dignity is that human beings have been called to communion with God" (GS 19, cf. 21), called, indeed, into "the everlasting communion of . . . incorruptible divine life" (GS 18), and the all-important section 22 of GS

5. Pope John Paul II, Discourse of February 27, 2000, in *L'Osservatore Romano*, English edition, February 28–29, 2000, 1.

6. Cf. Austin Flannery, OP, ed., *Vatican Council II*, vol. 1, new revised edition (Northport, NY: Costello Publishing Company, 1996), 922.

7. Norman P. Tanner, ed., *Decrees of the Ecumenical Councils* (London: Sheed and Ward; Washington, DC: Georgetown University Press, 1990), vol. 2, Trent–Vatican II, 1081.* Unless otherwise indicated, this translation is used for Vatican II documents in the current chapter.

specifies that "it is in Christ that the truths stated here find their source and reach their fulfilment." Christ himself has ended our individual isolation: "by his incarnation the Son of God united himself in some sense with every human being," and this communion of each now with Christ is doubly revelatory. In a sentence made tighter by the repetition of words, GS 22 says: "Christ, the last Adam, in the very revelation of the mystery of the Father and his love, fully reveals humankind to itself [literally: man to man himself] and brings to light its most high calling" (my translation). After quoting the second of the latter two extracts from GS 22 in *Sources of Renewal*, Cardinal Wojtyla says: "We seem here to have reached a key point in the council's thought" (SR 75), and italicizing them both for emphasis in his first encyclical, *Redemptor Hominis* (RH, 1979), Pope John Paul refers to *Gaudium et Spes* 22 as "this stupendous text from the Council's teaching" (RH 8–9). Echoes of the text abound in his later writings.

Recalling the final stages of work, in 1965, on the draft of *Gaudium et Spes*, Pope John Paul later said that, among all the bishops and theologians with whom he had the "good fortune" to work, he was "particularly indebted to Father Yves Congar and to Father Henri de Lubac," both of whom he subsequently nominated as cardinals. He specially singles out de Lubac: "I still remember today the words with which the latter [de Lubac] encouraged me to persevere in the line of thought that I had taken up in the discussion . . . From that moment on I enjoyed a special friendship with Father de Lubac."[8] De Lubac's own recollection of their meeting during the drafting of "Schema 13," which became *Gaudium et Spes*, is enlightening: "We worked side by side . . . It did not take long observation to discover in him a person of the very highest qualities. He knew my works, and we were soon on good terms."[9]

From late 1951 to 1953, Father Wojtyla was on leave in order to write a thesis on Max Scheler, the founder of modern personalism, as part of his qualification for university teaching. He spent some of that formative study period in Paris and probably became familiar with de

---

8. John Paul II, *Crossing the Threshold*, 159. Pope John Paul later explained that he had been speaking on "personalism," cf. John Paul II, *Rise, Let Us Be On Our Way* (London: Jonathan Cape, 2004), 165.

9. Henri de Lubac, *At the Service of the Church* (San Francisco: Ignatius Press, 1993), 171.

Lubac's writings at that time. He may well have heard of de Lubac earlier from the director of the doctoral dissertation that he wrote on St. John of the Cross at the Angelicum University in Rome, from 1946 to 1948. His director was Father Réginald Garrigou-Lagrange, a Dominican whose influence in Rome was already then stoking up suspicion of de Lubac, as a leader of what he termed the *nouvelle théologie.*[10]

De Lubac's controversial book *Surnaturel* (1946) had just appeared, in which *he* had used the term *"nouvelle théologie"* in criticism of the theory of "pure nature" expounded by neoscholastics such as Garrigou-Lagrange, that eradicated the intrinsic bond between human nature and the supernatural and, thereby, kept the church hermetically sealed off from the world at large. De Lubac showed that the theory, presented as the teaching of Aquinas, was in fact a catastrophic distortion of his authentic doctrine of the natural desire in every human being for the supernatural vision of God, which perfectly aligned with the famous words of Augustine at the start of his *Confessions,* "You have made us, Lord, for yourself, and our hearts are restless until they rest in you."[11]

The young Father Wojtyla was "disturbed . . . that Garrigou-Lagrange, his mentor, had turned on the New Theology . . . with uncontained rage," and he himself visited France (summer, 1947), became aware of the alarm felt there at the gap between the church and the world, and had great regard for the worker-priests who tried to bridge the gap.[12] *Gaudium et Spes* was an authoritative denial of any grounds for such a gap, and a reassertion, from its opening sentence, of solidarity between the church and the world. The primary cause of the alienation that had arisen was the theory of "pure nature," and GS 22 enshrined a vindication of de Lubac's unyielding opposition to it, showing thereby that it was Garrigou-Lagrange's *théologie* that was *nouvelle.* After quoting the above words of Augustine in GS 21, the council fathers simply and clearly stated in GS 22 that "in truth there is one ultimate calling, which is divine, for all people" (my translation).

10. Cf. de Lubac, *At the Service of the Church,* 60.

11. Cf. Paul McPartlan, *The Eucharist Makes the Church. Henri de Lubac and John Zizioulas in Dialogue* (1993; new ed., Fairfax, VA: Eastern Christian Publications, 2006), 25–49; also Joseph A. Komonchak, "Theology and Culture at Mid-Century: The Example of Henri de Lubac," *Theological Studies* 51(1990): 579–602.

12. Cf. Tad Szulc, *Pope John Paul II: The Biography* (New York: Scribner, 1995), 146–48.

Already in his first book, *Catholicisme* (1938), de Lubac gave voice to the traditional understanding that unites Augustine and Aquinas when he said, "the vision of God is a free gift, and yet the desire for it is at the root of every soul."[13] Then, directly foreshadowing the words of *Gaudium et Spes*, he explained that it is Christ who lays bare this desire:

> By revealing the Father and by being revealed by him, Christ completes the revelation of man to himself. By taking possession of man, by seizing hold of him and by penetrating to the very depths of his being Christ makes man go deep down within himself, there to discover in a flash regions hitherto unsuspected. It is through Christ that the person reaches maturity, that man emerges definitively from the universe, and becomes conscious of his own being. Henceforth, even before that triumphant exclamation: *Agnosce, O Christiane, dignitatem tuam*, it will be possible to praise the dignity of man: *dignitatem conditionis humanae.*[14]

Here are seeds, nurtured at Vatican II in *Gaudium et Spes* and in the council's Declaration on Religious Freedom, *Dignitatis Humanae* (DH), and richly harvested in the pontificate of John Paul II. In a sense, the whole program of his pontificate could be said to derive from de Lubac's foundational work on nature and grace. Because all human beings are graced with a call to a single destiny, which is divine, the church has a mission to all and must defend the dignity of people everywhere, including their right to religious freedom, not just as one right among others, but as the right that underpins all others.[15] At Vatican II, Archbishop Wojtyla was a persuasive advocate of clear teaching on the controversial subject of religious freedom.[16] As pope, he made over a hundred journeys to all parts of the world, bearing the Gospel and frequently speaking up for basic religious freedom and human dignity, and he greeted with "deep love and respect" the many representatives of Christian traditions and world religions who responded to his invitation to a World Day of Prayer for Peace held in Assisi on October 27, 1986. He paid

13. Henri de Lubac, *Catholicism*, trans. Lancelot C. Sheppard and Elizabeth Englund (San Francisco: Ignatius Press, 1988), 327.

14. Ibid., 339–40.

15. Cf. Jean-Georges Boeglin, *Les droits de l'homme chez Jean-Paul II* (Paris: Salvator, 2000), 53–58; also Herminio Rico, *John Paul II and the Legacy of* Dignitatis Humanae (Washington, DC: Georgetown University Press, 2002).

16. Cf. Rynne, *Vatican Council II*, 463.

the first ever papal visit to a mosque, in Damascus in 2001, and, in the aftermath of 9/11, held another gathering of world religious leaders in Assisi on January 24, 2002, to reject all use of violence in the name of religion.

Meanwhile, in his letter on preparation for the jubilee year 2000, *Tertio Millennio Adveniente* (TMA, 1994), Pope John Paul urged members of the church to repent of "the acquiescence given, especially in certain centuries, to *intolerance and even the use of violence* in the service of truth. From these painful moments of the past a lesson can be drawn for the future, leading all Christians to adhere fully to the sublime principle stated by the council: 'The truth cannot impose itself except by virtue of its own truth, as it wins over the mind with both gentleness and power' (DH 1)" (TMA 35). The liturgy of the Day of Pardon presided by the pope on March 12, 2000, the First Sunday of Lent, duly made sorrowful mention of the Crusades and the Inquisition.

The Day of Pardon also addressed "sins regarding relations with the people of the first Covenant, Israel: contempt, hostility, failure to speak out," words that were read not just publicly by a curial cardinal that day in St. Peter's Square but also in the intense privacy of prayer at the Western Wall in Jerusalem by Pope John Paul himself on March 26, 2000. Following custom at the Wall, he placed the paper containing these words and signed by him into the Wall itself, from where it was subsequently taken to the Yad Vashem Holocaust memorial.

A radical improvement of relations between the Catholic Church and the Jews was the principal concern of Vatican II's Declaration on the Relation of the Church to Non-Christian Religions, *Nostra Aetate* (NA), which specifically stated that, "Although the Jewish authorities with their followers pressed for the death of Christ, still those things which were perpetrated during his passion cannot be ascribed indiscriminately to all the Jews living at the time nor to the Jews of today" (NA 4). Having had close contact and friendly relations with Jews since his childhood in Wadowice, and coming from a country where the Jewish population of three million was almost wiped out by the Holocaust, Pope John Paul was remarkably qualified to understand and address the pain of the Jewish people, particularly the pain caused by the church. In 1986, in Rome, he became the first pope to visit a synagogue, and particularly singled out the following words from the Vatican II Declaration: "[the church] deplores the hatred, persecutions, and displays of anti-Semitism directed against the Jews at any time and by anyone" (NA 4). On April 7, 1994, on the fiftieth anniversary of the Warsaw Ghetto uprising, Pope John Paul invited around a hundred concentration camp survivors to the Vatican and spoke to them individually before attending, with the Chief Rabbi of Rome, a concert commemorating the Holocaust.

Lumen Gentium

Pope John Paul believed not only that human beings are revealed and known by their acts, but that the same is true of the church. He wrote that *Gaudium et Spes,* on the church's relationship to and activity in the modern world, complements and completes *Lumen Gentium* (LG), on the church's own life and structure (SR 35, 69), but specified that it does so "because it reveals what the Church essentially is. The redemptive work of Jesus Christ which determines the inmost nature of the Church is in fact the work of the redemption of the world." Consideration of *Gaudium et Spes* therefore *precedes* consideration of *Lumen Gentium* in his book *Sources of Renewal* (SR 69), and I observe the same ordering here. In short, for John Paul, the church was essentially outward looking, and *Lumen Gentium* simply described the inner reality of *such* a church. *"The Church is missionary by her very nature,"* he said with emphasis in his encyclical letter *Redemptoris Missio* (RM, 1987, 62), and this mission derives "from the profound demands of God's life within us" (RM 11).

The council emphasized that God's life is a *trinitarian* life of *communion,* and taught that the church is first and foremost a *mystery* (cf. chapter 1 of *Lumen Gentium,* "The Mystery of the Church") because it is "a people made one by the unity of the Father and the Son and the holy Spirit," as Cyprian said (LG 4). What is then distinctive of this people (cf. chapter 2 of *Lumen Gentium,* "The People of God") is that it is "a communion of life, love and truth" (LG 9). Cardinal Wojtyla wrote at length on the church as the People of God in *Sources of Renewal* (SR 112–200), but emphasized that "the link uniting the Church as People of God" is "communio" (SR 133–46). Thus, although, as the extraordinary synod of bishops held in 1985 to assess the impact of the council twenty years after its close acknowledged, use of the term "People of

God" for the church has waned, what has rather dislodged it is what Wojtyla regarded as the essential idea behind the term, namely the idea of the church as *communion*. To the people of Krakow, he said that, "both *ad intra* and *ad extra*," the church must "seek ways of realizing 'communion' among human beings" (SR 146). The synod itself reflected the same understanding when it said in its "Final *Relatio*": "The Church as communion is a sacrament for the salvation of the world."[17]

Communion is therefore what the church is and what it offers to the world, and Wojtyla drew a criterion from the council in this regard: "in the society of the Church itself all must measure their behaviour according to the principle of communion whose theological meaning and importance have been re-emphasised by Vatican II" (SR 146). Reflecting on the thirtieth anniversary of the beginning of the council, Pope John Paul said that Vatican II would "go down in history *primarily as an ecclesiological Council*," and that it was also "*profoundly trinitarian*," with an understanding of the church rooted in the mystery of the Trinity. He particularly highlighted the "exchange of gifts" that ought to characterize a trinitarian church set in a universe itself filled "*with the mystery of divine communion*," both *ad extra*, between the church and the world, and *ad intra*, between "the multiplicity of Churches spread over the face of the whole earth" that make up the one mystical body of Christ.[18]

By its highlighting of the trinitarian mystery of the church, not only in *Lumen Gentium* 4, but also in *Gaudium et Spes* 24 and in the Decree on Ecumenism, *Unitatis Redintegratio* (UR) 2, Vatican II played a significant part in the renewed appreciation of the Trinity that was a striking feature of many Christian traditions in the twentieth century.[19] We may identify two notable ways in which Pope John Paul sought to develop the trinitarian awareness instilled by the council: first, by the trinitarian trio of encyclical letters that he wrote and the trinitarian framework he gave to the years of preparation for the millennium, and second, by the many synods of bishops that he gathered, for an exchange of gifts among the local churches.

17. "Final *Relatio*," II, D, 1, in *L'Osservatore Romano*, English ed., December 16, 1985, 9.

18. Pope John Paul II, Christmas Address to the College of Cardinals, December 22, 1992, in *L'Osservatore Romano*, English ed., January 6, 1993, 6–7.

19. Cf. Geoffrey Wainwright, "The Ecumenical Rediscovery of the Trinity," *One in Christ* 34 (1998): 95–124.

In 1986, Pope John Paul recalled the trinitarian greeting taken from the letters of St. Paul and used in the celebration of the Eucharist: "The grace of our Lord Jesus Christ and the love of God and the fellowship of the Holy Spirit be with you all" (2 Cor 13:13), and said that he was now completing, in his encyclical on the Holy Spirit, *Dominum et Vivificantem* (cf. 2), the trinitarian program inspired by it and already begun with the encyclicals, *Redemptor Hominis* (1979) and *Dives in Misericordia* (1980). In 1994, he directed that the three years of immediate preparation for the Great Jubilee should be devoted to reflection on Jesus Christ (1997), the Holy Spirit (1998), and God the Father (1999), respectively (cf. TMA 30–54). He also announced that, following upon the special assemblies of the synod of bishops already held for Europe (1991) and Africa (1994), there would be further continental synods for the Americas, Asia, and Oceania, the first of which duly took place in 1997 and the remaining two in 1998. In the event, there was also a special assembly for Lebanon (1995) and a second special assembly for Europe (1999). The earlier particular synod for the Netherlands (1980) should also be recalled. Meanwhile, the regular program of ordinary assemblies of the synod continued throughout his pontificate, with synods on the Christian Family (1980), Penance and Reconciliation (1983), the Vocation and Mission of the Lay Faithful (1987), the Formation of Priests (1990), the Consecrated Life (1994), and the Ministry of the Bishop (2001). Before he died, Pope John Paul announced a further assembly of the synod to consider the Eucharist, duly held in October 2005.

In 1983, Pope John Paul promulgated the new Code of Canon Law, to which, together with the subsequent Code of Canons for the Eastern Churches (1990), he later referred as being, "in a certain sense . . . the last documents of Vatican II." He added that "something similar could be said (and perhaps even more rightly so) of the *Catechism of the Catholic Church*," which arose from the extraordinary synod of 1985 and was published in 1992.[20] The Codes are indeed intimately related to the council. When he announced the forthcoming council in 1959, Pope John XXIII also announced a complete revision of the church's canonical discipline. The existing Code for the West dated from 1917 and some provisions for the Eastern Churches had been promulgated in

20. Cf. Pope John Paul II, Christmas Address, 1992.

1948, but there was no complete Code for the Eastern Churches. The new Codes are therefore not only landmarks in the overall life of the church, but more specifically achievements of major importance for the implementation of Vatican II, by giving a legal framework for the life of the postconciliar church. We should associate with them also the Apostolic Constitution, *Pastor Bonus*, of 1988, which restructured the Roman Curia, building upon the initial reform undertaken by Pope Paul VI at the behest of the council.[21]

Writing on the synod of bishops with reference to the new Code, Cardinal Joseph Ratzinger specified that it "advises the pope; it is not a small-scale council, and is not a collegial organ of leadership for the universal church."[22] Such an organ might perhaps be envisaged in the ongoing implementation of Vatican II, to exercise the authority over the universal church that the college of bishops together with the pope has, as *Lumen Gentium* taught (cf. LG 22), but the synod as presently constituted is certainly not it. Synods are undoubtedly a most significant new feature of the postconciliar church, nurtured by Pope John Paul II, to the benefit of a real collegial spirit among the bishops, but their limited status must be recognized. Synods, even the regional assemblies, are held in Rome, and their deliberations are finally submitted to the pope, who in due course personally issues a post-synodal apostolic exhortation.

The distant origins of the Curia lie in the twelfth century, when it was formed to manage the papal territories at a time when the church was becoming much more centralized under a highly directive papacy. The Gregorian Reform, initiated by Pope Gregory VII (1073–85), culminated in the pontificate of Pope Innocent III (1198–1216), the first to style himself the "Vicar of Christ." Yves Congar, himself a Dominican, has shown how the rise of the new mendicant orders at that time, with their immensely influential theologians, the great scholastics, such as St. Thomas Aquinas and St. Bonaventure, contributed to a decisive shift away from the communional ecclesiology of local churches that had generally obtained beforehand toward a universal ecclesiology.

---

21. Cf. Vatican II, Decree on the Pastoral Office of Bishops in the Church, *Christus Dominus*, 9–10.

22. Joseph Ratzinger, *Church, Ecumenism, and Politics* (Slough: St. Paul Publications, 1988), 46.

As mendicants, the members of the new orders did not fit into the stable structure of local churches and were much criticized. "Clearly, they needed to justify themselves and they did so by invoking a canonical mission received from the bishops . . . or better, received from the pope. This entailed their developing the theology of a power of the pope amounting to a properly episcopal authority over all the faithful, whatever diocese they belonged to . . . All of the mendicant theologians developed these ideas," he says, "which, it must be admitted, became those of the catholic Church." The church, they maintained, is one people, with one head, not just invisibly in heaven, but visibly on earth. As each local church has a bishop at its head, so also the church as a whole has a bishop at its head. "Such an ecclesiology immediately entails an affirmation of the pope's universal jurisdiction."[23] Significantly, Cardinal Humbert, who excommunicated the Ecumenical Patriarch in Constantinople in 1054 (and was excommunicated in return) at the start of the schism of West and East, Catholic and Orthodox, was an early advocate of the idea of the pope as "universal bishop."[24]

The Orthodox have continued resolutely to resist such ideas, which they believe still to be operative in the Catholic Church. Pope John Paul's own practice of sending a letter to all the priests of the world on Holy Thursday each year (a practice not continued by Pope Benedict XVI) leaned in that direction. In his first such letter to all priests in 1979, Pope John Paul adapted famous words of Augustine and said: "For you I am a bishop, with you I am a priest."[25] Vatican I indeed declared that the pope has ordinary and immediate *episcopal* jurisdiction over all the shepherds and faithful of the church, but it bequeathed the difficulty of explaining how this power does not impede but rather confirms the ordinary and immediate episcopal jurisdiction that each bishop has in his own diocese.[26] Vatican II greatly improved on this drily juridical account by emphasizing once more the church's *eucharistic* life.

23. Yves Congar, *"De la communion des églises à une ecclésiologie de l'église universelle,"* in *L'Episcopat et l'Eglise universelle*, eds. Y. Congar and B. D. Dupuy (Paris: Cerf, 1964), 227–60, at 244–45.

24. Ibid., 238.

25. John Paul II, Letter to Priests, *Novo incipiente nostro* (1979), no. 1; cf. Augustine, *"Vobis enim sum episcopus, vobiscum sum christianus,"* *Serm.* 340, 1 (PL 38, 1483).

26. Cf. Vatican I, First Dogmatic Constitution on the Church of Christ, chap. 3, in Tanner, ed., *Decrees of the Ecumenical Councils*, vol. 2, 813*–814*.

The bishops are high priests, presiding at the Eucharist of their local churches (Constitution on the Sacred Liturgy, *Sacrosanctum Concilium*, SC 41; cf. LG 21, 26). They are *all* "vicars of Christ" (LG 27). Their collegiality (LG 22) fits with this renewed patristic understanding and is rooted in the eucharistic communion of their churches. The fundamental eucharistic ministry in the church is that of the bishops, whom priests, normally called "presbyters" by Vatican II, represent (SC 42; Decree on the Ministry and Life of Priests, *Presbyterorum Ordinis*, 5). It might be said that a thoroughgoing application of this idea would mean that a bishop would say to his presbyters not so much that he was a priest with them but that they were priests with him.

Although Vatican II wanted to show the Catholic Church's integration of eucharistic and universal ecclesiology, in order to refute Orthodox claims that these two models were incompatible,[27] the two were left rather juxtaposed in its documents.[28] The pontificate of John Paul II saw remarkable efforts, no doubt influenced by Cardinal Ratzinger, then prefect of the Congregation for the Doctrine of the Faith (CDF) and a consistent advocate of eucharistic ecclesiology, both to advance a eucharistic understanding of the church (most notably evidenced by Pope John Paul's own final encyclical letter, *Ecclesia de Eucharistia*, 2004), and also to integrate the papacy itself into such an understanding, as a service rendered amid the local churches to the overall harmony of their eucharistic witness. The 1992 letter from the CDF on the idea of the church as communion said that "the existence of the Petrine ministry . . . bears a profound correspondence to the eucharistic character of the Church,"[29] and the *Catechism of the Catholic Church* makes a similar connection (in para. 1369).

Ratzinger regretfully notes that the "most crucial development" that occurred in the Latin West as it entered the Middle Ages was "the increasing distinction between sacrament and jurisdiction, between liturgy and administration as such."[30] Most of the major divisions that still

---

27. Cf. Paul McPartlan, "Eucharistic Ecclesiology," *One in Christ* 22 (1986): 314–31, at 327.

28. Cf. Walter Kasper, "Church as *communio*," *Communio* 13 (1986): 100–117, at 111.

29. Congregation for the Doctrine of the Faith, Letter to the Bishops of the Catholic Church on Some Aspects of the Church Understood as Communion, *Communionis Notio*, 1992, n. 11.

30. Joseph Ratzinger, *Principles of Catholic Theology* (San Francisco: Ignatius Press, 1987), 254.

mark the church, beginning with that between Catholics and Orthodox, have occurred since that time and been related to this development. We can therefore see the prime ecumenical importance of removing the distinction, not only, as Vatican II did, with regard to bishops, but also with regard to the pope.

Against this background, two rather contrasting features of the pontificate of John Paul II stand out. First, he gave strong encouragement to the many "new movements" that have sprung up in the church in recent decades. Their rise at the end of the second millennium invites comparison with the rise of the mendicant orders at its start, for they too have a strongly universal focus in their ecclesiology and sometimes rather weak or strained relations with local bishops. Pope John Paul addressed a huge gathering of members of over fifty movements and communities, both great and small, on Pentecost eve 1998 in Rome. Second, however, in a quite unprecedented way, John Paul II placed his own ministry in the spotlight and, in his encyclical letter on ecumenism, *Ut Unum Sint* (UUS, 1995), invited leaders and theologians of other Christian traditions to engage in "a patient and fraternal dialogue" with him about it, in order to help him exercise it in a way that would be recognized by all as "a service of love" (UUS 95–96).

This encyclical testifies to the sustained commitment to ecumenism that is one of the principal ways by which Pope John Paul II implemented Vatican II, at which "the Catholic Church committed herself *irrevocably* to following the path of the ecumenical venture" (UUS 3, emphasis in original; cf. UR 1). Looking at the period since the council, he himself said: "the whole activity of the local Churches and of the Apostolic See has taken on an ecumenical dimension in recent years" (TMA 34). This was, in no small measure, thanks to his leadership. Ecumenical meetings were always an integral part of his international visits.

Sadly, largely for the reasons indicated above, Pope John Paul's greatest ecumenical desire, namely the restoration of full communion between the Catholic and (Eastern) Orthodox Churches, has not yet been achieved. Only a year after his election, he visited the ecumenical patriarchate in Constantinople and expressed his hope for full communion between Catholics and Orthodox by the dawn of the third millennium. Nevertheless, his pontificate saw great progress in theological dialogue between the two churches, resulting in four agreed statements at the international level,[31] and also many blessed moments, such as the visits to Rome of Ecumenical Patriarchs Demetrios (in 1987) and Bartholomew (in 1995 and twice in 2004). The international Catholic-Orthodox dialogue experienced increasing difficulties after the fall of communism in 1989/90 because of the resurgence of the Eastern Catholic Churches. The topic of "uniatism" dominated all discussion and the international dialogue reached an impasse in 2000. The fact that the dialogue resumed with new energy and resolve in 2005/6 owes much to two remarkable acts of reconciliation performed by Pope John Paul in his latter years despite his failing health: first, his trip to Athens in 2001, during which he begged forgiveness from the Lord for the sacking of Constantinople by the Latins in 1204 and for all the actions by which Catholics had sinned against their Orthodox brothers and sisters, and second, his return of the relics of Sts. John Chrysostom and Gregory Nazianzen to the ecumenical patriarchate in 2004.

Self-abandonment to God

Pope John Paul consistently wanted to apologize for past deeds of the church's members that "sullied her face, preventing her from fully mirroring the image of her crucified Lord, the supreme witness of patient love and humble meekness" (cf. TMA 35). Apologizing is essentially a process of purification, so as to reflect the image of Christ more faithfully in the world. It deeply accords with the opening of *Lumen Gentium*, which specifies that *Christ* is the light of the world, and that the church's desire is to let that light shine through it for the benefit of all. Apologizing is an essential part of the self-abandonment to God that, as we saw above, Pope John Paul regarded as the fundamental Christian attitude.

"In the lives of those who, while sharing our humanity, are nevertheless more perfectly transformed into the image of Christ (cf. 2 Cor 3:18), God makes vividly manifest to humanity his presence and his face." From these words of *Lumen Gentium* 50, we can readily understand how crucially important the saints were to Pope John Paul, as examples of

---

31. Cf. John Borelli and John H. Erickson, eds., *The Quest for Unity: Orthodox and Catholics in Dialogue* (Crestwood, NY: St. Vladimir's Seminary Press; Washington, DC: United States Catholic Conference, 1996).

the very self-abandonment that he regarded himself as called to foster in all. He clearly believed that a prime way of fostering it was to furnish the faithful with fresh examples of it. A striking feature of his pontificate is the vast array of hundreds of new saints and over a thousand new blesseds that he gave to the church around the world as patterns of self-abandonment. His own self-abandonment was amply reflected in his motto: *Totus tuus*.

It was perhaps especially to young people that John Paul II wanted to teach the message of Vatican II that, made as we are in the image of God, each human being can fully discover himself or herself "only in sincere self-giving" (GS 24). Millions gathered with him in different countries for World Youth Days, lastly in Toronto in 2002, and were challenged by him to find fulfillment in this way, with Christ as guide (cf. RH 13). It was a challenge communicated not just by Pope John Paul's words, but, to the very end, by the outstanding witness of his own life.

5

Understanding
John Paul II's Vision of the Church

James Voiss, SJ

"Santo Subito! Santo Subito!" Only a short time following the announce-ment of Pope John Paul's death, placards calling for his immediate can-onization made their appearance in Saint Peter's Square. They expressed admiration, affection, and appreciation for the personal holiness of the man whose charismatic leadership had shaped the course of Catholic life for over one quarter of a century. For many who grew up knowing no other pope, John Paul's vision of the church defined its essence. But others have found his vision troubling. Many who experienced the tran-sition from a pre–Vatican II to a post–Vatican II church and who enthu-siastically embraced the changes in practice and ethos in the early years following the council felt John Paul's leadership to be a step backward.

Now that John Paul is gone, these conflicting assessments define the terrain on which present battles over the future of the church will be fought. Yet in the disagreements that surface, it is not always clear that the various participants understand the late pope's ecclesial vision in the same terms. What was his vision? That is the question of this essay.

Sketching a response to that question poses certain challenges. First, John Paul did not develop a systematic ecclesiology. Nevertheless, eccle-siological themes pervade his papal writings, and they possess their own coherence. It will therefore be necessary to draw those themes from the breadth of his writings and indicate their interrelationships in his thought. Second, the volume of relevant literature published under the pope's name means that this essay will have to limit itself to sketching main themes. Some topics deserving attention cannot be treated here.

Third, unlike theologians working in academic settings, John Paul was in a position to put his vision of the church into effect. Therefore, if we are to understand his vision of the church, we must examine the vision of church articulated in his writings in relationship to the vision operative in his actual leadership.

These challenges set the parameters of this essay. In what follows I shall first sketch key elements of John Paul's ecclesiological vision as expressed in his writings. We shall then examine tensions that emerged in his pontificate at the intersection of that vision and his actual practice of leadership. Next I shall indicate some of the foundations of those tensions. This will yield a deeper insight into his *operative* ecclesiology before I finally offer some concluding observations on John Paul's vision of the church.

A Preliminary Sketch

From the time of his first published reflections on Vatican II in *Sources of Renewal*[1] until the end of his pontificate, John Paul consistently drew upon one dominant image to articulate his vision of the church: communion.[2] This term provided him with a way to speak of the church that integrates its many dimensions. But the language of communion is not univocal. There are many distinctive communion ecclesiologies.[3] When John Paul uses this language to express *his* integrated vision of the church, he emphasizes the theological basis of communion, the structures and dynamics of ecclesial life, and the church's mission. We must examine these emphases more closely.

---

1. Karol Wojtyla, *Sources of Renewal: The Implementation of the Second Vatican Council*, trans. P. S. Falla (San Francisco: Harper & Row, 1980), (hereafter, SR).

2. See, for example, Wojtyla, SR, 61, 120, 135. The notes below, drawn from John Paul's encyclicals, apostolic exhortations, and apostolic letters, provide numerous examples of his use of communion language. For additional information, see Joseph Ratzinger, "Some Aspects of the Church Understood as Communion," *Origins* 22 (June 25, 1992): 108–12. For further insight into John Paul's understanding of the church as communion, see Dennis M. Doyle, *Communion Ecclesiology: Vision and Versions* (Maryknoll, NY: Orbis, 2000), 72–84.

3. See, for example, J. M. R. Tillard, *Church of Churches: The Ecclesiology of Communion*, trans. R. C. De Peaux (Collegeville, MN: Liturgical Press, 1992); John D. Zizioulas, *Being as Communion: Studies in Personhood and the Church* (Crestwood, NY: St. Vladimir's Seminary Press, 1985).

Theological Foundations of Communion

John Paul points to the ecclesiology of communion as the unifying motif of the deliberations at Vatican II.[4] The theological grounding for that motif lies in God's own way of being as a communion of persons (SR 121; see also DeV 9). Father, Son, and Holy Spirit dwell together in a communion of self-giving love (see DeV 11, 22, 41, 64), which God then lavished upon the world and revealed in Christ for our salvation.[5] The Son, for his part, promised to send the Spirit (DeV 22) to enlighten his disciples and to unite them with the Father and the Son in a sharing of divine life and love (EdE 35–36). As John Paul observes, "[t]he reality of the Church as Communion is, then, the integrating aspect, indeed the central content of the 'mystery,' or rather, the divine plan for the salvation of humanity" (CL 19). Moved by the power of the Holy Spirit, the church is to be a communion of persons, united through faith in Christ to share in God's own life for our salvation. Therefore, the communion of ecclesial life must reflect the dynamics of God's own self-giving love.

Structures and Dynamics of Ecclesial Communion

In order to preserve and foster this communion, Christ bestowed on the church the gift of the Eucharist and a hierarchical structure.[6] The Eucharist celebrates participation in divine life here and now through sharing in the sacrament of Christ's body and blood.[7] It draws the community together in Christ and orients it toward the eschatological fulfillment of the communion it celebrates (EdE 19). But it also strengthens

4. See, for example, Wojtyla, SR, 120, 396–97. See also, John Paul II, "*Dominum et Vivificantem*," *Origins* 16, no. 4 (June 12, 1986): 64, (hereafter, DeV); John Paul II, "*Christifideles Laici*," *Origins* 18, no. 35 (February 9, 1989): 8, 17, 19, (hereafter, CL) and John Paul II, "*Ecclesia de Eucharistia*," *Origins* 32, no. 46 (May 1, 2003): 34, (hereafter, EdE) where John Paul indicates that *communio* was identified as the unifying theme at Vatican II by the extraordinary synod of bishops in 1985. See also, John Paul II, "*Novo Millennio Ineunte*," *Origins* 30, no. 31 (January 18, 2001): 42, (hereafter, NMI). Citations from ecclesiastical documents indicate paragraph numbers.

5. John Paul II, "*Redemptoris Missio*," *Origins* 20, no. 34 (January 31, 1991): 5, 10, 13, (hereafter, RM).

6. See, for example, John Paul II, EdE, 21, 35, 61; John Paul II, "*Pastores Dabo Vobis*," *Origins* 21, no. 45 (April 16, 1992): 28.

7. John Paul II, EdE, 23, 34, 41; John Paul II, "*Ecclesia in America*," *Origins* 28, no. 33 (February 4, 1999): 35, (hereafter, EAm); John Paul II, CL 18.

and orients the faithful for their life in fidelity to the gospel (EdE 22, 34). The celebration of the Eucharist draws the community into the sacramental-ritual enactment of Christ's sacrificial love so that the *communio* of the church might be continually transformed into the sign and instrument of Christ's redemptive work.

In John Paul's vision, the Eucharist is integrally related with communion in the church's "hierarchical order."[8] Both are given to build up ecclesial communion. As he explains, initially Christ appointed apostles to whom he entrusted the gospel.[9] These constituted a *collegium* with Peter as its head (RM 63). Continuing the mission of Christ, their task was to teach, sanctify, and govern the church guided by the Holy Spirit, to build up the *communio* of the church, preserving it in faith and holiness of life. As first witnesses to Christ, they exercised a magisterial function in the church, preserving the integrity of the gospel (LG 22, 23). The apostles then appointed others to succeed them in the *collegium* so that their ministry might continue.[10] Their successors now constitute the college of bishops with and under the pope as successor of Peter.

In addition to this *collegium*, early in the church's history others were appointed to assist bishops in carrying out their ministry. Priests and deacons serve the unity in faith of the church.[11] Thus, their ministries must be exercised in a spirit of communion—priests and deacons in communion with their bishops (PDV 17) and bishops in communion with one another and with the head of their college, the pope.[12] John Paul saw this hierarchically structured *ordo* of ministerial office as a divinely mandated *structural* and *structuring* element of ecclesial communion.

8. See, for example, John Paul II, EdE, 35, 38, 39; John Paul II, RM, 51; and John Paul II, EAm, 36.

9. See Pope John Paul II, "*Veritatis Splendor*," *Origins* 23, no. 18 (October 14, 1993): 27, (hereafter, VS).

10. See John Paul II, CL 22; John Paul II, "*Ad Tuendam Fidem*," *Origins* 28, no. 8 (July 16, 1998): 4 (hereafter, ATF); John Paul II, "*Apostolos Suos*," *Origins* 28, no. 9 (July 30, 1998): 2, (hereafter, AS); John Paul II, "*Catechesi Tradendi*," *Origins* 9, no. 21 (November 8, 1979): 11, (hereafter, CT).

11. John Paul II, "*Ut Unum Sint*," *Origins* 25, no. 4 (June 8, 1995): 55, 88, (hereafter, UUS).

12. John Paul II, EdE 28; John Paul II, "*Ecclesia in Asia*," *Origins* 29, no. 23 (November 18, 1991): 43, (hereafter, EAs); John Paul II, EAm 33; John Paul II, "*Ecclesia in Africa*," *Origins* 25, no. 16 (October 5, 1995): 1, (hereafter, EAf).

It provides institutional stability to preserve the church throughout the ages in fidelity to the gospel.

In the pope's perspective, hierarchical structure is essential. But it is not sufficient to make the church a *communio*. Structure facilitates the sacramentality of the church, the capacity of the church to be a sign and instrument of communion. It provides the visible, institutional organ for the mediation of that grace which draws the faithful into the communion of trinitarian life and love. To be this sacramental medium of communion, the structure must operate in the ways appropriate to communion. It must reflect and be moved by the life of God's own spirit (DeV 5, 25). But what does this mean in the concrete?

Two dynamics of ecclesial life figure prominently in John Paul's response to these questions because of their essential relationship to *communio* in the Spirit of Christ: obedience and dialogue. Obedience in this context does not mean "subservience." Rather it signifies openness to being moved on both the vertical and horizontal planes. On the vertical dimension, each individual Christian must remain open to and obedient to God. This implies a habit of prayerful listening to the movement of God's spirit in the life of the individual and in the life of the community.[13] This vertical dimension is the presupposition of ecclesial life and the foundation of communion on the horizontal plane (SR 321). On the horizontal plane, John Paul insists that the faithful must be obedient to the authoritative voice of religious authority within the church.[14] This is vital to preserving the *unity* of the church. But religious authority must also be obedient to the Spirit. It, too, must listen—as John Paul knew. And sometimes the Spirit of God speaks with the voices of those *not* called to hierarchical service. Or it may come from those at a lower rank in the *ordo* of church authority. By what means do members of the church call one another to deeper fidelity to God's spirit in building up the *communio*? John Paul's answer is "dialogue."

Vatican II emphasized that, at each level of ecclesial life, open communication is essential for the *communio* of the church and for its fidelity to and effectiveness in mission (LG 27, 37). John Paul builds on the council's perspective when he states, "the idea of dialogue is deeply

---

13. John Paul II, RM 51; CL 16, 58; NMI 33; PDV 26, 38.
14. John Paul II, PDV 28; AS 8; CL 30.

rooted in the content of faith—that content which Vatican II emphasized and illuminated with its own teaching" (SR 34). Dialogue is integral to the dynamic engagement of each individual with God. For this
reason it must also operate within the *communio* of the church. "Dialogue
is not a departure from the vertical dimension of the Church, as it is
sometimes thought to be: it is an effort which accompanies the profession and witness of the whole Church and every Catholic, in order to
discover and define the right place for every man in the response of faith
addressed to God" (SR 37; see also UUS 28). It is by dialogue within the
church that differences in understanding can be overcome and unity in
faith can be strengthened (SR 28).

Inevitably the contrasting imperatives of obediential openness and
dialogue lead to tensions. These must not be simply suppressed or
evaded by the appeal to institutional authority. For the sake of *communio*,
they must be negotiated with careful discernment. For, as John Paul
explains, "The order of grace is more fundamental to the constitution
of the People of God than is the order of authority on which the hierarchy of the Church is based. The order of grace is also the source of
the final equality of all members of the Church in regard to the reality
of salvation, to which all are equally called" (SR 144). And this order of
grace is the foundation of the ecclesial communion itself.

Communion and Mission

The dynamics of intra-ecclesial life mentioned above also pertain to
mission. As the socially constituted sacramental sign and instrument of
communion, the church continues the mission of Christ in the world.
As John Paul explains, "Communion and mission are profoundly connected with each other, they interpenetrate and mutually imply each
other to the point that communion represents both the source and the
fruit of mission: communion gives rise to mission and mission is accomplished in communion."[15] Moreover, "the Church is 'a sacrament, that
is sign and instrument' of this coming together of the two poles of creation and redemption, God and man. She strives to restore and

15. John Paul II, CL 32. John Paul elaborates on this point in the post-synodal, apostolic
exhortations for the synods for Africa and Asia. See EAf 29; and EAs 9, 25. See also, John
Paul II, RM 5, 49, 62.

strengthen the unity at the very roots of the human race: in the relationship of communion that man has with God as his Creator, Lord and Redeemer" (DeV 64). Thus, the mission of the church is to bear witness to communion in the life of the triune God as the deepest truth and fulfillment of human longing and salvation.[16] It is also to promote that unity-in-communion of the human race that reflects the trinitarian life of self-giving love revealed in and proclaimed by Christ as the kingdom of God (RM 15; EAm 33, 43). This is what it means for the church to be "sacrament."

This way of characterizing the mission of the church draws together two important aspects of John Paul's understanding of ecclesial mission. First, it situates mission in relationship to its ultimate end—union of all people with God. The mission given the church by Christ is for salvation understood in terms of that union.[17] Therefore, the action of the church in the temporal realm must always be oriented toward its eschatological fulfillment (RM 20). Second, as indicated above, John Paul distinguishes between vertical and horizontal dimensions of communion. The vertical relationship with God is always primary in the realm of grace and ecclesial communion (SR 84, 321). Only in the ambit of that prior, vertical relationship can one come to the communion intended by God on the horizontal plane—communion of humankind. Communion on the vertical axis expresses itself through the fostering of communion on the horizontal axis. But communion on the horizontal axis mediates the event of communion with God (vertical axis).

If the ultimate goal of mission is eschatological union with the triune God, the form of that mission is evangelization (CT 16, 68). Both in word and in way of life, Christians are to bear witness to God's saving action in Christ.[18] They are to labor for a transformation of culture in accord with the values of the Gospel.[19] The hierarchy helps guide the church, even as it negotiates the varying demands of mission in the wider world. Through its ministries of teaching, sanctifying, and gov-

16. See, for example, EAm 33.

17. John Paul II, EAm 74; DeV 7, 9; EdE 34–36; RM 23.

18. CL 14, 42, 62; EAf 2, 56, 77, 90; EAm 26, 39, 63; EAs 42, 43, 45, 46; RM 26; John Paul II, "*Dives in Misericordia,*" *Origins* 10, no. 26 (December 11, 1980): 13.

19. CT 53; CL 29, 44; EAf 59, 61; RM 52; John Paul II, "*Evangelium Vitae,*" *Origins* 24, no. 42 (April 6, 1995): 95, 96.

erning, it preserves unity of faith and life and proper order within the church so that it may be an effective sign and instrument of *communio*.

Tensions in John Paul II's Vision

Taken in the abstract, John Paul II's vision of the church as a communion of persons is quite beautiful—even compelling. But in the practical realm, some have experienced John Paul's actual leadership as conflicting with his articulated ideals. This critique emerges most consistently with his administration's approach to the intra-ecclesial dialogue that his writings suggest is necessary for communion. Often this has occurred when doctrine and church life intersect. John Paul's statements on the doctrinal status of the teachings on artificial contraception[20] and on the nonadmission of women to the presbyterate,[21] for example, were clearly directed toward ending discussion, even though many theologians felt that important questions had been left unresolved. Indeed, the inclusion of one's position on these issues in the "hidden criteria" of selection for episcopal office suggests the intensity of the pope's desire to end their discussion.[22] Theologians who ventured to discuss those teachings critically were disciplined for their writings, thereby suppressing public theological discourse.

Under John Paul's leadership, the church also witnessed an increasing centralization of decision making in Rome. This has fostered intra-ecclesial dynamics that hinder aspects of the communicative dynamics John Paul thought were so essential to ecclesial communion. Indeed, the former superior general of the Carmelite Order, Camilo Macisse, has charged John Paul's curial administration with "violence" against members of the church.[23] He cites several examples to support this claim, but their common thread is that the Roman Curia has exercised power in ways that manipulate or even prevent open communication (dialogue!). As Macisse indicates, "These days, the Church no longer employs physical

20. See John Paul II, The Role of the Christian Family in the Modern World (*Familiaris Consortio*) (Boston: St. Paul Editions, 1981), 13, 29, 31, (hereafter, FC).

21. John Paul II, "*Ordinatio Sacerdotalis*," *Origins* 24, no. 4 (June 9, 1994), (hereafter, OS).

22. Peter Hebblethwaite, "'Secret' Criteria Set Bishops' Appointments," *National Catholic Reporter*, February 4, 1994, 14.

23. Camilo Macisse, "Violence in the Church," *The Tablet*, November 22, 2003, 8–9.

coercion. But the other forms of violence—moral and psychological—continue, in an exercise of power which ignores both legitimate diversity in the Church and the Gospel insistence on dialogue."[24] Some voices get heard. Others are marginalized or even aggressively stifled.

One locus of this "violence," perhaps the most surprising, bears special attention. It is the extent to which the bishops participating in the special synods for their regions of the world found their own voices to be diminished or distorted at the synod. Many participants expressed frustration precisely because of the effect of synod practices on communication dynamics. In the preparatory phase, bishops of Africa and Asia, for example, protested that they had insufficient time to examine the *Lineamenta* for their synods.[25] This was especially problematic for Asian bishops who had to first translate the preparatory documents into their own languages.[26] Appeals for additional time were not granted. Asian bishops further observed that the issues identified in the *Lineamenta* were much too European in their outlook and did not take adequate account of the Asian contexts.[27] Calls for greater autonomy in adapting to local cultural challenges and the need for a non-Western approach to interreligious dialogue were downplayed in the formulation of the synod's agenda. Africans expressed similar concerns. It appeared that their synod was being arranged *by* Europeans *for* Europeans *about* Africans.[28]

Bishops also expressed reservations about the conduct of the synods themselves and about the formulation of the final documents. As reporter Peter Hebblethwaite observed, at the synod for Africa bishops were only allowed eight minutes to speak. "No bell is needed to stop them. After eight minutes the microphone is simply cut off. All this inhibits that spontaneity that is such an attractive feature of Africa. Nor

24. Ibid., 8.

25. See, for example, Robin Lubbock, "Can African Church Be Itself? Rome Synod May Hold Answer," *National Catholic Reporter* 30, no. 21 (March 25, 1994): 8; and Peter C. Phan, comp. and ed., *The Asian Synod: Texts and Commentaries* (Maryknoll, NY: Orbis, 2002), 17.

26. Phan, *Asian Synod*, 27, 28.

27. Gary MacEoin and Thomas C. Fox, "Synod Working Paper Skips Host of Concerns Asian Bishops Voiced," *National Catholic Reporter* 34, no. 24 (April 17, 1998): 14–15.

28. Peter Hebblethwaite, "Synod on Africa a World Away from Real-Life African Church," *National Catholic Reporter* 30, no. 23 (April 8, 1994): 8. Asian conferences of bishops expressed similar concerns. See, for example, the response of the Philippine bishops to the *Lineamenta* in Phan, *Asian Synod*, 39.

does it escape the Africans that the 20 heads of Roman dicasteries at the synod can speak as long as they like."[29] When bishops broke up into different language groups to discuss issues without the procedural constraints of the plenary sessions, the issues they were directed to address often did not correspond to the issues that they had indicated most concerned them.[30] Roman curial officials exercised a great deal of control over defining the topics for those conversations. They also controlled the formulation of the propositions on which the bishops were to vote for inclusion in the final documents. As a consequence, some of the bishops' strongest concerns were downplayed in the final documents or, in some cases, passed over completely.[31]

These reports about the synods create a cognitive dissonance when contrasted with John Paul's articulated vision of the church as a communion. They highlight two loci of tension. The first is the apparent conflict between the communicative ideal the pope articulated for the church and the dynamics of communication actually exercised under his authority. The second touches the relationship between the Roman curial administration and the college of bishops dispersed throughout the world. According to the bishops' complaints, the Roman Curia's mode of operation vitiated open communication between the bishops and the head of their *collegium*. If John Paul's administration of the church routinely allowed this to occur—and it appears that it did—then one must ask about the pope's understanding of communion. What does he *really* mean?

Foundations of Tension

It is important to note that the experiences just cited reflect three long-standing, polarized tensions in the church. They are not unique to John Paul II's pontificate. But when viewed in relationship to his language

29. Peter Hebblethwaite, "Everything Under Control in Rome, but not Quite," *National Catholic Reporter* 30, no. 26 (April 29, 1994): 10.

30. Thomas C. Fox, "In Tug of War at Synod, Curia Gets Last Word," *National Catholic Reporter*, May 29, 1998, 16.

31. Thomas C. Fox, "Asian Bishops Remain Politely Persistent," *National Catholic Reporter*, May 8, 1998, 13; Thomas C. Fox, "Propositions Blend Asian, Roman Views," *National Catholic Reporter* May 29, 1998, 16.

and practice of communion, they take on sharper focus. The first tension involves religious authority and its exercise. Should decisions be made at the highest level of authority (centralization)? Or should they be made at the level of competence nearest to the situation (subsidiarity)?[32] Concretely, this tension surfaced in the requests of Asian bishops for greater autonomy in taking initiatives within their cultural settings.

The second polar tension exists between the promotion of visible unity (sometimes understood as conformity to uniform modes of expression) and the impulse to pluriformity in accord with diverse cultural conditions (inculturation). This second tension is interrelated with the first. Asian and African desires for greater inculturation include by implication the desire for greater freedom to make decisions about how best to foster *communio* within their own regions. Exercising that freedom would produce a greater diversity of expression within the church.

The third tension arises between obedience as a motivation and mechanism for preserving institutional order on the one hand, and open dialogue as the means of achieving communion in understanding on the other. Explicitly, in the disciplining of dissenting theologians, and implicitly, in the administrative control of the dynamics of communication at the synods, the issue of obedience was at stake.

In the examples cited above, it appears that John Paul favored the first option of each polarity. In these cases, centralization trumps subsidiarity, visible unity (uniformity) is a higher value than cultural adaptation, and obedience supersedes dialogue.

But why? Why did John Paul take these options in these cases? And what nuance might the answer to that question lend to our own grasp of his vision of the church?

A thorough answer to these questions is beyond the scope of this essay. However, four interrelated elements in John Paul's thought can lead us to a deeper understanding: (1) his cultural heritage, (2) his intellectual formation, (3) the hermeneutic he applied to Vatican II, and (4) his perception of the context of ecclesial mission during his pontificate.

---

32. For a discussion of the reception of subsidiarity at the synods of 1967, 1969, and 1985, see John G. Johnson, "Subsidiarity and the Synod of Bishops," *The Jurist* 50, no. 2 (1990): 351–401. See also, Peter Huizing, "Subsidiarity," in *Synod 1985: An Evaluation*, ed. Giuseppe Alberigo and James Provost (*Concilium*, 1986), 118–23.

The Influence of John Paul's Cultural Heritage

Two aspects of John Paul's cultural heritage bear on his vision of church and his own role in it. First, he came from a country that had been partitioned and repartitioned by foreign powers. Catholic faith fused with Polish cultural identity in a manner that provided some stability in the face of foreign political domination. Within such a context, the person of faith, standing fast in the face of overwhelming contrary forces, understandably occupied pride of place as a Polish heroic ideal.[33] Second, as a man of letters, John Paul had imbibed the spirit of Polish Messianism, a tendency in nineteenth-century Polish poetry to interpret the sufferings of Polish Catholics through the lens of the "suffering servant."[34] As George Huntston Williams explains, these factors come together in John Paul's self-understanding as pope: "God in his providence had brought forth a Vicar of Christ out of the suffering Nation of the Messianic Poets, of the prophets and bards of Polish literature who had tried to fathom God's intentions in allowing his People, *semper fidelis*, to have been tripartitioned in the eighteenth century and bipartitioned in unspeakable ruthlessness in the twentieth century."[35]

John Paul's Intellectual Formation

John Paul II's intellectual formation also shaped his vision of the church. As Ronald Modras points out,[36] Karol Wojtyla was steeped in neoscholastic Thomism. That background continued to influence his thought even as he later engaged in dialogue with Max Scheler's phenomenology. One can see neoscholastic metaphysical realism underlying his ultimate rejection of Scheler's philosophy as insufficiently objective.[37] Significantly, Wojtyla valued Scheler's method for analyzing

33. See George Huntston Williams, *The Mind of John Paul II: Origins of His Thought and Action* (New York: Seabury, 1981), 28–29, for example, for a discussion of the place of St. Stanislaus in Polish consciousness.

34. See Williams, *Mind of John Paul II*, 23, 30, 42, 311, 314. See also the assessment in Adam Nowotny, "Fortress Catholicism: Wojtyla's Polish Roots," in *The Church in Anguish: Has the Vatican Betrayed Vatican II?* ed. Hans Küng and Leonard Swidler (San Francisco: Harper & Row, 1987), 37.

35. Williams, *Mind of John Paul II*, 314.

36. See his essay in chapter 3 of the present volume.

37. This is the assessment of Modras in Ronald Modras, "A Man of Contradictions? The Early Writings of Karol Wojtyla," in *The Church in Anguish: Has the Vatican Betrayed Vatican II?*

human experience, but rejected his appeal to feelings as a basis of moral norms. Such a foundation would be too relativistic. Objective truth, clearly grasped, provides the intellectual foundation that allows the heroic person of faith to withstand the moral decadence implied in relativistic or subjectivistic thought.

John Paul's Hermeneutics of Vatican II

A third influence on John Paul's vision of the church is his interpretation of Vatican II. In *Sources of Renewal* three distinctive lenses emerge which surface frequently in his later papal writings. First, Vatican II is primarily a pastoral council.[38] As such, its purpose is the spiritual renewal of the church, not change of structures. Second, John Paul reads the council documents according to a "principle of integration."[39] They are to be interpreted in a manner that emphasizes their continuity with prior councils.[40] Third, he found *Lumen Gentium*'s description of hierarchical distinctions giving order to ecclesial life (LG 13) to be "a concise summary of the whole" of the document.[41] One is to read the document on the church through the lens of its affirmation of hierarchical structure in its relationship to the dynamics of ecclesial communion.

The Context(s) of Ecclesial Mission

Finally, for John Paul the church has been constituted a *communio* on mission. That mission has been entrusted to it by God, but it is shaped by the context(s) in which it is to be carried out. John Paul saw the world

ed. Hans Küng and Leonard Swidler (San Francisco: Harper & Row, 1987), 42. See also, Nowotny, "Fortress Catholicism: Wojtyla's Polish Roots," 27–28; and Williams, *Mind of John Paul II*, 117–18, 131, 132.

38. Williams, *Mind of John Paul II*, 18.

39. See Williams, *Mind of John Paul II*, 39, 57. For a discussion of some of the limitations of this hermeneutic, see Modras, "A Man of Contradictions," 47.

40. For a critical appraisal of this hermeneutic from a historical perspective, see John W. O'Malley, "Vatican II: Did Anything Happen?" *Theological Studies* 67, no. 1 (2006): 3–33. For further discussion see, Stephen Schloesser, "Against Forgetting: Memory, History, Vatican II," *Theological Studies* 67, no. 2 (2006): 275–319; and Neil J. Ormerod, "'The Times They Are a Changin': A Response to O'Malley and Schloesser," *Theological Studies* 67, no. 4 (2006): 834–55.

41. Wojtyla, SR 137. I am grateful to Dr. Ronald Modras for drawing my attention to this statement.

as a battlefield in which totalitarian ideologies,[42] uncontrolled capitalism (PDV 7), and uncritical subjectivism threaten the church and all of humanity. These forces have relativized the objectively revealed values of the Gospel.[43] They have enslaved human beings to idols of their own making. The church, called to be the visible witness to the Gospel, is at war with what John Paul characterized as the prevailing "culture of death."[44] It must therefore be a clear "sign of contradiction" to the spirit of the age.

Implications for Understanding John Paul's Vision

These four factors form a matrix of meanings from within which John Paul viewed the church. Understanding their interrelationships will give us deeper insight into his ecclesiology. It will also help make sense of the tensions noted above.

Growing up under communist oppression gave Karol Wojtyla an appreciation for the ability of the church to sustain moral integrity and clarity of Polish national identity in the face of opposition. Strains of Polish Messianic thought gave meaning to hardship, casting the sufferings of a nation (and a pope) in the form of the redemptive mission of Christ. His introduction to neoscholastic metaphysics provided a philosophical framework for justifying claims to objective truth while revelation supplied a content deserving of such justification. The synthesis of these elements provided a stable worldview to counter the assaults of communist and other anti-Christian ideologies. And the encounter with Scheler's phenomenology provided him with a personalist vocabulary that could mediate the objective, revealed truths of faith to a wider (non-neoscholastic) world.

These aspects of John Paul's personal formation shaped his reading of the council. Interpreting the council in terms of the "principle of integration" helps to preserve the stability of church teaching over time. This emphasis coheres with John Paul's concern for objective truth.

---

42. CL 40; John Paul II, EAf, 117; EAm 71; Pope John Paul II, *"Fides et Ratio," Origins* 28, no. 19 (October 22, 1998): 46; Pope John Paul II, *"Tertio Millenio Adveniente," Origins* 24, no. 24 (November 24, 1994): 36.

43. EAm 53; ibid., 7, 52; VS 32, 34, 106.

44. CL 38; EAm 62; EAs 35, 38.

Vocabulary may change, but substance remains the same. Continuity is essential to maintaining the integrity of the identity of the church. And the church's hierarchical structure and institutional teaching authority provide stability and guard against distortion of that identity.

John Paul's perspective on the larger world—the context of mission—also comes into play in his sense of the church and of his own role as its leader. The pope feared that the pernicious effects of a relativistic, fractious zeitgeist had already infected the church. He saw evidence of this in the intra-ecclesial divisions and disagreements following the council. He therefore set out to restore visible, effective unity in conformity with right doctrine by exhorting to spiritual renewal and by disciplining those who strayed.

Against this background it becomes easier to make sense of the cognitive dissonances mentioned above. John Paul perceived theological disagreements about matters on which the magisterium had previously made pronouncements to be reflections of a disobedient, alien spirit. It is important to note here that John Paul II had no cultural category for dealing creatively with "loyal dissent" within the church. To him, dissenting voices threatened the identity of the church and the unity of the *communio* because they threatened the integrity of the tradition. They must be silenced.[45] Even those bishops calling for greater regional autonomy, well-intentioned though they may have been, appeared to him to be running the risk of relativizing the integrity of the church's traditions. Their initiatives could fracture visible unity by conformity to the dictates of their local cultures. It fell to him and his allies (like-minded bishops and the curial administration at his disposal) to restore what had been lost to postconciliar exuberance and to preserve the integrity of the church.

In his response to the perceived threats of his pontificate, we gain some understanding of John Paul's reasons for resolving the long-standing polar tensions in the church as he did. This, in turn, gives us deeper insight into his operative vision of the church. In order to preserve institutional communion in faith and practice, he judged it preferable to

45. See, for example, Peter Hebblethwaite, *Pope John Paul II and the Church* (Kansas City, MO: Sheed and Ward, 1995), 75–76, 205, 258; Williams, *Mind of John Paul II*, 214, 298–99.

enforce obedience to the magisterium rather than tolerate open debate and dialogue. He saw it as desirable to promote visible unity even if that meant diminishment of legitimate diversity. He found it more expedient to oversee decision making through a central administration rather than to trust the judgment of bishops in their own regions. In John Paul's operative vision, for the sake of ecclesial unity in the face of a world hostile to the Gospel, it was necessary to manage discourse within the church. All of this despite his extensive writings on the church as a *communio* and on the necessity of dialogue for building up that communion in faith. Thus, although his preferred idiom was that of *communio*, it becomes apparent that his *operative* vision was often hierarchical, institutional, and authoritarian.

Conclusion

This essay has attempted to gain deeper insight into Pope John Paul II's vision of the church by probing beyond his articulated statements about the church into a point of tension in his actual practice of leadership. This approach has brought to light an operative emphasis in his ecclesiology that could be missed or undervalued if one were to attend only to his written statements about the church as communion. Such an approach is useful; it can serve as a corrective to presentations of his ecclesial vision based solely on his writings. But it is also limited. There were many other areas of tension in his pontificate and there were many moments of profound pastoral wisdom. A more complete exposition of John Paul's understanding of the church will need to give greater attention to both.

6

"Defending the Faith": The Changing Landscape of Church Teaching Authority and Catholic Theology

Gerard Mannion

Introduction

This chapter explores developments and events relating to the official understanding and exercise of the teaching office of the church (i.e., magisterium*) during the pontificate of John Paul II, as well as exploring changing perceptions of the role of the Catholic theologian in the same period. What, if anything, was distinctive about developments pertaining to such during the pontificate of John Paul II?[1] The chapter seeks to consider a number of key representative documents, events, and incidents in order to illustrate and chart the story of the changing landscape of magisterium and the changing understanding of the role of the Catholic theologian between 1978 and 2005, an era which witnessed growing tensions between the Vatican and many Catholic theologians throughout the world. We will briefly touch upon the still very open debate concerning whether or not all these developments should be attributed to the leadership of John Paul II himself, or to particularly

---

* Note that when the term magisterium is preceded by the definite article (i.e. "the magisterium"), this denotes an understanding of magisterium that centers upon the role of the "official" church authorities, particularly Rome. Numerous debates enter the fray here. Suffice to signify here that they ultimately concern the fundamental notion of what (and not "who") magisterium is and who can and should exercise it. Although not entirely satisfactory, the term "the official magisterium" will be employed here when referring to such conceptions of magisterium so as to distinguish them from broader understandings.

1. For a brief historical survey, cf. Michael Fahey, "Concepts of Authority in Twentieth-Century Theology: An Ecumenical Overview," *Science et Esprit* 59, no. 2 (2007): 405–19. For a collection of texts on various topics, cf. Gerard Mannion, Richard Gaillardetz, Jan Kerkhofs, and Kenneth Wilson, eds., *Readings in Church Authority: Gifts and Challenges for Contemporary Catholicism* (Aldershot: Ashgate Press, 2003).

78

prominent curial officials, examining John Paul II's own statements and actions of relevance along the way.[2]

The Changing Landscape of Magisterium

Numerous studies rehearse the developments of how (or, for some, whether) Vatican II marked a period of opening to the world for the church. Attendant with such an opening came a new era where a degree of theological innovation and new inquiry were not simply tolerated but actively encouraged. The fruits of Vatican II were also very much the fruits of such theological "daring." It appeared that the church, by the close of the council, had come a long way since the normative understandings of magisterium and of the role of the Catholic theologian shaped by the pontificate of Pius IX and Vatican I, the backlash to the modernist crisis at the dawn of the twentieth century, and Pius XII's denunciation of the "new theology" in *Humani Generis*. Vatican II was supposed to usher in a new, more collaborative and communicative understanding of magisterium and also of the relationship between Rome and Catholic theologians. But somewhere along the way this new dawn did not quite materialize in the hopeful and cordial fashion that many of the council fathers had envisioned.

By the time John Paul II had settled into his pontificate, theologians were already coming into regular conflict with Rome, and the tone of documents issuing forth from the official magisterium was becoming more imperatival again in a way that was partly reminiscent of the

2. Key studies include Francis A. Sullivan, *Magisterium: Teaching Authority in the Roman Catholic Church* (Dublin: Gill and Macmillan, 1985) and Richard A. Gaillardetz, *Teaching with Authority* (Collegeville, MN: Liturgical Press, 1997). See also, Kenneth Wilson, ed., "Magisterium: the Church and its Teaching," chapter 2 of Mannion et al., *Readings in Church Authority*, 91–145; Michael A. Fahey's ecumenical summary, "Magisterium," chapter 29 of *The Routledge Companion to the Christian Church*, eds. Gerard Mannion and Lewis M. Mudge (London and New York: Routledge, 2008), 524–35; Yves Congar's two influential essays on the subject, "A Semantic History of the Term 'Magisterium'" and "A Brief History of the Forms of the Magisterium and Its Relations with Scholars," both now in eds. Charles E. Curran and Richard A. McCormick, *The Magisterium and Morality*, Readings in Moral Theology, no. 3 (New York: Paulist Press, 1982), 297–313 and 314–31. A most accessible introduction is Richard R. Gaillardetz, *By What Authority? A Primer on Scripture, the Magisterium and the Sense of the Faithful* (Collegeville, MN: Liturgical Press, 2003).

preconciliar days and yet also novel, given all the ecclesial and wider cultural and political events that had transpired since.[3]

From the late 1960s onward, many opposed to elements of how Vatican II was being interpreted and implemented throughout the church increasingly began to make their voices heard. The controversy over *Humanae Vitae* of 1968 and what some perceived as open rebellion against the official magisterium that ensued, along with the resignations from active ministry of a large number of priests, led to a hardening of attitudes among a number of those in positions of power, teaching, and influence in the church. Increasing and, to many, retrogressive steps against theological dissent were to follow.

In 1972 a number of those who wished to see Vatican II interpreted and implemented in a very different fashion set up the journal *Communio* (particularly to counter the viewpoints regularly expressed in the post-conciliar journal, *Concilium*, established in 1965—Joseph Ratzinger later remarking that it was as much a program as anything else).[4] Interestingly, this new journal, unlike its predecessor, appeared with a Polish edition from the outset.[5]

Postconciliar developments from the grass roots up to the level of national episcopal conferences (such as in the Netherlands) had set alarm bells ringing in certain quarters. Many believed the pace of reform was being handled badly (particularly in the case of the liturgy) or indeed was moving not only too fast but also in the wrong direction altogether.

Much of the blame for these perceived ills was laid at the door of theologians by disgruntled curial officials, bishops, and Catholic pressure groups of a more conservative ecclesial outlook and disposition, some sections of the media, and theologians of a different ilk to those perceived to be liberal. Their number would increasingly have the ear

3. The themes covered here are complementary to those that concern numerous other chapters in this volume, but particularly those on moral theology, collegiality, liberation theology, and other faiths. Where particular topics have been dealt with in sufficient detail elsewhere, we will, by and large, seek to avoid repetition here.

4. Joseph Ratzinger, "*Communio: Ein Programm*," *Internationale katholische Zeitschrift Communio* 21 (1992): 454–63. English trans., "Communio: A Program," *Communio* 19, no. 3 (1992): 436–49.

5. Peter Hebblethwaite, "Between Lucerne and Krakow: European Pluralism and the Church's *Magisterium*" in Karl-Joschef Kuschel and Hermann Häring, *Hans Küng: New Horizons for Faith and Thought*, 65–78 (London: SCM, 1993), 74.

of Paul VI and his advisers. Documents such as *Mysterium Ecclesiae* (1973, issued in particular reaction to Hans Küng's 1970 book, *Infallible*) were released, which again sought to set definite limits to theological and philosophical inquiry in the church. New investigations were instigated against both individual theologians and indeed specific approaches and methods of theology, most notably the theology of liberation (which would be investigated throughout the 1970s and 1980s), but also, in particular, against theologians who advocated further reforms in the church and new formulations and interpretations of key doctrines.

Tensions, then, were already to the fore during the latter stages of Pope Paul VI's pontificate. The International Theological Commission (ITC) had sought to offer some reflections and guidance in 1976 in twelve theses "On the Relationship between the Ecclesiastical *Magisterium* and Theology,"[6] which perhaps brought the need for further consideration of this relationship into sharper focus. Paul VI's eventual long-term successor would take charge of providing some solutions to difficulties in such relations. But the ITC would gradually become ever more subservient to the Congregation for the Doctrine of the Faith (CDF), and respected theologians such as Karl Rahner would resign from it as a result of its increasing subordination and consequent ineffectiveness. Hence, as one commentator put it in 1993, "the battle-lines of the future were drawn up in the 1970s."[7]

1978–83: A Reassertion of "Roman" Authority?

The election of John Paul II in 1978, and his later appointment of Joseph Ratzinger as prefect of the CDF in 1981, marked further defining moments of how magisterium would be understood and exercised, particularly vis-à-vis Catholic theologians, in the closing decades of the twentieth century.

Let us first explore this period through the eyes of one commentator who was very close to the events as they unfolded and whose writings communicate the feeling and reactions in the church at the time, as opposed to later reflections and analyses that benefit from hindsight. Peter

---

6. See *Gregorianum* 57 (1976): 548–63.
7. Hebblethwaite, "Between Lucerne and Krakow," 75.

Hebblethwaite, a veteran "Vaticanologist," evocatively opened his account of the changing face of magisterium in this early period of John Paul's papacy by juxtaposing three events that took place in Rome on the same day, December 15, 1979. The final one was an address by John Paul II on the role of theologians in the church delivered to the Gregorian University. The first was the signing of the minutes of a colloquium between the Belgian Dominican theologian Edward Schillebeeckx and members of the CDF. The meeting had been convened to put serious charges forward about the content of the first volume of Schillebeeckx's (eventual) trilogy on Christology. The second was the then-prefect of the CDF, Franjo Seper's, signing of the declaration that led to the removal of the license to teach, and hence official status as a Catholic theologian, of the Swiss theologian Father Hans Küng, who was based at Tübingen University in Germany.

So, by the end of 1979, not much more than a year into the pontificate of John Paul II, much debate and attention had already been focused upon the subject of the (official) magisterium and the relation between it and Catholic theologians.[8] Before Christmas that year, not only would John Paul II have provided some further insight into his own understanding of the role of the Catholic theologian in an address given at the Catholic University of America, but the media would focus attention upon the investigations into the work and standing of three prominent Catholic theologians—Jacques Pohier, OP (condemned for his book *Quand je dis Dieu*), being the third[9] in addition to Schillebeeckx[10] and Küng. The latter had been under investigation for the majority of his career, being particularly under suspicion for his ecclesiology in the late 1960s

---

8. Here space does not permit a detailed treatment of individual cases, although many excellent and illuminating studies are already in existence. I explore, in both a critical and constructive light, the wider ramifications of the debates relating to magisterium in this period and beyond in a forthcoming study, *A Teaching that Learns?*

9. Les Editions du Seuil, 1977. Cf. CDF, "Declaration regarding the book of Rev. Jacques Pohier *Quand je dis Dieu*" (April 3, 1979), *AAS* 71 (1979): 446–47. The aftermath of his condemnation is movingly recounted in Jacques Pohier, *God in Fragments* (London: SCM, 1985). Pohier was banned from teaching, presiding at the Eucharist, and also from preaching, the latter being a particularly harsh penalty for one called to the Dominican Order ("of Preachers") to bear.

10. Cf. Edward Schillebeeckx, *I am a Happy Theologian* (London: SCM, 1993), especially 32–40.

and his views on papal infallibility in the early 1970s prior to his official condemnation in relation to a wide and, as numerous commentators have illustrated, largely inaccurate or unjust list of charges in 1979.[11] In fact, Küng's major "crime," it would appear, was "a contempt for the *Magisterium* of the Church."[12] News would also emerge of ongoing investigation into further scholars, such as Charles E. Curran and John J. McNeill, SJ,[13] in the United States and Leonardo Boff in Brazil.[14]

The title of Hebblethwaite's book, *The New Inquisition?*,[15] will no doubt seem a touch dramatic to some today, but rereading it one must be mindful of the ecclesial atmosphere that the events which it relays gave rise to all those years ago while most of the wider Catholic world and beyond were still focusing upon this smiling, articulate, energetic, and peripatetic pontiff "from a far country."[16] Hebblethwaite's title was carefully and deliberately chosen to capture the chill that had descended in relations between Rome and Catholic theologians. Hebblethwaite, who had been based in Rome for some years and had impeccable sources throughout the Vatican and surrounding environs, was in no doubt that behind the condemnations of these three priest-theologians stood the full support of the new pope. The overwhelming majority of evidence would appear to suggest he is correct. In Hebblethwaite's opinion, Paul VI's control over what was going on in the Vatican may not have been particularly tight in his final years,[17] an ironic parallel with the latter years of John Paul II himself:[18] "Paul VI may have allowed the

11. Among many sources, cf. Hans Küng, *My Struggle for Freedom: Memoirs*, trans. John Bowden (London: Continuum, 2003).

12. Cf. CDF, "Declaration regarding certain aspects of the theological doctrine of Professor Hans Küng–*Christi ecclesia*" (December 15, 1979), *AAS* 72 (1980): 90–92; see also, Hebblethwaite, "Between Lucerne and Krakow," 75.

13. Cf. John J. McNeill, *Both Feet Planted Firmly in Midair: My Spiritual Journey* (Louisville, KY: Westminster John Knox Press, 1998).

14. See Mario Aguiler's essay in chapter 9 of the present volume and cf., also, Harvey Cox, *The Silencing of Leonardo Boff: The Vatican and the Future of World Christianity* (London: Collins Flame, 1988) and Rosino Gibellini, *The Liberation Theology Debate* (London: SCM, 1987).

15. Peter Hebblethwaite, *The New Inquisition? The Case of Edward Schillebeeckx and Hans Küng* (London: Fount, 1980), 9.

16. Cf. Mary Craig, *Man from a Far Country: a Portrait of Pope John Paul II* (London: Hodder and Stoughton, 1979).

17. Hebblethwaite, *New Inquisition?*, 40.

18 See also, ibid., 105–7, esp. 106.

CDF to start proceedings, but none were ever concluded. Under John Paul II the tempo has been speeded up, the workload increased, and there are no inhibitions about concluding. These differences depend partly on temperament and partly on previous convictions."[19] In a later essay still, Hebblethwaite concludes:

> We come now to the centre of the discussion. European theology is plu-
> ral, or it does not exist. Yet in central and Eastern Europe, *magisterium* is
> singular. It is most commonly referred to as *the magisterium* as though there
> were only one form of magisterium, the Episcopal or (in fact) papal *mag-
> isterium*. I will maintain that this "doctrine" (or *theologoumenon*) is charac-
> teristic of the pontificate of Pope John Paul II. It was not found in the
> pontificate of Paul VI. And this difference between the two popes of the
> late twentieth century explains why Hans Küng, though frequently criti-
> cized under Paul VI, had to wait until the pontificate of John Paul II to
> be "condemned."[20]

As Hebblethwaite observes, the Schillebeeckx case, in particular, brought such international protest that the actual issue under consideration of Christology was soon pushed into the background as the debate widened "to include academic freedom, the relationship between theologians and the *magisterium* (or the pastoral office of the Church), the spirit and methods by which theological conflicts should be resolved and, finally, the worrying direction taken by the pontificate of John Paul II" itself. He concludes: "One issue can unlock all issues."[21] Indeed. The legacy, i.e., the reception, implementation, and fulfillment, of Vatican II itself already seemed at stake,[22] and this debate about the "authentic" interpretation of the council, indeed all such issues, would remain constant topics of discussion throughout the pontificate of John Paul II.

Thus the tone for John Paul's stewardship of the church had been set. Following Vatican II, the Holy Office, as the CDF was previously known, had seen its influence, power, and central importance much

---

19. Ibid., 106.

20. Peter Hebblethwaite, "Between Lucerne and Krakow, 69.

21. Hebblethwaite, *New Inquisition?*, 27.

22. Ibid., 28. Hebblethwaite here means in the eyes of Dutch protesters, although this assessment spread rapidly and would become an increasingly accurate one during the coming years of the pontificate.

diminished thanks to the conciliar reforms and Paul VI's further changes, such as the establishment of the ITC and his reliance upon the Secretariat of State rather than the Holy Office for much of his reign. From early on during the papacy of John Paul II, the CDF would return center stage and eventually reassert itself as the most important curial department. Documents would increasingly be released by the official church, most often at the behest of the CDF, which once again appeared keen to assert the clear and absolute authority of the church's "official" (or "central") magisterium, and particularly of the papacy, in matters of faith and morals (even, on many occasions, in matters beyond these parameters). None of this could have taken place without the facilitation and active approval of the new pope.

To many across the church, it would come to appear that the lines of orthodoxy were being drawn more rigidly once again as theologians were expected to give their faithful assent and obedient service to the church's official teaching as defined by the interpretations prevalent in the Rome of the day. Many scholars believed that the very definition of magisterium and/or of its remit were being rewritten here. During John Paul's pontificate, documents would be issued from Rome that sought to define what was legitimate and permissible inquiry for scholars and what was not. Much debate eventually surrounded the theological interpretation of the so-called non-definitive magisterium and eventually that of what constitutes "definitive" teaching.

What particularly upset or met with the indignation of many was the modus operandi of these investigations of theologians, which were usually secretive and involved questionable methods of interpretation as well as presentation. Even the case for the defense on behalf of any suspect theologian was put by someone unknown to them and in a hearing during which they would not be present, being at that stage oblivious to the whole process. Needless to say, the accused would also not learn who had tabled the accusations in the first place. From the outset of this period in 1979, there were protests about fundamental human rights and due process of justice being ignored within the church.[23] Further flaws in the method of investigation would appear on many occasions. In particular, it appeared that passages from differing parts of the works

---

23. Cf. ibid., 40 and passim.

of the theologians under scrutiny were being taken out of context, lumped together, and presented as meaning something that their authors argued they patently did not mean. Worse still, some theologians were condemned or at least publicly criticized for things they had *not* said or had insufficiently emphasized, even if their works did not concern such doctrines or issues. Let us turn to consider how far such charges were circumstantial and how far they tallied with the ecclesial vision of the new pope.

Interpreting John Paul II on Theology and Magisterium

By 1963 Karol Wojtyla was convinced not only of the church's need for theologians, but indeed for *more* theologians, according to his lifelong friend Mieczyslaw Malinski, who was encouraged to progress from his philosophical studies to take up theology at the Angelicum by the then–auxiliary archbishop of Krakow. Poland had enough philosophers and now needed good theologians, Wojtyla told him, "And there's a new subject that is just beginning to develop as a result of the [Second Vatican] Council and is sure to become very important, and that is ecclesiology. I would like you to study it." [24]

Of course, it is always difficult to assess the mind of a pope on any given subject, so we would do well to consider but a few brief examples of what Karol Wojtyla's attitudes on such matters were both before his election to Peter's chair and in the years immediately following. As suggested, the evidence would support the contention that John Paul II believed in a strong central authority for the church in Rome, one in which the CDF played a leading role, and a church in which the teaching and writings of Catholic theologians came under close scrutiny. Both as cardinal (1967) in Krakow and as newly installed pope, this philosopher advocated loyalty and fidelity to the central magisterium, proffering (as one might not be surprised, given his own theological formation during the years of Pius XII) what commentators have deemed to be a particularly Polish take on the understanding of the role of the Catholic theologian as laid down by *Humani Generis*: one of faithful explication of

---

24. Mieczyslaw Malinski, *Pope John Paul II: The Life of Karol Wojtyla*, trans., P. S. Falla (New York: Crossroad, 1981), 149.

official teaching, where the core function was apologetic and where dissent and public disagreement were not viable options.

Pope John Paul provided a further indication of his appreciation of the value of theologians, but also, and in some detail, his understanding of the nature and limits of their role, in an Address to Presidents of Catholic Colleges and Universities (delivered at the Catholic University of America on October 7, 1979).[25] While upholding the necessity of scientific rigor, John Paul also, as Hebblethwaite observed, indicated a shift away from the priority of dialogue so dear to Paul VI.[26] Hebblethwaite is also in no doubt that John Paul II's attitudes toward magisterium and Catholic theologians since becoming pope reflected those he held beforehand as "His views on the subject [of theologians] were clear and oft-repeated."[27] One particularly illuminating document here was a 1971 address by Karol Wojtyla to the Polish Congress of Theology, "Theology and Theologians in the Postconcilar Church," which is almost exclusively concerned with the relation between theologians and "the" magisterium. Thus not only is this a subject matter which, I suggest, permeates Pope John Paul's pontificate in its entirety, but also, and regardless of one's assessment of the outcomes and implications of this for the church, constitutes one of his most significant and enduring legacies for the Catholic world.[28]

Indeed as early as the 1971 date of that address, Hebblethwaite contends, this was already *the* central question for Karol Wojtyla: "it obsessed him."[29] In that address, Wojtyla was already setting down his understanding of the *functional* role of the Catholic theologian as being

25. A contrast also discussed in Hebblethwaite, *New Inquisition?*, 25, 27, and chapter 6, "John Paul II and Theology," 103–28. The address can be found in the *AAS* 71 (1979): 1264.

26. Hebblethwaite, *New Inquisition?*, 25–27. On Paul VI and dialogue, cf. Mannion, *Ecclesiology and Postmodernity: Questions for the Church in Our Time* (Collegeville, MN: Liturgical Press, 2007) 105–23.

27. Hebblethwaite, *New Inquisition?*, 106ff, discussing Henryk Nowacki, *"La Teologia nella Chiesa postconiliare"* in *Studia in Honorem Caroli Wojtyla*, an issue of *Angelicum*, 56 (1979): 239–60.

28. Karol Wojtyla, *"Teologia I Theologowie w Kosciele Posoborowym,"* a commentary upon which was provided by Ronald Modras, "Solidarity and Opposition in a Pluralistic Church," *Commonweal* (September 14, 1979): 493–95, and is also discussed in Hebblethwaite, *New Inquisition?*, 106–7 and in "Between Lucerne and Krakow," 73–74.

29. Hebblethwaite, *New Inquisition?*, 107 and also Hebblethwaite, "Between Lucerne and Krakow," 75.

one of defending and teaching the faith as articulated by Rome: popes and bishops teach, theologians guard and interpret and explicate. The deposit of faith, of revelation, should not be tampered with. Anything more innovative risks confusing and alienating the faithful. Anyone who has read the church documents pertaining to the relation between theologians and "the magisterium" that issued throughout the middle period of John Paul II's pontificate will find these sentiments very familiar.

And, of course, such ideas were not, as Hebblethwaite further shows, very original—they echoed those of Wojtyla's sometime mentor, Cardinal Stefan Wyszyński who had particular contempt for the journal *Concilium* and its contributors.[30] He was far from being alone in such attitudes. The situation in the Poland of the Eastern Bloc at that time led Polish church leaders to foster unity through uniformity and fidelity to fundamentals. Thus a united front against the hostile atheism of the pseudo-communist state could better be preserved. Furthermore, many Polish theologians felt that, rather than embracing the fashions of modern Western theology, it was farther east and to the common Slav inheritance of the Orthodox communions that Polish scholars should be looking for inspiration.[31] Hebblethwaite contends that the busy bishop, Wojtyla, was not reading much contemporary theology by the 1970s in any case.[32] Such sentiments are echoed across other chapters in this present volume and elsewhere: Wojtyla was not a "professional theologian" per se,[33] yet he had received a considerable theological education and was certainly highly competent in the discipline. His dissertation at the Angelicum had been on St. John of the Cross and had been directed by Réginald Garrigou-Lagrange— both significant factors that would color his later theological understanding, along with the fact that this was undertaken from 1946–48.

30. Hebblethwaite, *New Inquisition?*, 108.

31. Cf. ibid., 108–9, and, for further brief contemporaneous perspectives on Wojtyla's Eastern Catholicism, see Modras, "Solidarity and Opposition," 494–95; Paul Thibaud, "The New Face of Spiritual Authority," also in *Commonweal* (September 14, 1979): 489–92; and, in the same issue, Edward Cuddy, "The Rebel Function in Catholicism," 495–97.

32. Hebblethwaite, *New Inquisition?*, 109, and see also, on the extension of this "Polish" theological outlook to the universal church, 123,

33. Note a somewhat different line was initially taken by Hebblethwaite both on this and the preceding point above in his earlier work, *Year of Three Popes*, 172. One of Karol Wojtyla's lifelong friends, however, also observes that he was not a theologian, although at Vatican II "he showed increasing ability to cope with theological problems," Malinski, *Pope John Paul II*, 169.

Wojtyla had served on the preparatory commission of one of the schemata that eventually flowered into Vatican II's *Gaudium et Spes*. Some credit him with putting forward the "compromise" form the document would take, i.e., its title as a *pastoral* constitution.[34] He also presided over the commission that produced the final declaration of the 1969 extraordinary synod of bishops that responded to the fallout from *Humanae Vitae*, made numerous interventions at the 1971 synod on ministry, and authored a position paper on the theological implications of evangelization for the 1974 synod on evangelization.[35] Although, as evident from his very first encyclical (March 4, 1979), he embraced the anthropological and personalist turn in modern theology, he never departed from his understanding of the theologian vis-à-vis "the" magisterium, indeed, such sentiments were also clearly present in that first encyclical, *Redemptor Hominis*.[36]

John Paul II continued to set the tone for the rest of his papacy with the release, on April 15, 1979, of *Sapientia Christiana* (On Ecclesiastical Faculties and Universities), an apostolic constitution which would oblige all who teach any aspect of the Catholic faith or morals in Catholic schools to obtain a mandate from the relevant chancellor (article 27, n. 1, n. 2), adding that they required the *nihil obstat* from the Vatican itself before they could either attain the rank of full professor or obtain a permanent contract.[37] This document made it clear that faithfulness, indeed deference, to the (official) magisterium was paramount, article 26, n. 2 stating that "Those who teach matters touching on faith and morals are to be conscious of their duty to carry out their work in full communion with the authentic Magisterium of the Church, above all, with that of the Roman Pontiff."[38]

---

34. Cf. Hebblethwaite, *Year of Three Popes*, 168, see also, Malinski, *Pope John Paul II*, especially 148–55 and 162–79, and brief personal reflections in John Paul II, *Crossing the Threshold*, 156–60. Others suggest his role in relation to the document has been exaggerated.

35. Cf. *Year of Three Popes*, 177. For surveys, see also, Ladislaus Örsy, *The Church: Learning and Teaching: Magisterium, Assent, Dissent, Academic Freedom* (Wilmington, DE: Michael Glazier, 1987); Michael Walsh, *John Paul II* (London: HarperCollins, 1994).

36. Cf., in particular, *Redemptor Hominis* 19. http://www.vatican.va/holy_father/john_paul_ii/encyclicals/documents/hf_jp-ii_enc_04031979_redemptor-hominis_en.html.

37. http://www.vatican.va/holy_father/john_paul_ii/apost_constitutions/documents/hf_jp-ii_apc_15041979_sapientia-christiana_en.html.

38. Ibid.

Addressing the plenary session of the ITC on October 26, 1979, John Paul left his listeners in no doubt that theologians teach not by their own authority but under a mission and mandate from the church itself—apologetics is their task.[39] The aforementioned address to the Gregorian University of December 15, 1979, spoke of "a loyal and docile openness to the suggestions of the *magisterium*."[40] Other speeches and addresses followed a similar pattern. One laudatory article of 1981 praised John Paul II's assertive stance, suggesting that he was ahead of, rather than behind, most intellectuals of the day.[41] In 1982 John Paul promulgated definitive statutes for the ITC in his Motu Proprio, *Tredecim Anni* (August 6, 1982)[42] which, in the opinion of many, further subordinated the ITC itself to the control of the CDF, thereby undermining the original intention of the fathers of the synod of bishops in 1967, which had called for the establishment of the ITC.[43] For example, as Francis Sullivan states, "The three qualifications mentioned by the Synod for the choice of members of the ITC were 'profound wisdom, distinguished repute, and outstanding scientific formation'; in the statutes the qualities required are 'eminent knowledge, prudence and fidelity toward the magisterium of the Church.'"[44] In effect, the ITC could publish nothing of its deliberations without papal and CDF approval (its president also being the prefect of the latter). Also in October 1982, speaking to the Bishops of Northern England, he offered an unequivocal summary of his position on these matters.[45]

---

39. http://www.vatican.va/holy_father/john_paul_ii/speeches/1979/october/documents/hf_jp-ii_spe_19791026_comm-teologica-intern_lt.html (accessed February 1, 2008), cf. Hebblethwaite, *New Inquisition?*, 114–20, esp. 120.

40. The passage in question is paragraph 2. See http://www.vatican.va/holy_father/john_paul_ii/speeches/1979/december/documents/hf_jp-ii_spe_19791215_universita-gregoriana_it.html (accessed February 8, 2008), trans. from the Italian by Hebblethwaite, *New Inquisition?*, 121, here referring to the Jesuit Order and Gregorian University in particular but, in the light of other events that day, with obvious, wider implications.

41. James V. Schall, "Of Inquisitors and Pontiffs: Criticizing John Paul II," *Homiletic and Pastoral Review* (June 1981).

42. *AAS* 74 (1982): 1201–5.

43. See Francis A. Sullivan, *Magisterium*, 174–218.

44. Ibid., 175.

45. "Address of Pope John Paul II to the Bishops of Northern England" on their *Ad Limina Apostolorum* visit (October 29, 1982), http://www.vatican.va/holy_father/john_paul_ii/speeches/1982/october/documents/hf_jp-ii_spe_19821029_nord-inghilterra-ad-limina_en.html, par. 6 (accessed February 1, 2008).

Perhaps a key question here comes to the fore: Was what began to take place in the church from the outset of John Paul II's papacy a conscious and well-planned strategy to rein in the perceived "liberal theological establishment"? Against the incredulous assertion of Archbishop Jérome Hamer, then of the CDF, that the proximity to one another of the 1979 denunciations was "pure coincidence," Hebblethwaite remarked in the immediate aftermath of the Schillebeeckx and Küng affairs, "To denounce one theologian may be a misfortune, to take on two in a week looks like an act of deliberate policy," despite further repeated denials of such by CDF and wider Vatican figures at the time.[46] For example, the "errors" that Küng was being accused of had been around for some time.[47] Indeed, by the middle period of this pontificate, which we shall shortly discuss, it seemed clear that there must have been a deliberate and well-planned strategy in place within the Vatican.

One of the most evocative statements that lends support to such a thesis is from a fellow traveler of the *Communio* project itself, which commends the Vatican's treatment of Küng and contrasts John Paul II's "flying start" very favorably in comparison to the perceived (by implication) failings of the previous regime: "John Paul II is safeguarding nothing less than the fundamental substance of Catholic faith. No one can deny that this was urgent after years of dogmatic, moral and liturgical permissiveness . . . Perhaps it is inevitable that the one should give the impression of Hercules cleaning out the Augean stables."[48]

So Pope John Paul II had, from the outset, embarked upon an exercise of the papal office where the "safeguarding of the faith," more specifically of doctrine itself, would be of preeminent importance and against all perceived foes, whether outside or inside the Roman Catholic Church itself. Thus Vatican II would henceforth be interpreted in a narrower sense as equally giving priority to and mandating such a defense of the faith.[49] And this despite the views of many (the earlier Hebblethwaite included) that John Paul would be steadfastly faithful to the open spirit of

46. Hebblethwaite, *New Inquisition?*, 78, and see also, 102, 123.

47. Ibid., 79. See also, Hebblethwaite, "Between Lucerne and Krakow," 75–76.

48. Hans Urs von Balthasar, cited in Hebblethwaite, *New Inquisition?*, 99; cf. also, Hebblethwaite, "Between Lucerne and Krakow," 71–77.

49. Cf. Hebblethwaite, *New Inquisition?*, 104, who draws attention to John Paul II's address to U.S. bishops in Chicago on October 5, 1979.

Vatican II, as suggested by his address the morning following his election.[50] A later Hebblethwaite was perhaps among the first, but was certainly not the last, to draw parallels with the Modernist crisis in the early twentieth century, both eras being characterized by a widely popular pope presiding over a period where theological innovation was frowned upon and individual scholars became scrutinized and condemned.[51]

The Triumph of Catholic Neoorthodoxy? 1984–94

By the mid-1980s it was obvious to scholars in the field that significant changes concerning the understanding and exercise of magisterium had taken place, and studies and surveys of such began to appear. In 1987 Ladislaus Örsy published an insightful article that captured superbly the climate which existed at that time in terms of relations between the official magisterium and Catholic theologians. But at its close Örsy, somewhat modestly, mentioned that his survey was "really an incomplete report on a scenery where deep changes have taken place."[52] Thus it was at this time that the particular issue of dissent from official teaching itself became a major issue.[53] It was also in this period that the clashes with liberation theology came to a head and resulted in the documentation and condemnations discussed in greater detail in chapter 8. It was the same period when Charles Curran was deprived of his license to teach in a Catholic institution and removed from his post at the Catholic University of America.[54] Later in this period, the outreach to homosexual Christians of Father Robert Nugent and Sister Jeannine Gramick was further condemned, as were these ministers themselves,[55] and John McNeil not only found himself once again reprimanded but this time

50. Hebblethwaite, *Year of Three Popes*, 186ff.

51. Hebblethwaite, *New Inquisition?*, 124.

52. Ladislaus Örsy, "Magisterium: Assent and Dissent," *Theological Studies* 48 (1987): 473–97, at p. 496. The same year saw the publication of a lengthier study by Örsy, *The Church: Learning and Teaching*.

53. Cf. Charles E. Curran and Richard A. McCormick, *Dissent in the Church*, vol. 6 of Readings in Moral Theology (New York: Paulist Press, 1991).

54. Cf. Curran and McCormick, *Dissent in the Church*, part 5, 357–539, and also Charles E. Curran, *Loyal Dissent* (Washington, DC: Georgetown University Press, 2006), *passim*.

55. CDF, "Notification regarding Sister Jeannine Gramick, SSND, and Father Robert Nugent, SDS," (May 31, 1999), *AAS* 91 (1999): 821–82; and also in *Origins* 29 (July 29, 1999): 133–36.

expelled from the Jesuit order. The issue of women being admitted to the ordained ministry was declared a closed question in this period and those such as Lavinia Byrne who refused to accept it as such were similarly censured.[56] Religious pluralism and the related debates concerning inculturation and complementarity of different faiths became issues that would preoccupy Rome well into the twenty-first century. The clear attempt to impose greater controls over Catholic faculties in church-linked universities and the question of priests being involved in active politics became further contentious issues, as were the numerous attempts to announce closure on further disputed doctrinal and moral questions.

In many ways this was the decisive period, when struggles between Catholic theologians and the (official) magisterium might have gone either way, as much support was mustered on behalf of individual scholars, methods, and movements under fire. Instead, it marks the decisive period primarily because the changes brought about in this period transformed the church and the wider understanding of magisterium throughout it, as the new official understanding and exercise of magisterium became more normative and accepted.

Protests about human rights within the church and about justice for theologians moved gradually from being the focus of the mass media and indeed of mass demonstrations by ordinary people and campus students, to more self-selecting circles of largely Catholic theologians with a particular research interest in the more specialized niche areas of ecclesiology and particular Catholic journals which earned themselves the growing ire of Rome and of the increasingly more conservative and hence "loyal" bishops that John Paul II had appointed throughout the church.[57]

A Decisive Turning Point?

And yet this was also the period when magisterium, dissent, and the role of the Catholic theologians became popular topics of study and discourse once again. Also of enormous significance in this period was the gradual implementation of the new Code of Canon Law (which had been

56. Who faced much pressure following the publication of her book *Women at the Altar* (London: Mowbrays, 1994).

57. On the latter development, see chapter 10 by Paul Lakeland in this present volume.

promulgated in 1983) and particularly those canons pertaining to Catholic theologians and the required assent and rejection of dissent contained therein. For example, Canon 812 of the revised Code now obliged Catholic theologians in *any* form of institution of higher studies to obtain a mandate from ecclesial authorities, despite the opposition of university and other leaders of higher education in the United States.[58] Canon 1371 laid down the norm that dissenters, even from non-infallible church teaching, should be punished if they persisted after a warning as to their conduct. As Charles Curran has commented, "These two canonical requirements were entirely new. In the meantime, the Vatican was appointing more conservative bishops throughout the world."[59] Books began to have the *Imprimatur* removed and new works would have it refused from the outset.

Thus the 1983 revision of the Code of Canon Law further centralized authority and dictated that such a method would prevail in the shaping, issuing, and enforcement of institutional church teaching authority (despite its allowing for provision of bodies of greater consultative value). Robert Ombres argues that increased codification

> has affected how authority is understood and exercised. It inevitably centralized authority and made it more firm, more enforceable universally, more standardized. A varied piecemeal *body* of canonical documents is more diffuse, less open to central control, more responsive to differences in time and place. Codification tends to favour the statement of what look like absolute and clear norms . . . Codified Canon law favours certainty, while in important respects a full theological understanding may not be available.[60]

Further developments followed of a similar character. In July 1984 Pope John Paul reaffirmed the teachings of *Humanae Vitae* at the same time that the Vatican was briefing against theologians it deemed to have

58. Cf. Curran, *Loyal Dissent*, 113f and n. 6.
59. Ibid., 113.
60. Robert Ombres, "What Future for the Laity? Law and History," in *Governance and Authority in the Roman Catholic Church: Beginning a Conversation*, eds. Noel Timms and Kenneth Wilson (London, SPCK, 2000), 92.

undermined the same with their dissent.[61] Less than a year later, in April 1985, the Congregation for Catholic Education released a first draft of a document making local bishops responsible for the orthodoxy of what is taught in Catholic institutions of higher education and obligating *all* teachers of theology to obtain a mandate from the church authorities.

Such attempts to exert ever greater control over who could teach in Catholic institutions, as well as over *what* they could teach and publish, along with a general attempt to bring theological inquiry in Catholic universities and seminaries under still closer scrutiny, came somewhat to a head on March 1, 1989, which saw the release of a new "Profession of Faith and Oath of Fidelity," which lecturers and teachers of philosophy and theology in Catholic educational institutions were expected to make. So, too, were new priests, rectors, and heads of religious communities obliged by the same. Protests soon followed, such as the Cologne Declaration that same year.[62] The Catholic Theological Society of America and the Canon Law Society of America took courageous action and deemed this new obligation to be "an untraditional extension of magisterial authority."[63] In particular, the new Profession and Oath appeared to demand assent, i.e., loyalty to and acceptance of teachings that had hitherto been considered open to discussion. The notion of what was to be considered definitive teaching had been considerably extended. Thus the joint report of the U.S. societies objected that such revealed "a theological misinterpretation of the nature of theological work and as another tendency toward excessive centralization and inhibiting control within the Church."[64]

A year later, in 1990, John Paul II issued a lengthy document on the nature and role of a Catholic University—*Ex Corde Ecclesiae*.[65] Passages that

---

61. John Paul expounded this reaffirmation in a five-month series of lectures and addresses that year. Cf. Curran, *Loyal Dissent*, 113f.

62. See *The Tablet* 243 (1989): 140–42, and from the CTSA, "Do not Extinguish the Spirit," *Origins* 20, no. 29 (1990): 462–67.

63. William C. Spohn, "The Magisterium and Morality: Notes on Moral Theology 1992," *Theological Studies* 54 (1993): 95–111, at 97.

64. *Report of the Catholic Theological Society of America and the Canon Law Society of America on the Profession of Faith and the Oath of Fidelity* (CTSA and Canon Law Society of America, April 15, 1990), 79, a passage also highlighted and discussed by Spohn, "The Magisterium and Morality," 98.

65. John Paul II, *Ex Corde Ecclesiae*, http://www.vatican.va/holy_father/john_paul_ii/apost_constitutions/documents/hf_jp-ii_apc_15081990_ex-corde-ecclesiae_en.html (accessed February 1, 2008).

sought to exert still further control over the work of theologians working in Catholic institutions caused much concern. In particular, the hardening of the obligatory demand that theologians apply for an official mandatum has subsequently caused a great deal of divisive debate and division, particularly in the United States and increasingly throughout Europe, with the Netherlands suffering especially sad divisions among its Catholic faculty.

A further development of great significance here was the new universal *Catechism of the Catholic Church*,[66] which was finally released in draft form by the CDF in 1989. Joseph Ratzinger had presided over its production. It set forth a presentation of Catholic teaching on faith and morals that was, by definition, fully intended to be taken as normative. However, as some commentators reflected, that did not necessarily mean its interpretation of teaching was to be accepted beyond question. As one put it, "Its spirit and content contrasted sharply with the message of the Vatican Council."[67] In different countries around the world, people began to criticize the language and tone of the text. In particular, the U.S. Conference's Ad Hoc Committee on the Catechism objected to the manner in which the Catechism appeared to differ from Vatican II on several key areas and also with how it failed to demarcate appropriately between church teaching of differing levels of authority and hence importance, as well as its seeming ignorance of the nature of the development of doctrine. The section on morality came in for especially fierce criticism. The CDF ignored the U.S. Bishops' request for a substantially revised text to be considered by all the bishops of the church.[68] In March 1993, the Catechism finally saw the light of day.

A "Blueprint" for Catholic Theologians?

One of the most decisive documents of all those issued throughout this period was released in 1990. A CDF document, *Donum Veritatis* (DVer), was an "Instruction on the Ecclesial Vocation of the Theologian"[69] and set down definite parameters to what constitutes legitimate areas of inquiry for

66. http://www.vatican.va/archive/catechism/ccc_toc.htm (accessed January 3, 2008).
67. Spohn, "The Magisterium and Morality," 96.
68. Ibid.
69. http://www.vatican.va/roman_curia/congregations/cfaith/documents/rc_con_cfaith_doc_19900524_theologian-vocation_en.html (accessed January 5, 2008).

Catholic theologians, as well as limiting the levels of permissible disagreement with official church teaching (dissent was unequivocally ruled out). It can be argued that this document crystallizes the various moves and developments toward redefining the role of the Catholic theologian per se that took place during John Paul's pontificate. This document "officially ratifies the extension of authority introduced in the second paragraph of the Profession of Faith," and different responses were to be outlined corresponding to different forms of teaching.[70] It was this document that gave birth to the highly controversial new category of teaching known as "definitive doctrine" (which is, nonetheless, *not* irreformable). Debates about such matters, as we shall see, would rage on well into the new millennium.

Donum Veritatis set forth a very particular understanding of the nature and exercise of the official magisterium. "The pastoral task of the Magisterium is one of vigilance. It seeks to ensure that the People of God remain in the truth which sets free. It is therefore a complex and diversified reality. The theologian, to be faithful to his role of service to the truth, must take into account the proper mission of the Magisterium and collaborate with it" (DVer 20). The instruction sets forth guidelines concerning the relation of theology and theologians to the (official) magisterium, including defining when it may be appropriate for theologians to raise questions about elements of magisterial teaching and when they cannot. In particular, the document focused upon the faithful *assent* the official magisterium demands of theologians and the CDF's understanding of what constitutes a legitimate concern and what constitutes erroneous and therefore forbidden *dissent* on the part of theologians. In essence, the document emerged from the various clashes with the theological community that had taken place during John Paul's pontificate to date. It sought to remove any doubt that those who felt that Rome was becoming more authoritarian were misunderstanding the context of the debates, as well as the nature and role of the Catholic theologian. It tackled head-on the major ecclesiological, moral, canonical, and methodological issues that numerous scholars had raised in objection to the developments witnessed thus far in John Paul's reign vis-à-vis theology and the official magisterium.

70. Spohn, "The Magisterium and Morality," 99. See also, Francis A. Sullivan, "The Theologian's Ecclesial Vocation and the 1990 CDF Instruction," *Theological Studies* 52 (1991): 51–68.

So, for example, the document reminds its readers that the church is *not* a democracy, and those theologians who apply the tenets of philosophical liberalism and political movements for greater democracy within the church are themselves in error. The document dismisses any claims that conscience can take precedence in discerning the truth of matters pertaining to the "communion of faith" (DVer 38). Nor, the document states, can any claim to the *sensus fidei* trump the authority of the official magisterium. Nor, even, can any claim to *religious* liberty (DVer 36).

Donum Veritatis set down four categories of church teaching and attempted also to indicate what appropriate responses on the part of Catholic theologians were due (namely, infallibly taught pronouncements, definitive propositions, non-definitive teaching, and "interventions in the prudential order," §§23–24). Here it was building upon the Profession of Faith but, as time would tell, rather than provide greater clarification on such matters, the result was greater controversy and much further debate and discussion among theologians, moralists, and jurists alike.

Furthermore, it appeared to be suggesting that matters of faith and morals were taught in the same fashion and hence demanded similar assent. Yet this went against the understanding of many scholars and much tradition that, with regard to morality, the quest for truth is a more complex matter altogether dependent upon numerous additional factors. Nonetheless, Pope John Paul's teachings on morality, particularly his encyclicals, appeared to endorse wholeheartedly such a rigid understanding of moral teaching. Indeed, this was so much the case that, in 1993, the esteemed moral theologian, Bernard Häring, following the publication of John Paul's *Veritatis Splendor*, was moved to issue an unfavorable comparison between John Paul's understanding of morality and that of his predecessor.[71]

Does this stand in contrast to the Polish bishop who told the fathers of Vatican II (debating Schema 13, one of two precursory schemata of *Gaudium et Spes*) that the church's job was not simply to teach the world from a position of authority, but "to co-operate with it in seeking right

---

71. Bernard Häring, "A Distrust that Wounds," in *John Paul II and Moral Theology*, eds. Charles E. Curran and Richard A. McCormick (New York: Paulist Press, 1998), 43 (originally in *The Tablet* 247 (October 23, 1993) 1378–79.

and true solutions to the difficult problems of human life and that the point to bring out was not that the Church already knew the truth, but how the world could be brought to recognize the truth and accept it".[72] Whatever the case may be, in 1995 John Paul replicated the tone and method of *Veritatis Splendor* in another encyclical, *Evangelium Vitae* (and such were again reflected in documents issued, such as the apostolic letter from 1998, *Apostolos Suos*), and, five years after the release of *Donum Veritatis*, its fundamental message was especially underscored in an address given by the pope himself. That address was actually to members of the CDF and bore the bold title "Magisterium Exercises Authority in Christ's Name."[73]

In it John Paul reinforced and made his own the message of the prevailing curial thinking concerning the authority and remit of "the" magisterium, *particularly* vis-à-vis Catholic theologians. In the light of reactions to *Donum Veritatis*, he especially reiterated and reinforced aspects of that document. Theology, he argued, is not a private enterprise and should never be divorced from the wider context of the life and vitality of the church. The power and authority of "the" magisterium are the power and authority of Christian truth. Indeed, this document actually asserted that the pope's own universal teaching office (understood in the nondefinitive sense) is exercised and fulfilled *through* the work of the CDF and like bodies which thereby share in the work of the office of the papal (ordinary) magisterium (DVer 43). On the one hand, this document could simply be interpreted as further confirming how John Paul was in agreement with, if not indeed primarily responsible for, the changing understanding and exercise of magisterium during the preceding seventeen years. But, on the other hand, given the date of its publication and the various health difficulties John Paul faced at the time, it may well be the point which marks another decisive shift in the exercise of magisterium during this pontificate, namely the point at which the CDF actually became the dominant power in the exercise of the magisterium itself. The address particularly seeks to emphasize that the remit of "the magisterium" in safeguarding this faith extends beyond those teachings which

---

72. As retold by Mieczyslaw Malinski, *Pope John Paul II*, 178.

73. Address to the CDF, November 24, 1995, trans. *L'Osservatore Romano*. English edition, November 29, 1995, 3.

are deemed to have been infallibly taught. However, as we shall see, further problems emerged when the CDF seemed to blur the distinctions between the status of teachings of different authority. Questions of gradations of authority and requisite assent came to the foreground of discussion. It is legitimate to consider, therefore, whether this address by Pope John Paul in 1995 marked some form of watershed, some handing on of the baton, as the CDF as opposed to Pope John Paul became the central point of focus and attention in the battle against dissent.

The Final Decade: The Baton Passes from Pope to Prefect?

Was this period the time when the direction in which the new understanding and exercise of the official magisterium began to be dictated less by Pope John Paul and more by the CDF? Certainly many who have written upon the subject would appear to offer evidence that it was. In February 2004, as his own health worsened, John Paul publicly "shook hands" with Cardinal Ratzinger in the "war on relativism" at the biennial plenary assembly of the CDF, reaffirming the CDF's role in defending the truth of the faith.[74] The evidence we have considered suggests that John Paul II was certainly aware of and involved in the direction in which the understanding and exercise of magisterium developed throughout the majority of his papacy. Such should be of little surprise, of course, as the pope would have to be present at final meetings to decide upon the denunciation of individual theologians and also would need to give some approval, at various stages, to different documents even when they were released under the name of the CDF.

And it appears obvious that in the earliest years of this papacy John Paul II was *very much* aware of and involved in these developments. This most likely also continued throughout much of the middle period of his pontificate, although a turning point was perhaps reached at some stage during those years. However, when we come to his final decade, the increasing influence of the CDF seems equally beyond question, with practicalities alone dictating such must have been the case in numerous instances.

74. "Pope and Ratzinger shake hands on war on relativism" (February 9, 2004), http://www.cathnews.com/news/402/41.php (accessed February 10, 2004).

Hence, from 1995 onward, John Paul's increasingly poor health placed severe limitations on the amount of actual hands-on involvement in church affairs that he could actually have had. Certainly by the second year of the new millennium there was increasing speculation that John Paul was no longer really in control of the church or was at least beyond penning and in his worst moments and toward the end perhaps even beyond consciously approving documents released from the Vatican. His decline was sad and painful to witness, no matter how bravely he faced it. This once athletic and energetic leader was now a shadow of his former self, and his own frustration with the limitations his condition placed upon him were equally evident. Indeed, John Paul's approval of documents during these later years probably requires a greater degree of hermeneutical investigation than the evidence currently available permits. Let us consider a few of the major developments in this final decade.

Defending the Faith or "Muzzling the Theologians"?

Perhaps one of the most decisive documents that illustrates the particular character of the understanding and exercise of church teaching authority under John Paul II, and yet one which was released in this crucial period when John Paul's health was in rapid decline, is the 1998 papal Motu Proprio *Ad Tuendam Fidem*, which should be considered along with the commentary upon the Profession of Faith (*Professio Fidei*) that the CDF issued around the same time. In effect, the papal document was designed to incorporate fully the 1989 *Professio Fidei* into canon law, particularly with regard to the juridical penalties relating to one clause of that profession.[75] Such were very much seen as attending to unfinished business. However, while some felt such business was a little tidying up of canon law, others surveyed the developments as being of a more ominous character.

Some commentators, such as Francis Sullivan, thought that *Ad Tuendam Fidem* was simply concerned with offering a canonical penalty for the rejection of propositions that, although not revealed truths, have been taught in a definitive way by the supreme magisterium of the church, and hence are to be held definitively by the faithful. As such, its provisions would be deemed unsurprising, as John Paul II had already

---

75. Joseph Ratzinger and Tarcisio Bertone, "Commentary on the Profession of Faith's Concluding Paragraphs," July 16, 1998, trans. *The Tablet* (July 11, 1998): 920–22.

introduced a penalty into the 1983 Code of Canon Law for the rejection of propositions taught by the official magisterium in a *non-definitive* way.

What was particularly novel, however, was the incorporation of the *second* clause of the profession of faith, this "oath of allegiance," into the Code of Canon Law.[76] The second clause concerned teachings "definitively proposed" by the church.[77] Problems arose because the commentary would appear to declare that the result of *Ad Tuendem Fidem* was to indicate as "definitive" teachings on matters which hitherto had been understood as being less settled.

In commenting upon this document, Richard Gaillardetz identifies two particular features of John Paul's defense of the unity of the faith that are distinctive. The first is this widening of what counts as "definitive doctrine" (clause 2) compared with the narrower understanding given at both Vatican I and Vatican II.[78] Such teachings were previously understood as non-revealed but required for the safeguarding and preservation of divine revelation. Both 1998 documents appear to broaden this understanding. The key part is their reference to teachings being considered to be definitive through their necessary connection to revelation in either a logical or historical manner. Gaillardetz observes how this is not only a broader but also a more ambiguous formulation than was previously seen in earlier documents issued during John Paul's pontificate, not least of all *Donum Veritatis*. The key point here is, of course, that not every teaching connected in some logical or historical way to revelation is something that is essential for the defense of the faith.[79] What enters into the landscape here is an arbitrary understanding and apportioning of definitive status to particular teachings.

The second novel development under John Paul that Gaillardetz also discusses is "*the manner* in which these definitive teachings are being proposed."[80] Thus, what took place during John Paul's pontificate is that

---

76. Cf. *Ad Tuendam Fidem*, 3 (http://www.vatican.va/holy_father/john_paul_ii/motu_propio/documents/hf_jp-ii_motu-propio_30061998_ad-tuendam-fidem_en.html (accessed January 4, 2008).

77. What Gaillardetz abbreviates to "definitive doctrines" in "Ordinary Universal Magisterium," 453.

78. Richard Gaillardetz, "*Ad tuendam fidem*: An Emerging Pattern in Current Papal Teaching," *New Theology Review* 12 (February 1999): 43–51, at 45–46.

79. Ibid., 46.

80. Ibid. (emphasis in original).

he or the CDF or another curial department would "confirm" that such a consensus of the bishops with regard to a particular teaching either existed across time or had been reached. Thus a confirmation of the status of the teaching was given.

The rub here, as Gaillardetz also points out,[81] is that the confirmation itself did not constitute something taught with the charism of infallibility, rather being at best an exercise of the pope's ordinary (and potentially fallible and reformable) magisterium or even a curial statement of much lesser weight. Further canonical subtleties in relation to the document were succinctly articulated by Hermann J. Pottmeyer. He believes *Ad Tuendam Fidem* confirms and further demonstrates that a "new form of papal teaching" has come to the fore in recent years—namely, one which seeks to define certain teachings as having been taught infallibly, but to define them as such, in *a fallible way*.[82]

To put this another way still, teachings can thus be proclaimed as "definitive doctrines" by appeal to the authority of the ordinary universal magisterium, and yet doubts exist as to whether the latter has consistently held a consensus on such particular teachings. What is thus further achieved through such changes is a downplaying of the long-standing recognition of the provisionality of some Catholic teaching.[83] And it is precisely such changes in the understanding and exercise of teaching that are confirmed and enshrined in canon law thanks to *Ad Tuendam Fidem* and the commentary upon the *Professio*. Did these developments constitute the completion, perhaps even the crowning achievement, of the changes to the understanding and exercise of magisterium in John Paul II's pontificate?

Concluding Remarks

David Stagaman closes his own study of authority with a plea that the church recognize and facilitate freedom and responsibility, as opposed

---

81. Ibid., 47–48.

82. Hermann J. Pottmeyer, *"Auf fehlbare Weise unfehlbahr? Zu einer neuen Form päpstlichen Lehrens,"* *Stimmen der Zeit* (April, 1999), English trans. "Fallibly Infallible? A New Form of Papal Teaching," from www.americapress.org, commentary by James S. Torrens in *America* (April 3, 1999): 19–20.

83. Gaillardetz, "An Emerging Pattern," 49.

to harsh censorship within its own confines. He takes as his inspiration this passage from a once lesser-known Polish moral philosopher:

> The attitude of opposition is a function, on the one hand, of that particular view one takes of the community and of what is good for it, and on the other, of the strong need to participate in the common existing and even more so in the common acting. There can be no doubt that this kind of opposition is essentially constructive; it is a condition of the correct structure of communities and of the correct functioning of their inner system. This condition, however, must be defined more precisely: the structure, the system of communities, must be such as to allow the opposition that grows out of the soil of solidarity not only to express itself within the framework of the community but also to operate for the benefit of the community to be constructive. The structure of human community is correct only if it admits not just the presence of a justified opposition but also that effectiveness of opposition which is required by the common good and the right of participation.[84]

It is ironic that the spirit of this passage, in the opinion of many commentators and in light of all the evidence considered in the foregoing, represents the exact opposite of the situation that prevailed throughout much of John Paul II's period as Supreme Pontiff.

We might describe this new understanding of magisterium as postmodern in character, for the evidence would suggest that the primary motivating factor behind its formation was the perceived need for the church to react in an authoritative fashion to the challenges posed to the church (both *ad intra* and *ad extra*) by this the postmodern age. In recent years it would appear that such an understanding has taken a still deeper root in the life of the church and naturally so, insofar as the pronouncements perceived to be authentic (i.e., authoritative and binding over all the faithful) continue to carry influence in the popular consciousness of Catholics, including an emerging generation of clerics, religious, and theologians.

The very understanding of magisterium and the core concepts pertaining to its operation and hence authority in recent times are, in themselves, not universally agreed upon by the episcopal, juridical, and

---

84. Karol Wojtyla, *The Acting Person*, trans. Andrzej Potocki (Dordrecht and Boston: D. Reidel, 1979), 286, in David Stagaman, *Authority in the Church* (Collegeville, MN: Liturgical Press, 1999), 138–39.

theological communities. We thus deal here with subjects that can only be discussed and researched in a tentative manner. This is especially so when we attempt to discern the relationship between magisterium and morality. Vatican II appeared to recognize and acknowledge this fact. The notion of magisterium of postmodern times, it would appear, is at pains to refute such an understanding or at least to set strict limitations upon the nature and range of discussions pertaining to certain subjects hitherto considered open to further debate.[85]

Now, of course, many would argue that the developments outlined in the foregoing are quintessentially *modern* in character as opposed to postmodern. I would suggest that perhaps a dialectical model might prove illuminating: out of the modern and dogmatic magisterium's meeting with and clashing with the more late modern or even early postmodern attempts to redefine and redirect the notion of magisterium, most notably the dialogical model that emanated from Vatican II, there emerges the restorationist reaction to the latter. This is something new, notwithstanding the fact that it moves away from and/or negates many features of both the modern and the Vatican II perceptions of magisterium: and it is this one might term "the" postmodern magisterium.

It is a realistic possibility that further ecclesial and theological divisions will follow unless necessary and open debates take place on these matters throughout the church. Most Catholics would agree that Pope John Paul II should not be criticized for his zeal to preserve and teach the deposit of faith. But the aspects of the manner in which the official magisterium during his pontificate safeguarded, defended, and policed that faith can and should be open to criticism. Michael A. Fahey ends his own recent study with two very pertinent questions that he believes are of central importance to the coming debates: "To what extent is the Roman Catholic understanding of magisterium purely doctrinal or largely cultural? And second, how can the exercise of magisterium be more integrated into the other dimensions of decision making so that it is more comprehensive?"[86] I would endorse such sentiments and add a

85. Cf., for example, Julie Clague, "Moral Theology and Doctrinal Change" in *Moral Theology for the 21ˢᵗ Century*, eds. Julie Clague, Bernard Hoose, and Gerard Mannion (London and New York: T and T Clark, 2008), 67–79.

86. Fahey, "Magisterium," 534.

plea for constructive, open, and truly critical dialogue here. The time for a new and wide-ranging hermeneutical engagement with the nature, understanding, and exercise of magisterium in the Roman Catholic Church has come. If such is entered into with a true spirit of charity and openness on the part of all participants, then faithful witness to, indeed a better living out of, the Gospel for these times will be the result.

7

John Paul II and Justice

Judith A. Merkle, SNDdeN

The church from her beginnings has called its members and the world to justice. After two millennia what can be added to this essential call of Christian faithfulness? This was the charge of John Paul II when he was elected pope on October 16, 1978. Karol Josef Wojtyla (b. 1920) was no stranger to the injustices characteristic of the modern world. He spent fifty-eight years living under a foreign government, either during the German occupation of Poland or in the face of the communist regime that followed.[1] The new pope believed that this life prepared him for the office of pope, where the charge to "strengthen the brethren" (Luke 22:32) meant leading the church to live in a world reeling from massive change. The church was not only to offer a spiritual and cultural resistance to all that crippled human flourishing but also to engage in areas that reflected its essential religious ministry yet also had direct social and political consequences. This involved four areas especially: the defense of human dignity, the promotion of human rights, the cultivation of the unity of the human family, and the provision of meaning to every aspect of human activity (GS 40, 42).[2] His inaugural sermon contained the signature words of his pontificate: "Be not afraid!" He affirmed that all human persons were to be active rather than passive before the forces of this global world. He also urged analysis of and action on issues that

1. George Weigel, *Witness to Hope: The Biography of Pope John Paul II* (New York: HarperCollins, 1999), 296–97.
2. J. Brian Hehir, "The Peace Pastoral and Global Mission," in *The Church and Culture Since Vatican II*, ed. Joseph Gremillion, 99–103 (South Bend, IN: University of Notre Dame Press, 1985).

were central to the struggle for international justice in this new world order. John Paul II's concern for the poor and call for the necessity of solidarity if human dignity is to be preserved and advanced in the world is expressed mainly in three social encyclicals: *Laborem Exercens,* On Human Work (1981), *Sollicitudo Rei Sociales,* On Social Concern (1987), and *Centesimus Annus,* On the Hundredth Anniversary of *Rerum Novarum* (1991). His approach to justice is certainly evidenced in these social encyclicals.[3] However, it is also contained in the philosophical and theological framework that shaped his understanding of action for justice. In this essay we will outline his approach to justice and observe the interplay between his philosophical/theological framework and his analysis of public and global affairs. Finally we will comment on the contributions and tensions present in the way he fostered the tradition of justice in the church and the world.

The Context of John Paul II's Approach to Justice

John Paul II framed his contribution to the justice tradition against a culture of communism, which influenced his early life, and liberal capitalism, which dominated during his pontificate. Liberal capitalism was like communism, in his view, in that both were economic systems and interpretations of the meaning of life. This reality necessitated a two-pronged approach to justice. On the one hand, he spoke out against issues that the market and its impact on politics created; on the other, he commented on the "deceits" regarding the meaning of human existence such a system institutionalized and fostered. As an alternative, he offered a rather cohesive philosophical and theological view of human identity that contradicted both the market model and socialism, both as styles of economy and visions of human flourishing.

John Paul II saw it as the role of the church to foster an alternative culture in society, especially before the more subtle influence of capitalism, and to offer people a vision of life's meaning that went beyond an

---

3. For all encyclicals, see *The Encyclicals of John Paul II,* ed. and intro. J. Michael Miller, CSB (Huntington, IN: Our Sunday Visitor, 1996). In this essay they will be referred to as LE (*Laborem Exercens*); SRS (*Sollicitudo Rei Sociales*); CA (*Centesimus Annus*). For an overview of these encyclicals see: Judith A. Merkle, *From the Heart of the Church: The Catholic Social Tradition* (Collegeville, MN: Liturgical Press, 2004), chapter 10.

"economic salvation." This articulation of the Gospel in our times had to be culturally positioned in opposition to mainstream thinking in society. The result was to be actively engaged in a new moral imagination that created more sustainable structures and systems in which the whole human and natural community could develop. His view of justice is countercultural without being otherworldly. Justice is more than a personal virtue that adds to personal moral rectitude. Justice requires a conversion process that evokes a new imagination that creates systems that are more interdependent in economic, cultural, political, and religious ways in our global society.

John Paul's view of justice, however, was different than his predecessors' views. While modern popes usually questioned the liberal market and an "economistic" view of the human person that limited the human drive for improvement to simply seeking more material things, John Paul II responded to a new form of capitalism, "monetarism." In Britain, the U.S., and, indeed, soon most nations of the West, the economy moved from its Keynesian, World War II style where government was a greater actor and restrainer in its functioning to an older style of the self-regulating market system. With this change came increasing deregulation, new free trade agreements, and a previously unheard of globalization of the economy. This new form of capitalism restructured the national economies of the U.S. and the U.K. according to a neoliberal vision of export-oriented development by market liberalization, the cutback and privatization of social services, and the reduction of the role of government to protection and service of the market.[4]

Developing countries became integrated into the world economy in the '70s as places of investment, however by the '80s they were in debt to the West. By the time of the Thatcher and Reagan governments, the economies of developing nations were restructured not to their own development but to serve the powerful interests of the first world. Because these major powers had control of the governing boards of the international lending organizations, neoliberal structural reforms could be demanded as the cost of loans for debt relief. The Structural Adjustment Programs (SAPs) oriented debt-ridden economies toward

---

4. James E. Hug, SJ, "Economic Justice and Globalization," in *Globalization and Catholic Social Thought*, eds. John A. Coleman and William F. Ryan (Maryknoll, NY: Orbis, 2005), 56.

participation in global markets to at least pay the interest on their loans. However, this required them to devote often their best lands for export crops whose earnings filled the pockets of the banks, governments, and multilateral institutions of the North.

For John Paul II this market system, with its lack of restraints and vision of human flourishing, fostered its own view of the meaning of the human person in this world. While socialist collectivism was weakening as a serious opponent of human freedom, laissez-faire capitalism carried its own insidious culture which shaped men's and women's vision of success and meaning and even affected their readiness to respond to God in faith. Individualism, desire for profit, thirst for power, those forces which ignore the fundamental equality of all and the purpose of creation and the goods of the earth were structures of sin that reside in cultural visions of what it means to be an adequate human being. John Paul II saw the structures they produced as not only unjust and harmful to the human community but rooted in personal sin, linked to the acts of individuals who socially reproduce them and make them difficult to remove (SRS 36). More importantly they formed a vision of human happiness which blinded people to the needs of the other and to their call as spiritual people.

The thirst for power and the desire for profit at any price make human attitudes absolute in a manner that is really religious in nature, argued the pope. They are a form of idolatry (SRS 36–37). He remarks that "hidden behind certain decisions, apparently inspired only by economics or politics, are real forms of idolatry: of money, ideology, class, technology" (SRS 37). Development in the global world is more than economic; it includes the trajectory of human growth toward otherness and depth.

John Paul II's assessment of his times led him to nuance the church's traditional stance against the eighteenth-century faith in the power of an unrestrained market to provide for universal human flourishing. The church's stance on justice had to be more than programmatic, calling for public norms and controls, labor unions, a culture of generosity and virtue to curtail the greed and excessive desire for profit which appeared indigenous to capitalism. It also had to be comprehensive, transforming the culture that blinded people's minds and crippled their wills to change their world. The Catholic community could no longer simply live in the world and practice its faith and pursue justice. Rather it must also transform the culture that fosters the continued draining off of the wealth of impoverished nations rather than invest in the development of the people. These global problems were real, but also symbolic of the spiritual crises of humanity. While John Paul II's philosophical and theological view of the human person has its own literature and commentary, I would argue that it is inseparable from his more issue-oriented focus in the social encyclicals. Public issues were icons of spiritual emptiness. Spiritual healing required action for justice.

From Spectator to Actor

Prior to Vatican II, the relationship between faith and justice was treated in a different context than that of our current, modern, pluralistic world. The setting of papal social thought from Leo XIII to Pius XII was an "organically Christian world."[5] Faith and justice were two parallel sources of order.[6] The form of natural law reasoning in the older social teaching relied mainly on universal concepts modified by their use in a Christian context. What was left less explicit was their connection with Christian theology. When the horizon of the thinking of the church is an organically Christian world, one simply presumes the foundations of its thinking. However, Vatican II addressed a different world, one of modern pluralism. In the face of pluralism, the church had to recover how its Christian belief served as the foundation of its arguments that people and the church should act for justice and the relationship between faith and justice.

In its document *Gaudium et Spes* (The Church in the Modern World), Vatican II grounded the church's social teaching in its understanding of Jesus Christ and the church. Later, in 1971, the synod of bishops advanced this teaching. "Action on behalf of justice and participation in the transformation of the world fully appear to us as a constitutive dimension of the preaching of the Gospel, or, in other words, of the Church's mission for the redemption of the human race and its liberation from every

5. Richard L. Camp, *The Papal Ideology of Social Reform: A Study in Historical Development 1878–1967* (Leiden: E. J. Brill, 1969).

6. John F. Cronin, SS, *Christianity and Social Progress: A Commentary on* Mater et Magistra (Baltimore and Dublin: Helicon, 1965), 7.

oppressive situation" (*Justice in the World*, 36). John Paul II follows the Vatican II tradition as he asserts that the foundation of the church's social teaching is the human person considered in the light of the mystery of the Incarnation and redemption (CA 53). This interest in foundational questions led him to approach questions of justice less as an ethicist seeking to analyze the precise nature of justice in a particular situation and more as a task of theological anthropology. Seeking justice is integral to the fulfillment of the human call to wholeness. By beginning with Christian belief about the nature of the human person, he attempts to reach out to all people of good will in their quest for human wholeness.

Perhaps distinctive to John Paul II's approach to justice is where he stood in the debates that ensued after the council regarding just how integral justice was to the practice of faith.[7] In contrast to those who felt that evangelization only really happens through actions for justice, John Paul II saw justice as part of faith, but faith as not exhausted by justice. The two are distinct but inseparable elements of a larger totality. However, his position on faith and justice separates his spirituality of the world from one in which spiritual growth could have validity *without* some action on behalf of the "other." On the contrary, as we find worth in our neighbor, respond to her or him as "other," we find God. The bonds formed in this way are deeper than the natural or human bonds we hope bind the world (SRS 40). These are the bonds of communion. This mix between a developed vision of the human person as constituted before God, called in faith to action yet also to union with God, and his view of the responsibility of the Christian and the church in society is a signature of John Paul II's stance on justice.

John Paul II integrated his ideas about justice to address a broader question, how the Christian message responds to the problems of modern experience. Karol Wojtyla explored extensively the meaning of human identity in the modern world. His foundational work, *The Acting Person*, attempts to lay a framework within which his theological understanding of the person can be understood.[8] Central to his view of the

---

7. Gerard Beigel, *Faith and Social Justice in the Teaching of John Paul II* (New York: Peter Lang, 1997), 3. I am grateful for Beigel's study, which I follow in part in the following section.

8. John Paul II, *The Acting Person*, trans. by Andrzej Potocki (Dordrecht and Boston: D. Reidel Pub. Co., 1979).

human person is his assertion that the human person is revealed through action. The person, through various aspects of consciousness, is able to reflect both on one's actions and the experience of these actions as one's own. We are both the subject and agent of our acts. In grasping this realization we become in touch with our transcendence, or the reality of our human freedom. Because we are free, we are consciously able to undertake action which is self-determining. The human person is not a static reality but one who is constantly called to a new realization and expression. Yet a deep and profound reality of "person" is also at the core of all these future developments.

Acts which are creative of the human person are ones which are freely chosen. When a person acts, they not only choose an action, but they determine themselves with respect to values, particularly moral value.[9] By choosing a value, we also allow that value to become part of our lives. Freedom is intrinsically related to an objective order of what is good and true. Freedom is not simply freedom to do what one likes but freedom to do what is right.[10] Self-determination is not simply the act of decision making, it is oriented to the truth. We become fully human by doing that which is true and worthy of human energy. Later in his pontificate he notes in *Centesimus Annus* that a notion of freedom that detaches itself from obedience to the truth absolves itself from the duty to respect the rights of others. Without a sense of the truth, one simply does what one has the power to get away with. The wars of the last century testify to this (CA 17).

In *The Acting Person* Wojtyla claims a truly human personal growth depends on participation in a transcendent order of truth, good, and beauty. Later he gives a more theological interpretation to this dynamic. The human person's existence is also a participation in God, and human action ought to deepen this participation. Since God is the supreme model of everything that exists, the normative order is rooted in the transcendent truth and goodness of God.[11] Duty arises because the discernment of truth about good takes place in the context of an exemplary

9. Beigel, *Faith and Social Justice*, 15.

10. Stephen Carter criticizes this cultural view of freedom in *Civility, Manners, Morals and the Etiquette of Democracy* (New York: Basic Books, 1998), 78.

11. Karol Wojtyla, "Ethics and Moral Theology," in *Person and Community: Selected Essays*, trans. Theresa Sandok (New York: Peter Lang, 1993), 103.

world which is charged not only with purposiveness but also with the dynamic tendency of all beings and goods to God their exemplar. We have a duty as humans to make judgments about what actions are true and good, because fundamentally we are called to imitate God. Values which hold high importance, unconditional values, carry with them an imperative, "I must," which is of a different moral order than simply "I want."[12]

John Paul II concludes that action is performed by a person and a person fulfills himself or herself through an action. The person is the fundamental value at stake in every human act. In other words, before we determine whether an act is right or wrong, we first have to note that in this action the person realizes himself or herself. This is why John Paul II can say later in *Laborem Exercens*, "the basis for determining the value of human work is not primarily the kind of work being done but the fact that the one who is doing it is a person" (LE 6). His moral theory has human flourishing as its core: "moral good is that through which the human being as a human being—as a person—becomes and is good, and moral evil that through which the human being as a human being—as a person—becomes and is evil."[13]

Authentic human action also involves participation with others. "Acting together with others" is an act of being a person, but also a participation in the realization of the fulfillment of others in community. The person not only comes to fulfillment acting together with others but also through the quality of their action in bringing about the common good. Since all persons need to act with others to bring about the common good, it is imperative that communities foster this kind of participation. Alienation is the antithesis of this participation.[14] However, community is more than a number of people acting together, rather it is the "specific unity of this multiplicity." A person has a lived experience of community, a consciousness of being in unity with others. This unity, however, neither dismisses the individual for the collectivity nor exaggerates his or her worth as the highest good, viewing others simply as obstacles. Solidarity, the readiness to accept one's share in the

12. Karol Wojtyla, "The Problem of the Theory of Morality," in *Person and Community*, 151.
13. Ibid., 149.
14. Karol Wojtyla, "The Person: Subject and Community," in *Person and Community*, 238.

community, and opposition, the capacity to work toward a better real-ization of the common good in community, are both virtues which build up community. Both require dialogue, a process of discernment and judgment wherein the community seeks the truth and acts together with others in realizing it.[15] Later he asserts that Catholic Social Thought not only has the task to condemn actual injustices in the light of an ade-quately understood concept of human dignity, but must also proclaim a meaningful new future (SRS 42).

John Paul II sees community concretely. In his words, "To partici-pate in the humanity of another human being means to be vitally re-lated to the others as a particular human being, and not just related to what makes the other (*in abstracto*) a human being. This is ultimately the basis for the whole distinctive character of the evangelical concept of neighbor."[16] Self-determination requires therefore a type of self-possession and self-governance that imply the capacity to make a "gift of oneself" in a disinterested way.[17]

While John Paul II grounds his approach to justice in these deep affirmations of the meaning of human persons, his ethic is not simply abstract or universalistic. He claims that such affirmations regarding the human person become too abstract if they do not sufficiently take into account the concrete, historical persons about whom the universal truth is proclaimed. "We are not dealing here with man in the 'abstract,' but with the real, 'concrete,' 'historical' man. We are dealing with *each indi-vidual*, since each one is included in the mystery of Redemption, and through this mystery Christ has united himself with each one forever" (*Redemptor Hominis* 14, as quoted in CA 53).[18] While the common good, key to a vision of justice, is particularly revealed in the social reality of community, this good embraces all the concrete dimensions of the per-son—his economic, social, political, and religious good—in the con-crete. We do not get a clear understanding of John Paul II's approach to justice looking only at his personalistic ethic; we must also examine his theology.

15. Wojtyla, *The Acting Person*, 283–88.

16. Wojtyla, "The Person: Subject and Community," in *Person and Community*, 237.

17. Karol Wojtyla, "The Personal Structure of Self-Determination," in *Person and Com-munity*, 194.

18. John Paul II, *Redemptor Hominis, The Encyclicals of John Paul II*, (hereafter, RH).

A Christocentric Anthropology

John Paul II's emphasis on the importance of human action in his anthropology is theologically confirmed in his focus on the person and act of redeeming love in the life and death of Jesus Christ. Specifically, it is the person of Jesus Christ and his act of redemption that carry universal significance for men and women and their self-understanding (GS 22). Christ opens to men and women the reality that their deepest reality is contained in the "mystery" of God's own plan of salvation. In Christ, we can rediscover our link with God that was lost through sin. The church needs to proclaim not only how God is revealed in Christ but also the dignity of the human person in face of the gift of the redemption. All men and women in the world, not just members of the church, are caught up and influenced by the mystery of the redemption. Through the work of redemption Christ "in a certain way united himself with each man" (GS 22).

Redemption is a reality directed toward men and women in the world, not just to their spiritual consciousness. The Holy Spirit in this sense offers to all the possibility of being made partners in this paschal mystery. The church, however, has a special participation in this work of redemption. The mystery of redemption "continues" and "abides permanently" in the church.[19] This constitutes the church as a sacrament—a sign and instrument—of communion with God and of unity among men (LG 1). The risen Christ continues to be active in his church through the power of the Holy Spirit. The reality of the redemption abides in the church above all because its effects are realized in men and women and in the world.

The individual participates in this mission through faith. The redemption reveals to men and women the deepest truth of their human dignity, their freedom, their capacity for communion, their orientation toward truth and love. This truth calls for an active response. "The man who wishes to understand himself thoroughly . . . must with his unrest, uncertainty and even his weakness and sinfulness, with his life and death, draw near to Christ" (RH 10). "Carrying out the truth in love" is the

---

19. Karol Wojtyla, *Sources of Renewal: The Implementation of the Second Vatican Council*, trans. P. S. Falla (San Francisco: Harper and Row, 1980), 65 and 85.

aspect of human activity in which the redemption of Christ bears fruit.[20]

John Paul II understands the human person in light of the redemption, through the lens of his philosophical interpretation of the core of humanity as truth, love, human dignity, and freedom. Christ reveals the interiority of these values and their integration within the human heart. Christ not only models this integration, but relationship with Christ brings about this integration in us. What results is more than a moral integration; it is a mystical one which draws the human person into the deepest mystery of his or her being, the human heart (RH 8.2).

The need of redemption central to his theological understanding of humankind finds a parallel in his analysis of the progress of the world. A type of "eschatological reserve" is exhibited. The immense progress of the last century is also "subject to futility" (RH 8.1). "The world of the new age . . . the world of the previously unattained conquests of science and technology—is it not also the world 'groaning in travail' (Rom 8:22)?" (RH 8.1). In the last half of *Redemptor Hominis* he continues this analogy. Human beings as never before are creative, yet inherent to their creations is their capacity to destroy people and civilization as a whole (RH 15.2). This paradox of globalization is an analogy of the paradox of the human situation.

Human progress has made the world better for all, yet he comes back to the question of "whether in the context of this progress man, as man, is becoming truly better, that is to say more mature spiritually, more aware of the dignity of his humanity, more responsible, more open to others, especially the neediest and the weakest, and readier to give and to aid all" (RH 15.4). Progress is more than economic; it includes personal growth toward otherness and depth. The full dimension of being human comes only as it tends "towards God" (RH 11). The person then enters into the realm of mystery where, as we work for a better world, we also understand the profound action of the "Redemption taking place in Christ Jesus" (RH 10). The anthropocentrism more familiar in modern culture is linked to a theocentrism in John Paul II's thought. While the culture sees these in opposition to one another, John

20. Ibid., 87.

Paul II links them in a deep way.[21] Wojtyla's assumption is that human beings are in a permanent state of experiencing existence, and God is fundamental to understanding the experience and explaining existence.[22] Awareness of self brings an awareness of God and a desire to act. This is the human experience of transcendence and that which elevates human existence. Justice is grounded in this experience.

Each person therefore is met with the challenge of acting in accordance with the dictates of his or her call to transcendence. Righteousness is that quality of action which is directed toward the good. Justice is righteousness acting within the context of community or the body politic. Because the world is both sinful and redeemed, the person, however, must act within the horizon of love: "Without the help of grace, men would not know how to discern the often narrow path between the cowardice which gives in to evil, and the violence which under the illusion of fighting evil only makes it worse. This is the path of charity, that is, of the love of God and of neighbor."[23] Love is what differentiates the person from other things, both animate and inanimate. Love reveals what human life is about and the meaning of human existence before God. Love also is a powerful force that transforms the hearts and acts of people in this world. Love is a choice and through it the person is linked directly to God. "The person is a being for whom the only suitable dimension is love."[24] Love then is inseparable from any act of justice.

The mystery of the love between the Father and Jesus Christ is the mystery into which we are invited through the outpouring of the Holy Spirit upon humanity (RH 9). The ordering of the love of the Trinity to human salvation is "mercy" since it is directed to saving humankind from sin. This mercy is at the heart of justice. "This love makes itself particularly noticed in contact with suffering, injustice and poverty, in contact with the whole historical 'human condition,' which in various ways manifests man's limitation and frailty, both physical and moral. It

21. Beigel, *Faith and Social Justice*, 43.

22. W. King Mott Jr., *The Third Way: Economic Justice According to John Paul II* (Lanham, MD: University Press of America, 1999), 134.

23. *Catechism of the Catholic Church*, Apostolic Constitution *Fidei Depositum*, John Paul, Bishop (St. Louis, MO: Liguori Publications, 1994), 1889:462.

24. John Paul II, *Crossing the Threshold of Hope* (New York: Alfred A. Knopf, 1994), 201.

is precisely the mode and sphere in which love manifests itself that in biblical language is called 'mercy.'"[25]

The order of justice therefore has its roots in merciful love. "True mercy is, so to speak, the most profound source of justice" (DM 14.4). The equality which justice effects "is limited to the realm of objective and extrinsic goods, while love and mercy bring it about that people meet one another in that value which is man himself, with the dignity that is proper to him" (DM 14.4). In addition, mercy elicits forgiveness, essential to a human society. A society which tries to eliminate forgiveness would be nothing but a world of "cold and unfeeling justice," in the name of which each person simply "claims his or her own rights vis-à-vis others" (DM 14.8). While justice involves equitable distribution of goods and fair compensation, mercy shapes mutual relationships between people. It is impossible to establish this bond between people if they wish to measure their mutual relationships solely according to the measure of justice (DM 14.6). Justice is therefore a first step of merciful love. Catholic social doctrine expresses the church's deep sharing with the people of our time a desire for a life in society that is just in every way (DM 12.2). However, programs that appeal to the idea of justice also paradoxically share in the same "shadow" existence as all forms of human progress, and human nature itself. "In such cases, the desire to annihilate the enemy, limit his freedom, or even force him into total dependence, becomes the fundamental motive for action; and this contrasts with the essence of justice, which by its nature tends to establish equality and harmony between the parties in conflict" (DM 12.3).

For John Paul II, justice is a multidimensional reality; justice alone is not enough. Only if a deeper power, that of love, is allowed to shape human life in its various dimensions, will justice overcome its tendency to lead to the negation and destruction of itself. Only mercy can satisfy the dignity of the person and serve as the foundation of a truly human society, because it is "the source of a life different from the life which can be built by man" (DM 14). It is the mercy of the Father, Son, and Holy Spirit that must be revealed at this stage of history and must be shown as present in our modern world. Only it is more powerful than evil, more powerful than sin and death (DM 15.6). Mercy addresses the

---

25 John Paul II, *Dives in Misericordia, The Encyclicals of John Paul II*, 3.3, (hereafter, DM).

value of the person as primary. It is the power within the person that enables the full actualization of the value of participation through the gift of self, not only in the lives of others and the affairs of society but also in the life of the Trinity. "Since authentic human fulfillment can occur only through the experience of God's mercy, mercy acquires a normative significance for human life" (DM 14).[26]

What difference might this emphasis on mercy make in John Paul II's approach to justice? It suggests an ethic of justice which must also hold in tension other Gospel values in its execution. If mercy establishes communion between God and human beings, it also has to lead us to seek communion while we are establishing justice in human relationships. In *Dives in Misericordia* 12, John Paul II asks, "Is Justice Enough?" Without a higher value than justice, namely love and mercy, efforts toward justice often fall into injustice (DM 12).

The integral relationship between mercy, love, and justice does not lessen the requirements of justice, rather it enhances them. John Paul II does not back away from the discernment of the ways and means of justice. A rule of discernment to be used in making choices between concrete options in society is the humanistic criterion. The humanistic criterion is

> the measure in which each system is really capable of reducing, restraining and eliminating as far as possible the various forms of exploitation of man and of ensuring for him, through work, not only the just distribution of the indispensable material goods, but also a participation, in keeping with his dignity, in the whole process of production and in the social life that grows up around the process.[27]

The order of mercy, however, constantly reframes what we understand as justice, calling us to forgive, calling us to invest, conferring "a new content" on justice through the introduction of that creative power of love "which is more powerful than sin" (DM 14).

In John Paul II's later writings he locates the hermeneutical function that mercy provides for justice in the relationships between freedom and

---

26. Beigel, *Faith and Social Justice,* 49.

27. John Paul II, "Address to the United Nations on the Declaration of Human Rights," *AAS* 1156, par. 17, as quoted in Donal Dorr, *Option for the Poor: A Hundred Years of Catholic Social Teaching* (Maryknoll, NY: Orbis, 1983), 275.

truth, human autonomy and community, and the role of transcendence in political life. He cautions that detaching human freedom from its essential and constitutive relationship to truth leads to contemporary relativist thought.[28] Failure to search for the truth of human dignity in its transcendent and permanent nature undermines the vision needed for essential political conditions in our world. Only a belief in the transcendent nature of human life, for instance, grounds openness in public administration, the rejection of illicit means in order to gain or increase power, and respect for the rights of political adversaries and others (VS 101).

Even though freedom must be related to truth and human autonomy has to be related to community, groups can also be blind to the truth, giving a cultural sense of truth or freedom an absolute value. Holy wars and "national security" mentalities all are distortions of the truth fed by need for identity and protection of the status quo. A greater truth is only accomplished through dialogue, openness to which is another evidence of the search for transcendence. Contrary to those who hold that religion is extraneous to public debate, John Paul II teaches it is central. Religion takes seriously that human beings have a transcendent goal. Without attention to the ethical relevance of transcendence, John Paul II cautions that society is at peril and justice simply leads to more injustice.

John Paul II and the Languages of Justice in Today's World

Justice is a question of human existence today which is worldwide in scope and is a moral requirement of all. John Paul II asserts that social justice concerns the social, political, and economic aspects of these challenges and, above all, the structural dimension of problems and their respective solutions (LE 2). What concerns John Paul II is the manner in which justice can easily be reduced to procedural questions or law alone and lose the fuller meaning that Christian anthropology can give it (SRS 39). Alone, justice is not enough.[29] Love, in this sense, presupposes and transcends justice. While justice is important in resolving

28. John Paul II, *Veritatis Splendor* (Vatican City: Libreria Editrice Vaticana, 1993) 4.8, (hereafter, VS).

29. John Paul II, Message for the 2004 World Day of Peace, *AAS* 96 (2004): 121.

conflicts and discerning reciprocal distribution of goods in an equitable manner, only love (including that love we call mercy) is "capable of restoring man to himself" (DM 14). Love in this sense takes on the style of social and political charity and is the highest and universal criterion of the whole of social ethics.

Certainly, the life of John Paul II militates against any criticism of his vision of justice as abstract, overly spiritual, and unrealistic in the modern age. He lived through more socially conflicted circumstances than most of his critics. Yet his desire to base social action in the church within a theologically grounded sense of the human person has made his contribution to the church's understanding of justice less programmatic and more foundational.[30]

A tension that does arise with his view of justice is in relation to his anthropology and whether it sufficiently speaks to the *varieties* of human identity in the modern world. As with much revisionist moral theology, the anthropology of John Paul II reflects a type of transcendental Thomism which focuses the structure of moral experience on the personal, intrapsychic becoming of the individual. While his anthropology has social and communal dimensions which are integral to his vision, it is less explicit when it must confront the effects of pluralism on human identity today. It shares with new theology after the council a positive edge. Through its reference to the individual, such theology can function in a world where the consensus model of universal principles has been displaced. However, before the multiple senses of self which exist in society today, we can ask, do its universalistic assertions include a diversity of people in their particularities?

Even though John Paul II recognizes the need to relate to human beings concretely, he has difficulty with the social theologies that define the moral self in a manner in which the structures of society impact self-understanding and human becoming. These theologies express in religious terms, even though imperfectly, current human expressions of the desire for emancipation. We have to ask how well John Paul's concept of justice deals with the particularities of these experiences, and what contribution it makes to the evolution of these expressions of Christian faith.

30. Merkle, *From the Heart of the Church*, 235.

The liberation theologies in Latin America, Asia, and Africa, along with black, feminist, and Hispanic theologies, affected Catholic life along the same time frame of the pontificate of John Paul II.[31] Primarily they articulated the experience of being human in modern society, which went beyond the classical and revisionist perspectives. Being human was influenced by social location, race, class, and gender. Human becoming depended on one's response not only to the traditional moral restrictions of the various forms of egotism but also to the social conditions that marked one's own or another's possibility of human flourishing. These theologies, which emerged from postwar emancipation movements across the globe, entered into the narratives of Catholic life, and further specified what it meant to be Christian in the face of the situation of one's neighbor. The following of Christ was not only an I–Thou relationship but involved response to the concrete quest for human emancipation arising in society and discernment of one's responsibility in regard to it.

The liberation theologies and the anthropology of John Paul II share a deep interest in this call to follow Christ as the foundation of the Christian moral life. The question is, how is this understood? John Paul II's Christocentric anthropology certainly relates the meaning of the redemption to the life of this world. The liberation theologies also seek to ground the quest for human emancipation in the doctrine of the redemption. They share a grammar but come to different conclusions. For the liberationists, the redemption is only understood as one engages in the transformation of whatever concrete alienation forms the starting point of theological reflection, whether it is race, class, gender, poverty, or violence. For John Paul II, the redemption can be understood and experienced prior to engagement in social action. However, social action centered in mercy, love, and justice brings one into the heart of the redemptive mystery and union with God.

The relationship of Christology to ethics and the mission of the church in society is the foundation of John Paul II's theory of justice. Yet when his theology comes into contact with thought that arises from reflection on concrete conflicts in actual social relations, the concrete-

---

31. Cf. also, chapter 8 of the present volume. One would also need to include the political theology of Johannes Metz, although that is beyond the scope of this paper.

ness of their assertions appears to him to reduce the redemptive mystery to too narrow a focus. For instance, black, feminist, Latin American, and to some degree pacifist theologians question how Christians understand the atonement central to the mystery of the redemption and its impact on understanding the Christian life. The kingdom of God is God's will for everyone, they argue, yet it is communicated in the Christian tradition in a manner in which the evils of racism, chattel slavery, abuse of women, patriarchy, national poverty, violence, and war can coexist with the salvation offered by Jesus Christ. They question a separation between the proclamation of salvation in Jesus Christ and the ethics of the converted life to which the Christian is called.[32]

John Paul II understands the relationship between salvation and social justice in a way that does not reduce salvation to a specific sociopolitical liberation process. Social justice is an essential part of the Gospel, yet the Gospel proclaims a salvation that is irreducible to social justice and its specific acts. "The Kingdom of God being in the world without being of the world, throws light on the order of human society, while the power of grace penetrates that order and gives it life" (CA 25). Social justice is more than an ethical deduction of the Gospel. When people act justly, they do so in a way which is informed by the very light and power of God's redeeming grace operating in the temporal sphere.[33] The divine realities give the light of the kingdom and the power of grace that gives life to the temporal sphere. Christian life is more than an emancipatory praxis or action; rather the Christian life is lived with the person of Christ as its center.

John Paul and those in emancipatory movements ask related questions but not the same question. People in emancipatory movements question how one can proclaim a salvation in Jesus Christ that can coexist with some of the worst socializations of evil since the origin of the

---

32. For example, Ignacio Ellacuria, "The Church of the Poor, Historical Sacrament of Liberation," in Mysterium Liberationis: *Fundamental Concepts of Liberation Theology,* ed. Ignacion Ellacuria, SJ, and Jon Sobrino, SJ (New York: Orbis, 1993), 543–64; J. Denny Weaver, *The Nonviolent Atonement* (Grand Rapids, MI: Eerdmans, 2001); Gustaf Aulen, Christus Victor: *An Historical Study of Three Main Types of the Idea of Atonement,* trans. A. G. Herbert (New York: Macmillan, 1969); James Cone, *God of the Oppressed* (New York: Orbis, 1997), 42–52. Rosemary Radford Ruether, "Christology: Can a Male Savior Save Women?" in *Sexism and God-Talk: Toward a Feminist Theology* (Boston: Beacon, 1983), 116–38.

33. Beigel, *Faith and Social Justice,* 100.

human race. They claim this happens when one methodologically places salvation prior to liberating praxis in such a way that one can assume the meaning of salvation can be grasped in a social situation which is blind to socially accepted evil. John Paul's question, however, is the opposite. He is concerned that emancipatory practice can be so identified with the Christian life, that one can practice it without the person of Christ and still call themselves Christian. The Christian life should be understood in a way in which consciousness of being a creature and in need of redemption, being a member of the Mystical Body of Christ, is logically prior to the horizontal emphasis of Vatican II on the People of God, which is often used as the ground of seeing the church as a movement of social reform.[34]

Liberation thinking in its depiction of sin can become so focused on a particular manifestation of sin that the reality of ontic evil, the fact of evil, is collapsed into moral evil, the evil people do. However, liberationists argue that without the particularity of sin denounced, sin and evil remain abstract and redemption an unnecessary addendum to a socially secure life protected by the status quo. The need therefore to maintain the inseparable unity between the particular and the universal is necessary in relating the redemption brought to us by Jesus Christ to contemporary visions of emancipation. The theological tensions in this question, however, are manifested in the multiple languages of justice that exist in the church today.

Those involved concretely in movements of emancipation might ask if John Paul II sufficiently develops his thinking to link Christ's redemption to concrete people in the movements which today express the human longing for emancipation. John Paul II avoids even the more common and moderate assertion that salvation is transcendental but is realized in specific sociopolitical options. Rather he states, "The Church well knows that no temporal achievement is to be identified with the kingdom of God, but that all such achievements simply reflect and in a sense anticipate the glory of the kingdom" (SRS 48).[35]

However, John Paul II's focus on Christ's redemptive mystery in his theory of justice adds impetus to overcoming social evils as an integral

---

34. Wojtyla, *Sources of Renewal*, 87.
35. On John Paul II and the kingdom of God, cf. also, chapter 13 of the present volume.

part of the Christian life. In no way is his redemptive theology indifferent to the concrete forms of evil in this world. He sees confronting evil in a manner that goes beyond an anti-worldview as fallen creation alone. His is more positive, based on the redemptive mode of God relating to the world. This mode "sees the nature of the international order in the persistent struggle to bring the human oneness established in Christ to transforming historical concreteness in the relationships that actually exist among human beings and their groups."[36] Obstacles to development have to be noted, but prophetic denunciation is not enough. John Paul II claims, "the church must strongly affirm the possibility of overcoming the obstacles which . . . stand in the way of development." And she must affirm her confidence in a true liberation "based on the Church's awareness of the divine promise, guaranteeing that our present history does not remain closed in upon itself but is open to the Kingdom of God" (SRS 47).

However time measures John Paul II's contribution to the church's tradition of justice, we know because of the theological grounding of his approach that he stands in the center of one of the most important theological questions of our time. In the words of Walter Kasper, "it is a fundamental question for modern Christology to decide the relation between redemption understood in a Christian perspective and emancipation understood as the modern age understands it."[37] Some may question whether John Paul II's thought, because of its foundational and theological tone, reflects a general tendency in the Catholic social tradition to be too vague and moralistic to have an impact on concrete problems.[38] Yet the former Soviet president Mikhail Gorbachev testifies to the role John Paul II played in the collapse of communism. He remarks, "everything that happened in eastern Europe during these last few years would not have been possible without the presence of this

---

36. Johann Verstraeten, "Catholic Social Thinking as Living Tradition that Gives Meaning to Globalization as a Process of Humanization," in *Globalization and Catholic Social Thought*, ed. John A. Coleman and William F. Ryan (New York: Orbis, 2005), 42.

37. Walter Kasper, *Jesus the Christ* (London: Burns and Oates; New York: Paulist Press, 1976), 42.

38. John A. Coleman, "Global Governance, the State and Multinational Corporations," in *Globalization and Catholic Social Thought*, 242.

pope, without the leading role—the political role—that he was able to play on the world scene."[39]

Perhaps John Paul II simply shared with the world in his thoughts on justice the fruits of a life well lived. His journey in a conflicted political world was marked by a deep and abiding faith. What for some becomes an occasion of escapism, was for him a call to investment. What the world can take in, hear, and act on from the legacy he left might mark the direction of its future.

39. As cited in Donal Dorr, *Option for the Poor* (Maryknoll, NY: Orbis, 1992), 342.

8

The Sources of Moral Truth
in the Teaching of John Paul II

Charles E. Curran

This essay considers the sources of moral truth used by Pope John Paul
II in his encyclicals.[1] For John Paul II the truth about the human person
constitutes the basis for his understanding of morality and moral theology. He later described his first encyclical, *Redemptor Hominis,* as addressing the subject of "the truth about man" (DM 1.2). John Paul II wrote
three social encyclicals—*Laborem Exercens* (1981), *Sollicitudo Rei Socialis*
(1987), and *Centesimus Annus* (1991). In the latter encyclical he points out
that "the guiding principle of Pope Leo's Encyclical and of all of the
Church's social doctrine, is a *correct view of the human person* and of his
unique value" (11.3). The title of his encyclical on moral theology is
Splendor of Truth. J. Michael Miller has pointed out that "obedience
of freedom to truth" is the first key theme of that encyclical, *Veritatis
Splendor,* and further appears as the central theme in many of John Paul
II's writings.[2]

---

1. The thirteen encyclicals written by John Paul II are the following: *Redemptor Hominis*
(RH), 1979; *Dives in Misericordia* (DM), 1980; *Laborem Exercens* (LE), 1981; *Dominum et Vivificantem* (DV), 1986; *Redemptoris Mater* (RMA), 1987; *Sollicitudo Rei Socialis* (SRS), 1987; *Redemptoris Missio* (RM), 1990; *Centesimus Annus* (CA), 1991; *Veritatis Splendor* (VS), 1993; *Evangelium
Vitae* (EV), 1995; *Ut Unum Sint,* (UUS), 1995; *Fides et Ratio* (FR), 1998; *Ecclesia de Eucharistia*
(EE), 2003. The encyclicals can be conveniently found in J. Michael Miller, ed., *The Encyclicals of John Paul II* (Huntington, IN: Our Sunday Visitor Press, 2001). Future references to
the papal encyclicals will be given by their initials in the text followed by the paragraphs as
found in the Miller book. This essay is based on my monograph—Charles E. Curran, *The
Moral Theology of Pope John Paul II* (Washington, DC: Georgetown University Press, 2005).

2. Miller, *Encyclicals of John Paul II,* 575.

The centrality of the truth about human beings as the basic corner-stone of John Paul II's moral teaching is thus evident. But then the question arises: What are the sources of moral wisdom and knowledge that he uses to arrive at the truth about human beings? In keeping with the Catholic tradition, John Paul II recognizes both divine and human sources for the truth about the human person. The encyclical *Fides et Ratio* (Faith and Reason) well illustrates his approach.

The theological grounding for this role of reason comes from the doctrine of creation. Some Protestants have seen sin as destroying or almost totally destroying the goodness of the human in general and reason in particular. But the Catholic tradition, in addition to affirming reason, has always insisted that grace does not deny human nature, but rather grace perfects human nature and brings it to its perfection. John Paul II in *Veritatis Splendor* insists that neither sin nor the darkness of error can take away from human beings the light of God the Creator. In the depth of the human heart there always remains a yearning for absolute truth and a thirst to attain full knowledge of it (FR 1.3).

The more theological encyclicals such as the three on the Trinity focus, in particular, upon Christ who fully reveals the human person to oneself (RH 10.1). In these encyclicals John Paul II emphasizes sin and the fact that humanity today is in crisis because it has exalted freedom over truth. These encyclicals dealing with faith aspects do not reflect upon the very Catholic theological tradition of human reason as a ve-hicle for bringing persons toward the apprehension and understanding of truth. The ad hoc nature of these encyclicals and their dealing with particular topics of a doctrinal nature help to explain to some degree the absence of the role of human reason in arriving at moral truth. But at times the emphasis on sin seems to leave no place for human reason.

One would expect the two encyclicals dealing with moral theology—*Veritatis Splendor* and *Evangelium Vitae*—to develop the role of reason as a source of truth. *Veritatis Splendor* strongly relies on the role of reason as developed in Catholic natural law theory, while the very beginning of *Evangelium Vitae* maintains that the gospel of life has a profound and pervasive echo in the heart of every person who can come to recognize the natural law written in their hearts (EV 2.2). But *Evangelium Vitae* emphasizes the dramatic conflict between the culture of death and the culture of life (EV 50.2). The struggle is a veritable war and conspiracy against life (EV 12). Logically one who accepts a basic goodness of the human and human reason cannot see contemporary existence in terms of a war between the culture of life identified with the church and the culture of death identified with the world. The pope's emphasis on the evils of abortion and euthanasia in light of the growing approval of movements throughout the world supporting these evils obviously colored his culture of life vs. culture of death approach, but that creates theological tension if not opposition with his holding on to human reason as a source of moral wisdom and knowledge.

The three social encyclicals constitute a whole and continue the tradition begun by Pope John XXIII of addressing not only Catholics but also all people of good will. These encyclicals call for all humanity to work together and thus emphasize reason and the human sources of moral wisdom and knowledge. In *Sollicitudo Rei Socialis*, John Paul II adroitly recognizes the problem of writing to two different audiences. In fact, he addresses one chapter of the encyclical to a theological reading of modern problems (SRS 35–40). The obstacles to authentic human development such as the all-consuming desire for profit and the thirst for power truly constitute moral evils and structures of sin that Christians through conversion are called to overcome, especially by practicing the virtue of solidarity. Solidarity is not just a vague feeling of compassion but a firm and persevering determination to commit oneself to the common good, to the good of all and each individual, because we are all responsible for all (SRS 38.6).

The pope hopes that even those who do not share his faith can recognize the need to change spiritual attitudes in view of the higher values of the common good and of the full development of the individual and of all people (SRS 38.3). So even while addressing Christians the pope also appeals to those who do not share the Christian faith. His choice of the word "solidarity" helps to support his appeal to all human beings. The pope does not choose a distinctively Christian term such as grace or agape or the kingdom of God. John Paul II insists that solidarity is undeniably a Christian virtue, but it has appeal to non-Christians as well.

All Catholic theologians agree with the need for Catholic theology to use both faith and reason as sources of moral truth. This essay will now develop in greater detail three significant sources for moral truth as found in the moral teaching of Pope John Paul II—Scripture, church teaching, and natural law. Not all Catholic moral theologians agree with the way in which John Paul II has used these three sources.

Scripture

The encyclical *Veritatis Splendor* highlights the principles of a moral theology based on Scripture and the living Apostolic Tradition (VS 5.3). Sacred Scripture remains the living and truthful source of the church's moral doctrine, for as Vatican II pointed out, the Gospel is the source of all saving truth and moral teaching (VS 28–29). John Paul II thus carries out the mandate of Vatican II in having a Scripture-based moral teaching.

How does John Paul II use Scripture in developing his moral teaching? In the mid-twentieth century Catholic biblical scholars accepted a more critical approach to Scripture. Biblical scholars pointed out, for example, the different levels in New Testament writings—sayings of the historical Jesus, the understanding of the early church, and the way in which each evangelist used his sources to develop his own narrative.[3] John Paul II does not generally allude to the findings of critical biblical scholarship and does not mention any contemporary Catholic scholars. In fairness to the pope, contemporary Catholic moral theologians generally do not employ critical biblical scholarship in their writing. A tension exists between this critical biblical scholarship and the work of moral theology. Scholars correctly point out there is no such thing as *the* biblical moral teaching but rather the teachings of many different authors working in many different circumstances, times, and cultures. Moral theologians have the function of proposing how Christian people should live and act today. The different perspectives, approaches, cultures, and time frames in the biblical moral teaching make the task of contemporary moral theologians much more difficult.

How then does John Paul II use Scripture in his moral teaching? He tends to consider Scripture as a unified whole and often employs what can best be described as a contemplative, meditative, and even homiletic approach to Scripture. Such an approach is similar to the way in which

3. William C. Spohn, *What Are They Saying about Scripture and Ethics?* rev. ed. (New York: Paulist Press, 1995).

the early Christian authors used Scripture. The encyclical *Dives in Misericordia* well illustrates such an approach. The encyclical devotes one chapter to the understanding of mercy in the Old Testament employing different genres and texts (DM 4). The chapter on the New Testament concentrates on the parable of the Prodigal Son and points out how the teaching of Christ makes the image inherited from the Old Testament at the same time both simpler and more profound (DM 5.2). Meditating on this parable the pope develops its meaning for today. Love is transformed into mercy when it goes beyond the precise and narrow form of justice (DM 5.6). The father in the parable is faithful to his fatherhood and faithful to his love, thus illustrating the mercy of God (DM 6.1). The parable expresses in a profound and simple way the reality of conversion, the most concrete expression of the working of love and of the response of mercy in the human world (DM 6.5). A subsequent chapter understands merciful love as revealed in the paschal mystery of Jesus (DM 7.1–9.6).

The major issue in using Scripture in moral theology is how one moves from the author of a particular scriptural passage to the horizon of the contemporary interpreter (i.e., hermeneutics). The great danger resulting from this fusion of horizons is the possibility of inegesis or eisegesis, which is using Scripture to support one's own presuppositions. The horizon of the contemporary author is bound to affect the way in which Scripture is employed, and this does not necessarily involve misuse of Scripture. John Paul II cites Genesis 1 and 2 more than any other texts in the Hebrew Bible.[4] The central theme in John Paul II's moral theology is the dignity of the human person, so it is only natural for him to insist on using the scriptural understanding that human beings are created in the image and likeness of God. His encyclicals cite John more than any other New Testament evangelist.[5] Jesus Christ plays a very significant role in all of his encyclicals, especially the more doctrinal ones. John Paul II sees Jesus Christ primarily as the Word of God who becomes incarnate and brings about our redemption and the new creation. Such a Christology from above, stressing the preexisting Logos and the Incarnation, finds its strongest biblical support in John and not

4. Miller, *Encyclicals of John Paul II*, 28.
5. Ibid.

in the Synoptic Gospels, which tend to take a "lower" Christology beginning with the human Jesus. There is no doubt that John Paul II's theological presuppositions have strongly influenced the scriptural texts that he uses, but such a use does not necessarily distort the Scriptures.

Veritatis Splendor employs Scripture to support its fundamental thesis—the reaffirmation of the universality and immutability of the moral commandments, particularly those that prohibit always and everywhere intrinsically evil acts (VS 115.3). The bishops of the church have the office of leading the faithful to God, just as Jesus did in the story of the rich young man in Matthew 19. The first chapter of the encyclical is a long meditation on the story of the rich young man who asks Jesus the question of what he has to do to have eternal life. Jesus reminds him of the moral commands already found in the Old Testament, and he indicates their spirit and deepest meaning by inviting the young man to follow him. "This 'answer' to the question about morality has been entrusted by Jesus Christ in a special way to us, the Pastors of the Church" (VS 114.3). The encyclical also insists that the moral prescriptions found in the old covenant, which attained their perfection in the new and eternal covenant in the very person of the Son of God made human, must be faithfully kept and continually put into practice. The task of interpreting these prescriptions was entrusted by Jesus to the apostles and their successors with the special assistance of the Spirit of Truth (VS 25.2).

Two problems stand out in John Paul II's use of the story of the rich young man. First, he basically distorts the original meaning of the story. The rich young man responded to Jesus that he had kept all these commands. Jesus then told him to sell his possessions, give them to the poor, and come follow Jesus. The rich young man went away sad for he had many possessions. The clear thrust of the story is the danger of riches. But *Veritatis Splendor* uses this text to support its basic thesis about the need for the faithful to obey the moral commandments taught by the hierarchical magisterium.

A second distortion involves the going from Jesus' proposing commandments to the rich young man to the hierarchical magisterium's teaching about absolute moral norms today. Such an approach fails to realize the difference between the moral commandments taught by Jesus and the concrete moral teachings of the papal office. The Old Testament and Jesus knew nothing about commandments against contraception or direct abortion and never deal with the intricate questions of the difference between the use of extraordinary and ordinary means of medical treatments.

On a more specific level *Veritatis Splendor* uses Scripture to support papal teaching on intrinsically evil acts and the condemnation of proportionalism. The heading of the discussion on intrinsic evil comes from Romans 3:18: "It is not licit to do evil that good may come of it" (VS 79.1). But this text is much too generic to prove that the contemporary papal teaching on intrinsic evil is correct and that proportionalism's approach is wrong. *Veritatis Splendor* goes on to assert that in teaching the existence of intrinsically evil moral acts the church accepts the teaching of Scripture. The Apostle Paul emphatically states: "Do not be deceived: Neither the immoral, nor idolaters, nor adulterers, nor sexual perverts, nor thieves, nor the greedy, nor drunkards, nor revilers, nor robbers will inherit the Kingdom of God (1 Cor 6:9-10)" (VS 81.1). But 1 Corinthians talks about persons and their vices and not about intrinsically evil acts as understood by the encyclical.

Church Teaching

Anyone familiar with the Catholic tradition knows that church teaching constitutes a very important source of moral wisdom and knowledge in the Catholic Church. There are two related questions about church teachings as a source of moral knowledge. The first concerns how John Paul II in his writings employs earlier church teaching; the second concerns how he understands the way in which the teaching office of the church functions.[6]

Use of Previous Church Teaching

One rightly assumes that John Paul II as Bishop of Rome would frequently cite previous teachings of the hierarchical magisterium. As in the use of Scripture, a primary question concerns the fusion of the two horizons—the horizon of the original text and the horizon of John Paul II himself. Here, too, John Paul II uses the earlier teachings to sup-

6. See also chapter 6 of the present volume.

port his particular interests and purposes without, however, distorting the meaning of the original text. But at times he also uses the earlier hierarchical teaching in a way that definitely distorts the meaning of the original.

Pope Wojtyla cites Vatican II documents in his encyclicals more than any other nonbiblical source. The pope saw his primary task in this moment of history as interpreting the teaching of this great council (DM 1.4). The pope himself, however, has recognized the existence of different interpretations of the council (RH 3.1). The dispute about the proper interpretation of Vatican II lies beyond the narrow limits of this study, but many commentators point out that the pope, in numerous ways, did not follow the real spirit of Vatican II.[7]

The pope often cites *Gaudium et Spes* 22 (three times in his first encyclical, *Redemptor Hominis*, 8.2, 13.1, 18.1): "The truth is that only in the mystery of the Incarnate Word does the mystery of man take on light." This emphasis fits with his insistence that Jesus Christ, the Redeemer, fully reveals the human being to himself (DM 1.3, RH 10.1). Others might not cite this paragraph as the most significant paragraph in *Gaudium et Spes*, but such a paragraph is in keeping with a primary emphasis of John Paul II's and does not distort the meaning of the original text.

However, there are instances when he uses Vatican II in an unwarranted way. *Veritatis Splendor* insists that certain human actions by reason of their object are intrinsically evil; that is, always and everywhere wrong. To support this position, John Paul II cites over one hundred words of *Gaudium et Spes* 27 (VS 80.1). But the text of *Gaudium et Spes* does not come out of the same framework as the pope with his insistence on intrinsically evil acts. In fact the citation never mentions the words "intrinsically evil." In addition, three of the actions mentioned in *Gaudium et Spes* 27—slavery, torture, and attempts to coerce the spirit—at times have been accepted and not condemned by the church. Logically the pope cannot claim that such acts are intrinsically evil if at one time they were accepted in the church. In a broader perspective, Mary Elsbernd maintains that *Veritatis Splendor* has reinterpreted *Gaudium et Spes* in light of an older Catholic moral theology with its insistence on a legal frame-

---

7. E.g., Hans Küng and Leonard Swidler, eds., *The Church in Anguish: Has the Vatican Betrayed Vatican II?* (San Francisco: Harper and Row, 1986).

work or methodology, an individualistic anthropology, and a downplaying of human initiative.[8]

Again, one would expect the three social encyclicals of John Paul II to cite frequently the other papal documents in the series, beginning with Leo XIII's *Rerum Novarum* in 1891, which John Paul II refers to as the social teaching or doctrine of the church. But here too the pope purposely reinterprets the earlier letter of Paul VI, *Octogesima Adveniens.* The Dominican French scholar Marie-Dominique Chenu, in a significant little book in the late 1970s, maintained that in *Octogesima Adveniens* Paul VI no longer accepts the social teaching of the church (Chenu calls it an ideology) with its emphasis on abstract and prefabricated concepts claiming to be based on the eternal and natural law and replaces it with a more inductive approach based on historical consciousness and with emphasis not on the eternal and the unchanging but on the particular and the local.[9] Chenu also notes that in this letter and in immediately previous documents before Paul VI (*Pacem in Terris* and *Gaudium et Spes*) the term "the social doctrine of the church" does not appear.[10]

John Paul II uses the encyclical *Sollicitudo Rei Socialis* to refute the Chenu thesis without explicitly mentioning him by name. *Sollicitudo* resurrects and gives great importance to the concept of the social doctrine of the church and insists it is not an ideology (SRS 41.7). The Latin text of *Centesimus Annus* uses the term "social doctrine of the church" about twenty times and insists on continuity in Catholic social teaching. The English translation of the encyclicals sometimes translates the Latin word *doctrina* as "doctrine" and sometimes as "teaching." The terms "Catholic social doctrine" or "Catholic social teaching" are thus often used interchangeably to refer to the teaching found in these documents of the hierarchical magisterium.

Sollicitudo in three places refers to the continuity in Catholic social teaching as principles of reflection, criteria of judgment, and directives for actions, with footnotes in all three cases to *Octogesima Adveniens* 4 (SRS 3.2, 8.4, 41.5). Thus, John Paul II claims that *Octogesima Adveniens* adopted

8. Mary Elsbernd, "The Reinterpretation of *Gaudium et Spes* in *Veritatis Splendor,*" *Horizons* 29 (2005): 225–39.

9. Marie-Dominique Chenu, *La "doctrine sociale" de l'Église comme idéologie* (Paris: Cerf, 1979).

10. Ibid., 87–96.

the same methodology that he uses—applying unchangeable principles in different historical and cultural circumstances. But Paul VI in *Octogesima Adveniens* did not follow such a methodology beginning with agreed upon principles, criteria, and directives. *Octogesima Adveniens* begins with the experience of the local Christian community attempting to discern the options and commitments that are called for to bring about the urgently needed social, political, and economic changes. In the same early paragraph Paul VI explicitly acknowledged it was neither his ambition nor his mission to put forward solutions that have universal validity.[11] Thus John Paul II proposes a more classicist and even deductive methodology in contrast to the more historically conscious and inductive methodology of *Octogesima Adveniens* and even claims that his approach is in continuity with *Octogesima Adveniens*.

The Role of the Teaching Church

In a consistent way from his very first encyclical, John Paul II sees the church through the gift of the Holy Spirit as guarding and teaching in its most exact integrity the truth about human beings revealed by Jesus (RH 12.2). How does John Paul II understand the church? The church has a divine-human constitution (DV 61.1). In light of this constitution the shortcomings, failures, and sins arise from the members of the church but not from the church itself (UUS 3.1). To his great credit, more than any other pope, John Paul II has recognized and apologized for the sins of the members of the church. But John Paul II's ecclesiology does not allow him to say that the church *itself* is sinful and has done wrong.[12]

Many contemporary Catholic theologians have a different understanding of the church, recognizing with Vatican II that the church is the people of God and a pilgrim church. A pilgrim church is a church that always falls short and is never perfect. One can and should even speak of a sinful church. If the church is the people of God, then one

---

11. Pope Paul VI, *Octogesima Adveniens* 4, in *Catholic Social Thought: The Documentary Heritage*, ed. David J. O'Brien and Thomas A. Shannon (Maryknoll, NY: Orbis, 1992), 266.

12. John Paul II, *Teretio Millennio Adveniente* 133–36, *Origins* 24 (1994): 401ff.; *Incarnationis Mysterium* 11, *Origins* 28 (1998): 450–51; "Jubilee Characteristic: The Purification of Memory," *Origins* 29 (2000): 649–50.

cannot so easily make the distinction between the sins of the members of the church and the holiness of the church. It thus seems evident that John Paul II has too triumphalistic an understanding of the church.[13]

This triumphalistic understanding of the church might also help to explain why John Paul II in his encyclicals never addresses the question of how the church "acquires" the truth. Of course, one cannot expect disparate encyclicals written in response to particular issues and topics to fully develop in depth all the concepts that are used. But the fact of the matter is that the church has to learn the truth before it teaches the truth. The encyclicals mention the deposit of faith that has been entrusted to the care and protection of the church, but the deposit of faith cannot be understood as a deposit of verbal propositions that the church defends, protects, and applies. The Catholic insistence on Scripture and tradition means that the church must understand, appropriate, bear witness to, and live out Scripture in light of ongoing historical circumstances. The early councils of the church well illustrate what it means to be a living tradition. These councils dealt with the basic beliefs of Catholic faith—who is God and who is Jesus Christ. The councils taught that in God there are three persons and in Jesus there is one person and two natures. But the concepts of nature and person are not found in Scripture. The early church used these concepts that originated in Greek thought to arrive at a more adequate but never perfect understanding of the Trinity and of Jesus Christ. History reminds us that only through a somewhat difficult and prolonged process did the church itself come to this understanding of the Trinity and of Jesus Christ.

Such a learning process is even more evident in the moral teachings proposed by the church. Many of the controversial issues discussed today, such as contraception, abortion, the use and threat of nuclear weapons, and the rightness of economic and political systems, are not found in Scripture. Scripture itself does not explicitly condemn slavery. Thus the teaching church has had to learn its moral teachings before it could teach them.

13. John Ford, "John Paul II Asks for Forgiveness," *Ecumenical Trends* 27 (December 1998); 173–75; Francis A. Sullivan, "The Papal Apology," *America* 182, no.12 (April 8, 2000): 17–22; Aline H. Kalbian, "The Catholic Church's Public Confession: Theological and Ethical Implications," *The Annual of the Society of Christian Ethics* 21 (2001): 175–89.

What about the assistance of the Holy Spirit? Yes, the Catholic tradition recognizes the gift of the Spirit to assist the church in arriving at truth. The ultimate question is how the Spirit works in the church. The Catholic tradition, to its great credit, has been characterized by its emphasis on mediation—the divine is mediated in and through the human. The assistance of the Spirit does not do away with all the other ways of arriving at truth, such as the experience of people living under the Spirit, human reason, and a dialogue with all people of good will. There can be no doubt that the church has to learn the truth before it can teach it.

In passing, John Paul II recognizes many voices in the living tradition of the church—the words of the fathers and doctors of the church, the practice and lives of our saints and martyrs, and the liturgy. However, the task of *authoritatively* interpreting the Word of God according to Vatican II belongs only to the bishops, the church's living magisterium, who exercise their teaching function in the name of Jesus and with the assistance of the Holy Spirit (VS 27).

The magisterium helps the formation of conscience by declaring and confirming the principles of the moral order that derive from human nature itself. The magisterium thereby does not impose truths from the outside but brings to light the truths that the human conscience already possesses. Especially in more difficult questions, consciences are able to "attain the truth with certainty and to abide in it" (VS 64.2). Thus the magisterium provides certitude to the Christian conscience on those moral teachings based on human nature.

Veritatis Splendor discusses the hierarchical magisterium also in the context of the role of moral theologians and theological dissent. Moral theologians who work in communion and cooperation with the magisterium should give loyal assent both internally and externally to the moral teachings of the hierarchical magisterium. Moral theologians can contribute by developing a deeper understanding of the reasons supporting the teaching and clarify more fully the biblical foundations.[14] The encyclical strongly condemns dissent understood in the narrow sense of carefully orchestrated protests and polemics carried on in the media (VS 109–13).

---

14. Again, cf. chapter 6 of the present volume.

Neither *Veritatis Splendor* nor any of the other encyclicals explicitly distinguish between infallible teaching and non-infallible teaching. Pope John Paul II inserted into the Code of Canon Law a category of teaching between infallible teaching of the divinely revealed truth and the non-infallible teaching to which the faithful owe a religious *obsequium* of intellect and will. The new category inserted into the code is *definitive* (i.e., infallible) teaching by the magisterium of a doctrine concerned with faith and morals that is not directly revealed but is necessarily connected with revelation. This is a new category in canon law, but it has similarities to what older Catholic theologians called the secondary object of infallibility.[15] But the encyclicals do not explicitly and directly refer to these different types of teaching and explicitly claim the same certitude for all their teachings. *Veritatis Splendor* does recognize the possible limitations of the human arguments proposed by the magisterium, but apparently this does not affect the certitude of the proposed teaching (VS 110.2).

Even though the encyclicals of John Paul II do not explicitly recognize any *degrees* of certitude with regard to the moral teachings of the magisterium, there are strong reasons in the Catholic tradition for insisting on degrees of certitude with regard to the moral teachings of the papal magisterium. Some of the moral teachings are not absolutely certain and in fact might even be wrong. First, past papal moral teachings have changed in the course of time. Think of the teachings on slavery, usury, the right to silence, democracy, the ends of marriage, and the role of women in society.[16] That such changes have occurred proves that these teachings were not certain and in fact at some stage, although they continued to be taught, were wrong. Second, all have to admit that the majority of moral teachings of the papal magisterium belong to the category of non-infallible church teaching. By definition, such teachings are fallible.

Third, Catholic tradition, as illustrated in the work of Thomas Aquinas, has recognized the difference between speculative truths and moral truths. Speculative principles, such as the assertion that a trian-

---

15. John Paul II, "*Ad Tuendam Fidem*," *Origins* 28, no. 8 (July 16, 1998): 113–16.

16. Charles E. Curran, ed., *Change in Official Catholic Moral Teachings*, Readings in Moral Theology 13 (New York: Paulist Press, 2003).

gle's angles add up to 180 degrees, are always and everywhere true. Moral principles, however, involving secondary principles of the natural law, oblige generally and in most cases but not always. Deposits should be returned, but if someone has deposited a sword with you and returns raving drunk threatening to kill someone, you should not return the deposited sword. Moral principles differ from speculative truths with regard to their truth and certitude precisely because new circumstances can arise in complex and specific situations that cause the principle to no longer be true and obliging.[17] Thus the Catholic tradition recognizes different levels of certitude with regard to many of its moral teachings. One might argue that the papal encyclicals should not become involved in such intricate points of Catholic theology, but still the true understanding of the Catholic tradition requires some recognition of different levels of truth and certitude with regard to the moral teachings of the papal magisterium.

Natural Law

Veritatis Splendor was written to deal with the genuine crisis that many moral theologians in the church disagree with some of the hierarchical teaching by reasserting "the traditional doctrine regarding the natural law and the universality and the permanent validity of its precepts" (VS 42). The encyclical, unlike all the others, is not addressed to a general audience of Catholics and all people of good will but to the bishops of the church, and it develops in an in-depth manner the foundations of moral theology and the teachings especially on disputed issues (VS 5).

John Paul II rejects both autonomy (the human person alone determines what is morally good) and heteronomy (the human person is ruled by some outside source). He proposes participated theonomy by which human self-determination participates in the wisdom and providence of God. How is this accomplished? Natural law is the answer (VS 41).

Natural law, according to Thomas Aquinas, is the participation of the eternal law in the rational creature. The eternal law is the plan of God for the world. God gave human beings reason by which human beings reflecting on human nature and what God has made can determine

17. Thomas Aquinas, *Summa Theologiae*, 4 vols. (Rome: Marietti, 1952), *Ia IIae* q. 94, a. 4.

what God wants human beings to do (VS 43). Without using the term "intrinsic morality," the encyclical insists that morality is intrinsic—something is commanded because it is good for us and fulfills our human nature. The natural law is not in opposition with true human freedom. The pope insists that the body is part of the human and rejects the charge of biologism or physicalism. Revisionist Catholic moral theologians have criticized the neoscholastic natural law theory for identifying the physical aspect of the act with the moral aspect. For example, the physical act of marital intercourse must always be present and cannot be interfered with either to prevent or to promote conception. The encyclical sees natural law as based on the natural inclinations of human nature to specific God-given ends. These natural inclinations determine the moral assessment of particular acts (VS 43–44).

Since John Paul II in *Veritatis Splendor* insists so much on natural law as the foundation for Catholic moral theology and moral teaching, one would expect that he would at least mention and refer to natural law in other encyclicals dealing with human action and human reason. As noted above, *Evangelium Vitae* does base its condemnations of direct killing, direct abortion, and euthanasia on natural law (EV 57.4, 62.3, 65.4). One would also expect the social encyclicals to insist on natural law as the basis for the teaching proposed there for all human beings. Earlier papal documents of Catholic social teaching heavily emphasized the natural law foundation for their teaching, which enabled them to speak to all human beings and not just to Catholics or Christians. But the social encyclicals do not develop the theory of natural law and, in fact, the three encyclicals do not even mention natural law.

One would also expect *Fides et Ratio*, which was written after *Veritatis Splendor* and *Evangelium Vitae*, to discuss in some detail the natural law as the basis for Catholic moral teaching based on human reason. The encyclical does insist on the need for metaphysics to move beyond the crisis in contemporary philosophy (FR 83.4). But *Fides et Ratio* mentions human nature only five times (FR 3.1, 29.1, 68.1, 80.3, 102) and never uses the term natural law.

Why the silence about natural law in many of the other encyclicals? The ad hoc nature of the encyclicals and the fact that they are not as theoretical as *Veritatis Splendor* help to explain the absence. But the failure even to mention natural law in the other encyclicals seems quite odd in light of the Catholic tradition in moral theology and the pope's heavy insistence on natural law in *Veritatis Splendor.*

Veritatis Splendor has not convinced most Catholic moral theologians who earlier expressed disagreement with the theory and application of natural law to some controversial issues in the life of the Catholic Church. Many would accept in general a natural law approach but not the specific approach developed in the encyclical. This essay is not the place to discuss once again in any detail the reactions to and criticisms of the natural law theory and its applications as found in *Veritatis Splendor.* It will suffice just to mention some of these aspects.

Fides et Ratio insists that the church has no philosophy of its own and does not canonize one particular philosophy in preference to another (FR 49.1). But *Veritatis Splendor* has clearly canonized the neoscholastic natural law theory. Revisionists continue to criticize this theory for a number of reasons: its failure to appreciate historical consciousness, its physicalism, its unwillingness to recognize with Thomas Aquinas that the secondary principles of the natural law are not always obliging, its emphasis on inclinations of human faculties and powers rather than on the person as a whole, and the failure to give some role to the social location of persons.[18] John Paul II's use especially of church teaching and of natural law as sources of moral truth continues to be controversial in the eyes of some Catholic moral theologians.

In keeping with the Catholic tradition, John Paul II has insisted on the need for both sources based on faith and sources based on human reason to arrive at moral truth. This essay has analyzed and criticized three sources of moral truth found in the encyclicals of John Paul II: Scripture, church teaching, and natural law.

18. Michael E. Allsopp and John J. O'Keefe, eds. Veritatis Splendor: *American Responses* (Kansas City, MO: Sheed and Ward, 1995); Joseph A. Selling and Jan Jans, eds., *The Splendor of Accuracy: An Examination of the Assertions Made in* Veritatis Splendor (Grand Rapids, MI: Eerdmans, 1995); John Wilkens, ed., *Understanding* Veritatis Splendor (London: SPCK, 1994).

9

John Paul II and
Theologies of Liberation

Mario I. Aguilar

Throughout John Paul II's long pontificate and particularly during the
1980s, the papacy and the Latin American Bishops with their theologians seemed to be constantly colliding. The appointment of Cardinal
Joseph Ratzinger, currently Pope Benedict XVI, as head of the Sacred
Congregation for the Doctrine of the Faith (CDF) brought new misun-
derstandings and new dialogues between Ratzinger and distinguished
theologians such as Gustavo Gutiérrez and Leonardo Boff, while others
such as Juan Luis Segundo, SJ, and Jon Sobrino, SJ, remained under
doctrinal scrutiny.

This chapter outlines some of the history of those theological encounters that involved Cardinal Ratzinger as the theological arm of John
Paul II. It is my central argument that the theological disputes about
doctrine were not only about the social role of the Catholic Church in
Latin America, or the use of Marxism as a heuristic device by the theologians being questioned, they had a central crux related to a slightly
different interpretation of the spirit of Vatican II.[1] Thus John Paul II

---

1. Solange Lefebvre, "Conflicting Interpretations of the Council: The Ratzinger-Kasper
Debate," in *The New Pontificate: A Time for Change?* eds. Erik Borgman, Maureen Junker-
Kenny, and Janet Martin Soskice, *Concilium* 2006/1 (London: SCM), 95–105. For a collection of Vatican II's major documents see Austin Flannery, OP, *Vatican Council II: The Conciliar
and Post Conciliar Documents*, rev. ed. (Northport, NY: Costello, 1992); for the history of the
council see Giuseppe Alberigo, ed., *History of Vatican II*, vol. 1, *Announcing and Preparing Vatican
Council II: Toward a New Era in Catholicism* (Maryknoll, NY: Orbis, 1995), vol. 2, *The Formation
of the Council's Identity: First Period and Intercession October 1962–September 1963* (Maryknoll, NY:

understood tradition and doctrine with some changes as the right implementation of the council, while the Latin American theologians, following Karl Rahner, understood the implementation of the council as a new and fresh break with tradition, creating a new relation between the Latin American churches and the traditional European theological constructions symbolized by the John Paul II/Ratzinger school of thought.

The Development of Liberation Theologies

Following the completion of Vatican II in 1965, the Latin American Bishops' Conference headed by the progressive Chilean Bishop Manuel Larraín scheduled a general meeting of Latin American Bishops at Medellín (Colombia) that took place in 1968. The meeting coincided with a time of questioning about poverty and injustice in Latin America and with the start of a period in which military regimes became more the norm rather than the exception.[2] The preparations at a local diocesan level for Medellín were intense and those leading the deliberations at the continental level were not the theologians but the pastoral bishops who, in the case of Brazil, were already experiencing a systematic violation of human rights. Within this difficult political context, the Latin American countries were responding to the implementation of Vatican II with enthusiasm and with a committed Catholic laity that had been heavily influenced by John XXIII's *Pacem in Terris* (1963) and Paul VI's *Populorum Progressio* (1967). The ideas contained in both encyclicals spoke of the possibility of a just order in society, but an order that had to consider development rather than armed struggle as its core value for an economic stability that provided the possibility of restoring dignity to all nations and to all human beings.

The genesis of Latin American liberation theology coincided with developments within a theology of inculturation in Africa and the Christian dialogue with world religions in Asia.[3] However, within those

---

Orbis, 1997), vol. 3, *The Mature Council: Second Period and Intercession September 1963–September 1964* (Maryknoll, NY: Orbis, 2000).

2. For a detailed analysis of the relation between church and state at the period and within different Latin American countries, see Jeffrey Klaiber, SJ, *The Church, Dictatorships, and Democracy in Latin America* (Maryknoll, NY: Orbis, 1998).

3. At the theological level African and Latin American theologians encountered each other through the Ecumenical Association of Third World Theologians (EATWOT) and

globalized developments a Peruvian priest, Gustavo Gutiérrez, became the face of liberation theology and helped other priests reflect vis-à-vis the implementation of Vatican II. Those priests were trying to develop a systematic framework that connected the life of the Latin American poor, development theory, and a divine sense of history, all under an umbrella of theological and material liberation.[4] *A Theology of Liberation* (1971), an expanded version of Gutiérrez's seminal conference to Peruvian priests, became the classic theological monograph; however, many other theologians started working on Christology, ecclesiology, soteriology, history of the church, and the role of the basic Christian communities.[5] The final documents of Medellín supported that theological program by reiterating the materiality of God's salvation and by encouraging an ecclesial immersion in the life of the materially poor, the marginalized, and those who were the victims of social injustice due to the fact that societies had created unjust structures included by the Latin American bishops under the umbrella of "structural sin."[6]

the first period of their work was coordinated by Enrique Dussel and François Houtart; see a useful historical overview in Enrique Dussel, "Theologies of the 'Periphery' and the 'Centre': Encounter or Confrontation?" in *Different Theologies, Common Responsibility: Babel or Pentecost?* eds. Claude Geffré, Gustavo Gutiérrez, and Virgil Elizondo, *Concilium* 171, 1984/1 (Edinburgh: T and T Clark, 1984), 87–97; see also EATWOT, *The Emergent Gospel* (Maryknoll, NY: Orbis, 1976). For a theological overview see Theo Witvliet, *A Place in the Sun: An Introduction to Liberation Theology in the Third World* (London: SCM, 1985). An Asian Christianity as a Christian project was more problematic; numbers of Christians in Asia, with the exception of the Philippines, remain small, and the post–Vatican II discussions on salvation within the world religions created more than an impasse between those who adhered to a Christ-centric option (exclusivists) and those who understood the world religions as places where God could save (inclusivists) (see Paul F. Knitter, *No Other Name? A Critical Survey of Christian Attitudes toward the World Religions* [London: SCM, 1985]).

4. For historical data on his life see Sergio Torres, "Gustavo Gutiérrez: A Historical Sketch," in *The Future of Liberation Theology: Essays in Honor of Gustavo Gutiérrez*, eds. Marc H. Ellis and Otto Maduro (Maryknoll, NY: Orbis, 1989), 95–101.

5. Gustavo Gutiérrez, "Toward a Theology of Liberation," July 1968, in Alfred T. Hennelly, ed., *Liberation Theology: A Documentary History* (Maryknoll, NY: Orbis, 1990), 62–76, and *Teología de la liberación: Perspectivas* (Salamanca: Ediciones Sígueme [16th ed.], 1999; Lima: Centro de Estudios y Publicaciones, 1971); for a full review of the theological works of eighteen Latin American theologians see Mario I. Aguilar, *The History and Politics of Latin American Theology*, vols. 1–2 (London: SCM, 2007).

6. See Second General Conference of Latin American Bishops 1968, *The Church in the Present-Day Transformation of Latin America in the Light of the Council, II: Conclusions* (Washington, DC: United States Catholic Conference USCC, 1970).

The development of Latin American theology is enormously complex, but its genesis can be traced to the European reflection by Gustavo Gutiérrez and Juan Luis Segundo, SJ in France, where both studied at the time when John XXIII had called the council and had spoken of "a church of the poor." Juan Luis Segundo, SJ and Gustavo Gutiérrez had a different pastoral experience, and that experience shaped what Segundo called "two kinds of liberation theology": a first one that arose out of the experience of the poor and a second one that was the product of reflection and study by Catholic-educated elites.[7] Thus for Gutiérrez and his life in the slums, the poor and the marginalized were at the center of God's work because they represented the incarnation of God, while theology as a reflection was a "second act." The option for the poor is a theological option that, as explained by Gutiérrez, emphasizes Jesus' life attitude toward others. Within Jesus' Gospel portrait he showed a real closeness to the poor and marginalized and liberation theology arose out of "our better understanding of the depth and complexity of the poverty and oppression experienced by most of humanity; it is due to our perception of the economic, social, and cultural mechanisms that produce that poverty; and before all else, it is due to the new light which the word of the Lord sheds on that poverty."[8] For Segundo, who had experienced pastoral work with the educated, liberation theology remained within the realm of the educated theologians who through their pastoral ministry passed some fresh ideas about the implementation of Vatican II to the laity and to the Catholic faithful in parishes. Those ideas reflected Segundo's own work with reflection groups, university students, and young professionals, and his own commitment to a systematic investigation of theological themes at the service of the church.

There is no contradiction between the role of the theologian in Gutiérrez and Segundo's work, but certainly Gutiérrez's work triggered numerous theological writings that used Marxism as a hermeneutical tool in order to explore social realities. Within the context of the 1970s, Christians and Marxists had encountered each other in the same project

7. Juan Luis Segundo, SJ, "Two Theologies of Liberation," delivered at Toronto, March 22, 1983, in Hennelly, *Liberation Theology: A Documentary History*, 353–66.

8. Gustavo Gutiérrez, "Option for the Poor," in Mysterium Liberationis: *Fundamental Concepts of Liberation Theology*, eds. Ignacio Ellacuría, SJ, and Jon Sobrino, SJ (Maryknoll, NY: Orbis; North Blackburn, Victoria: Collins Dove, 1993), 235–50 at 250.

of challenging unjust social structures: Christians following the values of the kingdom of God, Marxists following the ideals of a revolution in which the people and the masses—would both become entwined through revolutions inspired by the Cuban Revolution (1959). The radicalization of the Latin American theologians coincided with the rising of Christians that equated the Gospel with a socialist political project, the so-called Christians for Socialism, and the consequent persecution of pastoral agents by the military in Brazil, Chile, Argentina, Uruguay, Paraguay, El Salvador, and Guatemala. The Christian communities worked together with Marxists in order to save lives and protect the rights of the persecuted, and John Paul II started getting worried about these unholy alliances. After all, the Polish pope had had the opposite experience of socialist, Marxist-oriented, Soviet-protected totalitarian regimes in Eastern Europe and particularly in his native Poland.[9] Thus the questioning of liberation theology took two main avenues: a questioning of their use of Marxism and a questioning of their ecclesiology in which the Petrine office appeared weak and simply a principle of unity rather than a given divine institution through communion with which all other local churches gain their legitimacy.

Theology and Marxism

The first public confrontation between John Paul II and the theologies of liberation came in the early 1980s, immediately after the Latin American Bishops Conference in Puebla (1979), when Gustavo Gutiérrez was asked to account for some errors in his writings and had to prepare a defense of his theological thinking. Gutiérrez had produced several other theological works; however, his literary corpus cannot be consid-

---

9. The position of John Paul II vis-à-vis communism was understandable, as the Catholic Church in Poland had to deal with communist imposed regimes; however, and as remarked by the historian Eric Hobsbawm, "In some countries of 'real socialism,' as for instance Poland, it was possible to avoid the Party in one's dealings with colleagues and friends," Eric Hobsbawm, *Interesting Times: A Twentieth-Century Life* (London: Abacus, 2003), 147; for an assessment of John Paul II's influence on the perception of a unified Europe see Patrick Michel, "John Paul II, Poland and Europe," in *Rethinking Europe*, eds. Alberto Melloni and Janet Martin Soskice, *Concilium* 2004/2 (London: SCM), 124–28.

ered systematically and chronologically ordered, as is the case with Leonardo Boff or Juan Luis Segundo, SJ.[10]

The call for Gutiérrez to defend his work can only be related to the genesis of a papal dissatisfaction with Latin American theology and with the leftist accusations of many of its practitioners by the military regimes of that time. The 1979 meeting of Latin American Bishops in Puebla (Mexico) had developed a "preferential option for the poor" and the ideas of liberation, while technically suppressed by John Paul II in his visit to Mexico, grew stronger, particularly due to the full support by the strong and prophetic Brazilian episcopal conference. Indeed, the position of Paul VI had been very different, so that when Bishop Pedro Casaldáliga was under attack by the Brazilian authorities Paul VI expressed very directly to the Brazilian government that an attack on Casaldáliga and his pastoral work with the poor in the Brazilian Amazonia would be considered a direct attack on the church, the Vatican, and the pope. John Paul II was just a year in office when the Sandinista revolution took over the government in Nicaragua, and the Vatican had to deal with the involvement of three priests, Ernesto Cardenal as Minister for Culture, Fernando Cardenal, SJ as National Youth Coordinator, and Miguel D'Scoto as Foreign Minister.[11] Their political commitment was questioned by John Paul II when he visited Nicaragua in 1983, but Ernesto Cardenal stated clearly that as a monk and a priest he saw his role as minister as a sacrifice for love of people. However, if the Vatican embarked upon its theological scrutinizing of the liberation theologians in private, in public and on arrival in Managua for the papal visit, John Paul II pointed his finger directly at Ernesto Cardenal, who was at the

10. Gutiérrez's theological periods within the original Spanish texts are clearly chronological, and they follow theological reflections that arise out of preparations for the meeting of Latin American Bishops at Medellín, Puebla, and Santo Domingo. These periods are more difficult to isolate within the published works in English due to the fact that Gutiérrez has not published everything he has ever written and that not everything published in other languages has been translated into the English language. Frei Betto has suggested, "It is quite likely that he is the author of more unpublished texts, known only to a small circle of readers, than of published works. Usually he does not even sign the mimeographed texts, which include an excellent introduction to the ideas of Marx and Engels and their relationship to Christianity," Frei Betto, "Gustavo Gutiérrez: A Friendly Profile," *The Future of Liberation Theology: Essays in Honor of Gustavo Gutiérrez* (Maryknoll, NY: Orbis, 1989), 31–37, at 35.

11. Teófilo Cabestrero, *Ministers of God, Ministers of the People: Testimonies of Faith from Nicaragua* (Maryknoll, NY: Orbis; London: Zed, 1983).

airport among the welcoming party of ministers of the revolutionary government. Cardenal interpreted this as "a humiliating gesture," a sign of annoyance by John Paul II because Nicaragua's was a Latin American revolution that did not persecute the church and in which Christians and Marxists, including priests, worked together for the good of society and "the theology of liberation was in power."[12]

In March 1983 the CDF made ten observations on the theology of Gutiérrez arguing that it provided "extreme ambiguity" and that "Gutiérrez accepts the Marxist conception of history, which is a history of conflict, structured around the class struggle and requiring commitment on behalf of the oppressed in their struggle for liberation."[13] Further, the CDF stated that "the influence of Marxism is clear both in the understanding of truth and the notion of theology. Orthodoxy is replaced by orthopraxy, for truth does not exist except within praxis—that is, in the commitment to revolution."[14] Gutiérrez defended himself, outlining his commitment to tradition and the fact that a historical analysis of social realities had always been part of the magisterium, including papal encyclicals and the whole corpus of the social doctrine of the church. The humiliation of Gutiérrez at the Vatican triggered a strong wave of support by academic institutions, including the University of Lyons where Gutiérrez had studied, an institution that, following an oral examination on Catholic doctrine, conferred Gutiérrez a doctorate in theology.

Karl Rahner also felt the need to defend Gutiérrez's work and, in a letter to the Cardinal of Lima (Juan Landázuri Ricketts), he wrote: "I am convinced of the orthodoxy of the theological work of Gustavo Gutiérrez. The liberation theology he represents is thoroughly orthodox and is aware of its limits within the whole context of Catholic theology. Moreover, it is deeply convinced (correctly, in my opinion) that the voice of the poor must be listened to by theology in the context of the Latin American church."[15]

---

12. Ernesto Cardenal, *La Revolución Perdida: Memorias*, vol. 3 (Mexico: Fondo de Cultura Económica, 2005), 288–301.

13. Congregation for the Doctrine of the Faith, "Ten Observations on the Theology of Gustavo Gutiérrez," in Hennelly, *Liberation Theology: A Documentary History*, 348–50, par. 2.

14. Ibid., par. 7.

15. Karl Rahner, SJ, "Letter to Cardinal Juan Landázuri Ricketts of Lima, Peru," Innsbruck, March 16, 1984, in Hennelly, *Liberation Theology: A Documentary History*, 351–52; Ger-

However, Cardinal Joseph Ratzinger continued his admonitions against the theology of liberation and in March 1984 he published a paper carefully constructing his case against this new Latin American theology.[16] Ratzinger compared the development of liberation theology with the hermeneutical challenges posed by the rise of New Testament criticism; however, he argued consistently that he was referring to those theologians of liberation who had embraced a Marxist hermeneutics and the class struggle. The only theologian attacked directly within the paper was Jon Sobrino, SJ, and Ratzinger writes: "Love consists in an 'option for the poor,' that is, it coincides with an option for class struggle. Theologians of liberation underline very strongly, in opposition to 'false universalism,' the partiality and partial character of the Christian option; to take sides is, according to them, a fundamental requisite for a correct hermeneutics of the biblical witness."[17] It is the last sentence in the paper by Ratzinger that initiated a full-frontal doctrinal attack on all Latin American theologians, including Juan Luis Segundo, SJ. Ratzinger concluded that: "if one thinks how radical this interpretation of Christianity that derives from it really is, the problem of what one can and must do about it becomes even more urgent."[18] On that possible ecclesiastical threat the board of the journal *Concilium* issued a statement in support of theologians of liberation. This was an influential statement coming out from those associated with the journal that had developed the whole theological enterprise of Vatican II.[19]

On August 6, 1984, the CDF published *Libertatis Nuntius* (Instruction on Certain Aspects of the Theology of Liberation) in which Ratzinger writes: "The present instruction has a much more limited and precise

man text available in Norbert Greinacher, *Konflikt um die Theologie der Befreiung: Diskussion und Dokumentation* (Cologne: Benziger Verlag, 1985), 184–86.

16. Joseph Ratzinger, "Liberation Theology," March 1984, in Hennelly, *Liberation Theology: A Documentary History*, 367–74, also available in *The Ratzinger Report: An Exclusive Interview on the State of the Church* (San Francisco: Ignatius Press, 1985), 174–86.

17. Ratzinger, "Liberation Theology," 373.

18. Ibid., 374.

19. Editorial Board of *Concilium*, "Statement of Solidarity with Liberation Theologians," June 24, 1984, in Hennelly, *Liberation Theology: A Documentary History*, 390–92; published in *Origins* 14 (July 26, 1984): 134–35. This section of this paper is taken from a larger analysis of Juan Luis Segundo's theology in Mario I. Aguilar, *The History and Politics of Latin American Theology*, vol. 2 (London: SCM, 2007), chapter 3: "Juan Luis Segundo, SJ."

purpose: to draw the attention of pastors, theologians, and all the faithful to the deviations and risks of deviation, damaging to the faith and to Christian living, that are brought about by certain forms of liberation theology which use, in an insufficiently critical manner, concepts borrowed from various currents of Marxist thought."[20] Leonardo Boff and Gustavo Gutiérrez responded publicly against the accusations by the Vatican.[21] However, the most consistent, well-argued, lesser-known theological engagement with John Paul II on these issues came from the Jesuit Juan Luis Segundo, one of the most intellectual theologians from Latin America, a man not in the trenches of the slums or the revolutions, but a man who defended human rights in Uruguay with his knowledge, his writings, and his systematic thought.[22]

Segundo's text, published under the title *Theology and the Church*,[23] is rather symptomatic of Segundo's theological training not only in that he apologized for some personal stories within the text but also in that he responded to his critics as he always did: he retired to his desk, read, reflected, and wrote about the matter as if it were a new theological problem to be evaluated and expanded. However, as well as reading and writing, he discussed many of those ideas with the groups he was journeying with.

Segundo intended to evaluate the theological themes raised by *Libertatis Nuntius* vis-à-vis the writings of Latin American theologians, but in doing so he produced a draft in which he wanted also to protect the authors of different streams of thought from further questioning by John Paul II. That would have contravened his golden rule of never writing without acknowledging authors and writers. As a result, the book became

20. Congregation for the Doctrine of the Faith, "Instruction on Certain Aspects of the Theology of Liberation," Vatican City, August 6, 1984, in Hennelly, *Liberation Theology: A Documentary History*, 393–414, at 394. The full text is also available in Juan Luis Segundo, *Theology and the Church*, 169–88.

21. Leonardo Boff, "Vatican Instruction Reflects European Mind-Set," Folha de São Paulo, August 31, 1984, in Hennelly, *Liberation Theology: A Documentary History*, 415–18; Gustavo Gutiérrez, "Criticism Will Deepen, Clarify Liberation Theology," September 14, 1984, in Hennelly, *Liberation Theology: A Documentary History*, 419–24.

22. See, for example, Juan Luis Segundo, SJ, *Signs of the Times: Theological Reflections* (Maryknoll, NY: Orbis, 1993).

23. Juan Luis Segundo, SJ, *Theology and the Church: A Response to Cardinal Ratzinger and a Warning to the Whole Church* (London: Geoffrey Chapman, 1985).

a more personal evaluation of the situation and the only example of such a personal approach in Segundo's works. Indeed, if one wanted to know in one single work what Segundo stood for within the theological world, this is the work to read rather than his classic *Liberation of Theology*. Segundo's argument is very clear throughout his examination of themes such as liberation and secularism, liberation and hermeneutics, popular church and political church. Segundo argues that: (1) *Libertatis Nuntius* equates Marxism with a political party rather than with a philosophical system developed within Western Civilization, and (2) the purpose of *Libertatis Nuntius* is to halt and destroy any possible advancement of the Spirit as embodied within Vatican II. For Segundo presumed that *Libertatis Nuntius*, published before the 1985 synod of bishops, was sending a very clear signal to those within the Catholic Church who believed in a model of unity in diversity. Therefore, Segundo is not concerned with developments within theology, but he is concerned with the lack of theological and philosophical precision by the superstructure of the Vatican and the power over canon and dogma exercised by Cardinal Ratzinger as the right-hand man of John Paul II.

The paradox of this first wave of this investigation and scrutiny of liberation theology by John Paul II is that it was actually those who were more pastorally oriented and not those at the extreme liberal wing of Latin American theology who were being investigated. The questioning was severe in tone and nature and did not allow for a dialogue with John Paul II but rather took the form of a doctrinal "examination" by a very competent German theologian, Cardinal Joseph Ratzinger. Nevertheless, the theological questioning, while focused on Gutiérrez as a theologian, opened questions about the theological progression and the implementation of Vatican II by the Latin American Bishops, the bishops representing the most energetic and Roman Catholic part of the universal Catholic Church. It was an attack on the pastoral and social role of the Latin American Catholic Church, for John Paul II an offshoot of the Roman Church led by the Bishop of Rome, for the Latin Americans a fruit of the collegiality and episcopal solidarity between sister churches. It was the New Testament controversy between Peter and Paul about custom and development of the early church revisited again, and on this occasion Peter rather than the apostle to the Gentiles had the upper hand. It is not surprising that the following period of theological disputes was to be concerned not with social hermeneutics and the use of Marxism but with the very nature of the church.

Ecclesiology and Liberation

The following major attack on liberation theology took place in 1984 when Leonardo Boff came under the close doctrinal scrutiny of the CDF.[24] Boff's book, *Church, Charism and Power*, previously researched as his doctoral dissertation, had questioned the reading of the tradition, as understood by John Paul II and Cardinal Ratzinger, in that it had brought the whole issue of ecclesial collegiality under the scrutiny of New Testament texts and the practices of the early church, concluding that a centralized Roman ecclesiology had been a historical development vis-à-vis the Christian Church and the developments of the Christian states/empires.[25] The CDF believed that the conclusions of the book contained an implicit undermining of the Petrine office, which had already been challenged by the biblical interpretation of European reformers in the sixteenth century, and a challenge to the office of bishops as teachers and interpreters of doctrine within the church.

The development of Boff's doctrinal investigation was triggered by doubts about his doctrinal fidelity to Catholic tradition within his doctoral work, completed and defended with the highest distinctions under the supervision of his fellow Franciscan Bonaventura Kloppenburg and with the second supervision of Joseph Ratzinger.[26] Kloppenburg, who had become a critic of liberation theology, wrote a review of the book suggesting that Boff was forwarding heresies.[27] Boff was surprised and

24. See Congregation for the Doctrine of the Faith, "Notification Sent to Fr. Leonardo Boff regarding Errors in His Book *Church, Charism and Power*," March 11, 1985, in Hennelly, *Liberation Theology: A Documentary History*, 425–30. Leonardo Boff had appeared in front of Ratzinger at the Vatican on September 7, 1984, and had defended his theological position, see "Leonardo Boff, 'Defense of His Book, *Church, Charism and Power*,'" September 7, 1984, in Hennelly, *Liberation Theology: A Documentary History*, 431–34. See also, Harvey Cox, *The Silencing of Leonardo Boff: The Vatican and the Future of World Christianity* (Oak Park, IL: Meyer-Stone Books, 1988).

25. Leonardo Boff, *Igreja—carisma e poder: Ensayos de eclesiologia militante* (Petrópolis: Vozes, 1981).

26. Robert McAfee Brown, "Leonardo Boff: Theologian for All Christians," *Christian Century* (July 2 and 9, 1986): 615.

27. Kloppenburg was editor of the *Revista Eclesiástica Brasileira* and an advocate of ecumenism after Vatican II; however, he was responsible for a report on liberation theology for

decided to send a copy of the book to Cardinal Ratzinger as his former teacher. Instead of a complimentary note, Ratzinger sent Boff a six-page letter summarizing the errors within Boff's book and summoning him to Rome to explain his ideas. Ratzinger suggested that Boff had distorted old Christian doctrines by reinterpreting them using a contemporary context, i.e., ideological perspectives from history, philosophy, sociology, and politics, perspectives that were not fully informed by theology. Ratzinger questioned if Boff was guided by faith or by other principles of an ideological nature, and he indicated serious problems within three areas covered by Boff's book: (1) Boff seemed to suggest that Christ has not determined the specific form and structure of the church, thus implying that other models could be as valid as the Roman Catholic one; (2) Boff seemed to suggest that doctrine and dogma could be mediated by contemporary readings "led by the Spirit," an idea that could lead to the legitimization of fashionable trends over "timeless truths"; and (3) Boff used Marxist analysis in order to assume that few within the church owned the means of production (forgiveness and the sacraments), and he proposed a model in which theological privileges were not concentrated in the few. It appeared that the Vatican was not so much worried about the use of Marxist analysis as about the "ownership" of the Holy Spirit that within Boff's writings goes out from the hierarchical church into the basic Christian communities.[28] In other writings Boff had also challenged Vatican II's use of the term "people of God" and, relying on the sociological analysis by the Brazilian Pedro Riberio de Oliveira, had added a sixth characteristic for the church as "the Church of the poor" or "the popular Church" (*Igreja dos pobros ou a Igreja Popular*).[29]

As a result of the CDF doctrinal investigation, Boff had a meeting in Rome with Cardinal Ratzinger, in September 1984, and was given a year to reexamine his writings. Until 1986 he was forbidden from teach-

---

the military that alerted them to the fact that there were Marxists and subversives within the Catholic Church. He served at the Latin American Episcopal Conference (CELAM) and was ordained as a bishop in 1982.

28. This section of this paper is taken from a larger analysis of Leonardo Boff's theology in Mario I. Aguilar, *The History and Politics of Latin American Theology*, vol. 1 (London: SCM Press, 2007), chapter 7: "Leonardo Boff."

29. Leonardo Boff, "A Theological Examination of the Terms 'People of God' and 'Popular Church,'" in Leonardo Boff and Virgil Elizondo, eds., La Iglesia Popular: *Between Fear and Hope* (*Concilium* 176, 1984/86), 89–97 at 89.

ing, publishing, giving conferences, or serving on editorial boards associated with the Catholic Church.[30] It is possible to suggest that Boff might well have been suspended indefinitely by John Paul II if Cardinal Alois Lorscheider, head of the Brazilian episcopal conference, had not traveled with him to support his work for the church in Brazil. Boff, a prolific writer, continued writing after his return to public teaching in 1986. However, the commencement, in 1992, of a new investigation into his writings by the Vatican eventually led, on June 26, 1993, to Boff's resignation from the active priesthood. Nonetheless, he continued his teaching and writing as a layperson and took up a post at the University of the State of Rio de Janeiro where he became professor of ethics, philosophy of religion, and ecology. Boff's theological consistency with the framework of the New Testament and with the tenants of liberation theology makes his analysis of the base communities rich in social and theological meaning to the point that his writings appeared to have posed a "threat" to the the Eurocentric perception of John Paul II and those around him.

Theological Suspicion

After the suspension of Leonardo Boff, the Vatican had to face enormous criticism, particularly within the European Union, because of the European-assumed right to freedom of expression. Due to such pressures Boff's silencing was lifted and John Paul II encouraged a public statement prepared by the CDF related to liberation theology dated March 22, 1986, with the title *Libertatis Conscientia* (Instruction on Christian Freedom and Liberation).[31] *Libertatis Conscientia* was much more positive than *Libertatis Nuntius* in its assessment of liberation theology, and it certainly sought to ground the notion of "true" human liberation upon Christ, warning that the church had witnessed, from Luther and the Protestant Reformation onward, attempts to find just orders of liberation for society and for human beings that, for the most part, had not delivered "true" liberation (LC 6). In particular there was a gentle warning about the reliance upon the (natural) sciences as the path toward

---

30. Cf. Harvey Cox, *The Silencing of Leonardo Boff*.

31. Text available in Hennelly, *Liberation Theology: A Documentary History*, 461–97. See also, R. Gibellini, *The Liberation Theology Debate* (London: SCM, 1987).

human liberation (LC 21). Further, a balanced way of understanding Jesus' preference for the poor was offered, whereby "he also wished to be near to those who, though rich in the goods of this world, were excluded from the community as 'publican and sinners' for he had come to call them to conversion" (LC 66). Within this doctrinal analysis, detachment from riches becomes a value and "the special option for the poor, far from being a sign of particularism or sectarianism, manifests the universality of the church's being and mission" so that "this option excludes no one"; however, "the church cannot express this option by means of reductive sociological and ideological categories which would make this preference a partisan choice and a source of conflict" (LC 68). In its final part the document assumes a theology of liberation as part of the Christian message but warns strongly against a materialistic anthropology that equates particular historical processes with the liberation expressed by the Gospels in the following terms:

> Thus, a theology of freedom and liberation, which faithfully echoes Mary's Magnificat preserved in the church's memory, is something needed by the times in which we are living. But it would be criminal to take the energies of popular piety and misdirect them toward a purely earthly plan of liberation, which would very soon be revealed as nothing more than an illusion and a cause of new forms of slavery. (LC 98)

The positive disposition toward liberation theology as an ecclesial force coming out of the commandment of love and embedded within the social doctrine of the church was newly expressed in John Paul II's letter to the Brazilian bishops that followed the doctrinal pronouncements on liberation theology.[32] In that letter John Paul II addressed some of the issues discussed during the Brazilian bishops' visit to the Vatican, and regarding liberation theology he mentioned that "the theology of liberation is not only timely but useful and necessary. It should constitute a new state—in close connection with former ones—of the theological reflection initiated with the apostolic tradition."[33]

It is possible to argue that *Libertatis Conscientia* expanded the doctrinal reflection on liberation and, in accordance with the philosophical for-

---

32. John Paul II, "Letter to Brazilian Episcopal Conference," Vatican City, April 9, 1986, in Hennelly, *Liberation Theology: A Documentary History*, 498–506.
33. Ibid., 503.

mation of John Paul II, as well as the theological standing of Joseph Ratzinger, it expressed very clearly the manner in which human liberation was understood by the (official) magisterium. Nonetheless, it is not possible to argue *either* that John Paul II accepted the centrality of liberation theology *or* that he condemned this theological movement. John Paul II instead embraced a contextual theological development provided it followed the development of the Christian tradition. Whenever particular theologians, in the opinion of John Paul II, did not follow the magisterium, they were to be questioned by the CDF, as occurred in the less-publicized case of Jon Sobrino, SJ, and his Christological writings. It is interesting that Gustavo Gutiérrez welcomed John Paul II's engagement with liberation theology and *Libertatis Conscientia* was assumed by some commentators as representing "a synthesis of the teaching of Pope John Paul II."[34]

In conclusion it can be argued that John Paul II, a philosophically minded bishop and later pope, did not fully agree with the centrality of context and politics; instead he preferred to practice Christianity within the philosophical realms of essences/accidents and of a Christian anthropology centered in Christ. Thus, his eventual acceptance of the hope of liberation came about through his visit to Latin America, where he experienced the newness and freshness of the Christian communities. Nevertheless, he remained unconvinced that liberation theologians were the prime movers of Latin America's pastoral revival, an assessment upon which, finally, Latin American theologians and John Paul II could agree.

---

34. Alfred T. Hennelly, SJ, "The Red-Hot Issue: Liberation Theology," *America* (May 24, 1986): 425–28, in Hennelly, *Liberation Theology: A Documentary History*, 507–13, see 508.

10

Mixed Messages: John Paul II's Writings on Women

Susan Rakoczy, IHM

In contrast to all other popes preceding him, Pope John Paul II often wrote and spoke about women. Some of his thought is new and ground-breaking, but much of it sends mixed messages to Catholic women.

While asserting that women are truly created in the image of God, he constructs an anthropology based on the biological differences between men and women, leading to an essentialist position. His interpretation of women's presence in society is predicated on his perspective that mothers should be at home with their children. There is little good news for Catholic women when he speaks of women in the church, and he closes the door unequivocally to women's ordination.

Women's Equality and Dignity

In his writings on Christian anthropology and specifically on women, Pope John Paul II strikingly breaks with Christian tradition by affirming woman's equality and dignity as a human being. In 1963 Pope John XXIII in his encyclical *Pacem in Terris* acknowledged the increasing role of women in society as one of the signs of the times, pointing out that

> it is obvious to everyone that women are now taking a part in public life
> . . . . Since women are becoming ever more conscious of their human
> dignity, they will not tolerate being treated as mere material instruments,

but demand rights befitting a human person both in domestic and in public life. (PT 16)[1]

The documents of the Second Vatican Council (1962–65) have little to say about women. On the one hand, the bishops insisted that "any kind of social or cultural discrimination in basic personal rights on the grounds of *sex*, race, color, social conditions, language or religion, must be curbed and eradicated as incompatible with God's design"[2] (GS 29, emphasis added), but in speaking of women's involvement "in nearly all spheres of life" they stressed that "they ought to be permitted to play their part fully according to their own particular nature" (GS 60), implying that women had a different "nature" than men.

The twentieth century inherited the teachings of Augustine of Hippo and Thomas Aquinas on how woman is to be understood as an image of God. Both positions are deficient in terms of asserting woman's dignity and equality. Augustine (d. 430) argued that only the male is created in the image of God. Woman becomes the image of God when she is joined to her husband:

> The woman with her husband is the image of God in such a way that the whole of that substance is one image, but when she is assigned her function of being an assistant, which is her concern alone, she is not the image of God, whereas in what concerns the man alone he is the image of God as fully and completely as when the woman is joined to him in one whole.[3]

Thomas Aquinas (d. 1274) builds on Augustine's thought and asserts that the male possesses the image of God in a different and superior way to that of woman. He identifies her essence as her sexuality and, using the perspective of the mind-body dualism inherited from Greek philosophy, argues that she has a weaker and more imperfect body which then affects the mind and intelligence.[4] Following Aristotle, Aquinas describes

1. Pope John XXIII, *Pacem in Terris* (Peace on Earth) (Pretoria: The Southern African Catholic Bishops' Conference, n.d.), no. 16, p. 10.

2. Austin Flannery, OP, *Vatican Council II: The Basic Sixteen Documents* (Northport, NY: Costello Publishing Company, 1996), 194.

3. Augustine of Hippo, *The Trinity* (12.10), trans. Edmund Hill, OP (Brooklyn: New City Press, 1991), 328.

4. Thomas Aquinas, *Summa Theologiae* (II–II. q. 70, a. 3, reply), vol. 10, trans. Fathers of the English Dominican Province (London: Burns Oats and Washbourne Ltd., 1929), 270.

the female as a defective human being since she was conceived because of an accident to the male sperm due to a south wind or the presence of a full moon.[5]

These perspectives continued to exert authority in Catholic theology into the twentieth century. In 1912, the *Catholic Encyclopedia* described women "as inferior to the male sex, both as regards the body and soul."[6]

In striking contrast, John Paul II asserts that "both man and woman are human beings to an equal degree, both are created in God's image" (MD 6).[7] Writing in 1995, at the time of the Fourth World Conference of the United Nations on Women held in Beijing, he phrases this conviction as "the inherent, inalienable dignity of women."[8] The image of God, shared equally by man and woman, means that "he or she is a rational and free creature capable of knowing God and loving him" (MD 7).

In his exegesis of the creation texts in Genesis 1 and 2 in *The Theology of the Body*,[9] John Paul II affirms "the homogeneity of the whole being of both" (TB 44). He sees this homogeneity in terms of the body, the somatic structure. But there is also the recognition by the man: "This at last is bone of my bones and flesh of my flesh" (Gen 2:23). The man recognizes the humanity of the woman.

While many of his writings on women present a "biology is destiny" perspective and a romantic sense of the "feminine," John Paul II's conviction that women are fully equal human beings with men represents a new and official teaching in the Catholic tradition.

---

5. Thomas Aquinas, *Summa Theologiae* (I. q. 92, a. 1, reply 1), vol. 13, trans. Edmund Hill, OP (London: Blackfriars, 1964), 37.

6. Quoted in Lisa Isherwood and Dorothy McEwan, *Introducing Feminist Theology*, 2nd ed. (Sheffield: Sheffield Academic Press, 2001), 40.

7. John Paul II, *Mulieres Dignitatem* (On the Dignity and Vocation of Women) (Kampala: St. Paul Publications-Africa, n.d.), 18.

8. John Paul II, *The Pope Speaks to Women* (Nairobi: Paulines Publications Africa, 1996), 5.

9. John Paul II, *The Theology of the Body* (Boston: Daughters of St. Paul, 1997), (hereafter, TB). This book is composed of 129 general audience addresses divided into four themes: "Original Unity of Man and Woman" (September 5, 1979–April 2, 1980), "Blessed are the Pure of Heart" (April 16, 1980–May 6, 1981), "The Theology of Marriage and Celibacy" (November 11, 1981–July 4, 1984), and "Reflections on *Humanae Vitae*" (July 11–November 28, 1984). Cf. George Weigel, *Witness to Hope: The Biography of Pope John Paul II* (New York: Harper Perennial, 2005), 335–36.

Von Balthasar's Influence on John Paul's Thought

George Weigel, biographer of the pope, asserts that Hans Urs von Balthasar (1905–1988) was "an important influence on John Paul's thinking."[10] Von Balthasar's interpretation of the relationship between men and women, and the distinct roles of each, are clearly echoed in many aspects of John Paul's thought, as will be developed below.

For von Balthasar, nature has determined the relationships and roles of men and women, and it is injurious to each and to society as a whole if there are "incursions of one sex into the other's natural role," since this "damages a critical balance, with baleful consequences."[11] This is a position of essentialism and it is expanded in many ways.

Von Balthasar does assert that both women and men are the image of God: "both man and woman *individually* (and not only *together*) constitute an 'image of God'; thus each has a guaranteed access to God."[12] Woman "is oriented to the man, yet has equal rank with him, sharing in the same free human nature."[13] Both man and woman are "seeking complementarity and peace in the other pole."[14]

Much of his language about the relationship of man and woman is a romantic abstraction, but one with significant consequences for women in society and the church. Woman is "the help, the security, the home man needs; she is the vessel of fulfillment designed specially for him."[15] Woman's "essential vocation [is] to receive man's fruitfulness," and her response is "reproduction."[16]

10. Weigel, *Witness to Hope*, 565.

11. Corinne Crammer, "One Sex or Two? Balthasar's Theology of the Sexes," in *The Cambridge Companion to Hans Urs von Balthasar*, eds. Edward T. Oakes, SJ, and David Moss (Cambridge: Cambridge University Press, 2004), 95.

12. Hans Urs von Balthasar, *Theo-Drama: Theological Dramatic Theory*, vol. 3: Dramatis Personae: The Person in Christ, trans. Graham Harrison (San Francisco: Ignatius Press, 1992), 286. (Emphasis in original.)

13. Ibid., 297.

14. Hans Urs von Balthasar, *Theo-Drama: Theological Dramatic Theory*, vol. 2: Dramatis Personae: Man in God, trans. Graham Harrison (San Francisco: Ignatius Press, 1990), 355.

15. Von Balthasar, *Theo-Drama*, 3:285.

16. Ibid., 3:286. Von Balthasar refers to Karl Barth's (*Church Dogmatics* III/1, 312) commentary on Genesis 2 "which speaks of man and woman as such, not on fatherhood and motherhood" (286).

There is a hierarchy of relation between man and woman and man has priority:

> The apparent paradox that men and women are equal but men have priority and headship may have its resolution in what has been described as the rule of "subordination in the order of creation and equality in the order of redemption."[17]
>
> In other words, men and women are equal before God, but this equality is limited in the creaturely realm because of Man's natural priority. Although Balthasar asserts the equality of the sexes before God, he appears to regard equality in the created order as a threat to sexual difference and as contributing to the excesses of an overtly masculinized, overtly technological, technocratic society.[18]

For von Balthasar, man's definite priority is "maintained by the Scriptures of the Old and New Testaments,"[19] since man has a monadic character—oriented to woman—while woman has a dyadic character of orientation to the man and to the child.

Woman's character is that of "receptivity, obedience, disponibility and willing consent to the action of another," while "leadership is identified as masculine."[20] Although he does maintain that receptivity and obedience are qualities of all persons before God, they are particularly feminine qualities. Thus Mary is "the archetype of the feminine," for she "displays the paradigmatically feminine qualities as a model for all Christians in relation to God, although she also serves as a model for women in particular."[21]

For von Balthasar, men are doers and makers, leaders who are focused on goals and achievement. Women are receptive vessels of the man; in sexual intercourse (he maintains that man always initiates sexual activity because of his primary fruitfulness[22]) and in life, man represents and woman receives. Thus ordination to the priesthood is impossible for

17. Karl Lehmann, "The Place of Women as a Problem in Theological Anthropology," *Communio* 10 (1983), 222. Cited in Crammer, "One Sex or Two?" 108n9.

18. Crammer, "One Sex or Two?" 96.

19. Von Balthasar, *Theo-Drama*, 3:292.

20. Crammer, "One Sex or Two?" 98.

21. Ibid. John Paul's very forthright Mariology is certainly linked with von Balthasar's thought. In many of the papal statements about women, a separate section links women's roles with Mary's obedience and receptivity.

22. Ibid., 99.

woman since her role is "being" while man's is that of representing Christ, who is male, and woman "is not called upon to represent anything that she herself is not."[23]

Von Balthasar's thought is clearly essentialist, emphasizing that women and men have a clear essence which perdures throughout history and is the same in every cultural and historical context. This position is the basis of the kinds of sexual stereotyping of women which have been addressed and critiqued in various ways since the middle of the nineteenth century, from the right of women to vote to women's leadership in business, government, and the church.

Corinne Crammer comments on the implications of von Balthasar's theological perspective: "Given the historical experiences of women, a theology of the sexes that is so insistent on the priority of Man and that associates divinity with Man while associating creatureliness and subordination with Woman is inimical to social equality between the sexes and lends support to male-female relationships marked by dominance and subordination."[24]

John Paul II's interpretation of woman as person, of the relationship of man and woman, and of women's roles in church and society is not an exact parallel with von Balthasar's thought, but there are many clear similarities.

Woman as Person

The assertion of woman's equality with man is the good news in John Paul II's anthropology. Humanity is one since both women and men "were created in the image and likeness of the personal God" (MD 6), and this image is human rationality. In view of the ecological crisis now confronting humanity, the statement, "Thanks to this property, man and woman are able to 'dominate' the other creatures of the visible world (cf. Gen 1:28)" (MD 6), while a traditional interpretation, shows the unfortunate anthropocentric character of theology that has brought humanity to the precipice of an uncertain planetary future.

---

23. Ibid., 100. This position on women and priesthood is clearly shown in John Paul II's thought. See the section below on the ordination of women.

24. Ibid., 107.

But much of the papal anthropology is decidedly mixed and often detrimental to women. John Paul's emphasis on the biological differences between men and women, which of course are true, often leads to a position of "biology is destiny" for woman and an extrapolation of the physical to the psychological.

In his meditations on Genesis 1 and 2 in *The Theology of the Body*, John Paul II traces the creation of male and female. The original solitude of the male, "It is not good that the man should be alone" (Gen 2:18),[25] leads to the creation of woman. While he asserts the original unity of man and woman as the image of God, the language used prepares the way for the link of woman's body with her destiny as mother. The original unity "is based on masculinity and femininity, as if on two different 'incarnations,' that is on two ways of 'being a body' of the same human being created 'in the image of God' (Gen 1:27)" (TB 43).

In the second creation account in Genesis 2:18-25, the image of sleep is used during which woman is created. The man recognizes the woman as "a second self" (TB 44), not another self. The first self is the primary self. The pope states that the "circle of the solitude of the man-person is broken, because the first 'man' awakens from his sleep as 'male and female'" (TB 44). The language of the Genesis text, that the woman is "a helper fit for him" (Gen 2:18, 20), introduces the subordination of woman to man that has been seen throughout human history. Although John Paul II stresses the unity of the communion of persons of male and female as the image and likeness of God (TB 46), there is much in the papal writings that demonstrates that the two different "incarnations" are not really equal since the male is the norm.

In asserting the central importance of the body in the creation of humanity—we are embodied as male and female—John Paul states that the "theology of the body is bound up with the creation of man in the image of God" and "becomes, in a way, also the theology of sex, or rather the theology of masculinity and femininity, which has its starting point here in Genesis" (TB 47).

---

25. Because the English translations of John Paul's writings use exclusive language, the use of "man" for humanity at times obscures his thought by sometimes conflating man and male.

An early example of the relation of male and female is present in the language of male power over woman. The consequences of the Fall in Genesis are more serious for woman than for man since "he will rule over you" (Gen 3:16). John Paul sees this domination as breaking the original unity of male and female, "especially to the disadvantage of the woman" (MD 10). Indeed, throughout history this text has been interpreted as justifying male oppression of women, rather than indicating that the original unity of male and female has been broken to the detriment of both.

The pope interprets this domination both in terms of marriage, in which both bear the inclination to sin, but also "indirectly they concern the different spheres of social life: the situations in which the woman remains disadvantaged or discriminated against by the fact of being a woman" (MD 10).

The Female Body

In his descriptions of the female body, John Paul II presents a foundation for the view that "biology is destiny." The body "which expresses femininity manifests the reciprocity and communion of persons" (TB 61–62), but it is also a body made for self-giving. As the woman

> "is given" to man . . . she is accepted by man as gift . . . At the same time, the acceptance of the woman by the man and very way of accepting her, becomes, as it were, a first donation. In giving herself (from the very first moment in which, in the mystery of creation, she was "given" to the man by the Creator), the woman "rediscovers herself" at the same time. (TB 71)

The biological differences become the basis for psychological differences.

Self-giving is then the essence of woman, since the second creation narrative "has assigned to man 'from the beginning' the function of the one who, above all, receives the gift" (TB 71). While John Paul II stresses the mutual relationship of man and woman, in which the man also gives himself, it is the woman who in her self-giving "reaches the inner depth of her person and full possession of herself" (TB 71).

In the papal view, the female body is formed for motherhood: "Maternity manifests this constitution internally, as the particular potential of the female organism. With creative particularity it serves for the conception and begetting of the human being, with the help of man" (TB 81). This is a traditional interpretation of woman's role in society: she is first a mother; all else is secondary. It ignores the fact that many women are not mothers, by choice and by circumstance, and that the potential for physical motherhood encompasses only a percentage of a woman's life, for example ages fourteen to forty-eight in an average life span of eighty years.

By stressing the maternal role of women, the pope reinforces traditional gender roles of women and men. Even though in other writings he supports woman's role in society, there is always the perspective that her primary place is at home with the children.

Idealization of Women

There is a great deal of idealization of woman as person in John Paul's writings. In his reflections on Christ's injunction on adultery and lust (Matt 5:27-28), he uses the phrase the "eternal feminine"[26] in describing how "the woman—who owing to her personal subjectivity exists perennially 'for man,' waiting for him, too, for the same reason, to exist 'for her'" (TB 150). Adultery and lust make woman into an object, but woman's very identity is as one who exists "for the other," not for herself.

He speaks of the "genius of women" which flows from Mary's "feminine genius."[27] The language both exalts and isolates. This "genius" is a "specific part of God's plan which needs to be accepted and appreciated"[28] both in society and in the church.

In his Angelus address of July 23, 1995, John Paul II elaborates the meaning of the "feminine genius." Women and men are not to be compared with one another since they hold much in common in terms of fundamental dimensions and values. He qualifies this by stating, "However, in

26. This perspective has links with C. G. Jung's concept of the feminine in which he "sees the feminine as a psychic element quite apart from its biological or cultural existence" (Ann B. Ulanov, *The Feminine in Jungian Psychology and in Christian Theology* [Evanston, IL: Northwestern University Press, 1971], 141). The scientist and theologian Pierre Teilhard de Chardin, SJ (1881–1955) wrote of the "eternal feminine" as born in creation: "I issued from the hand of God—half formed, yet destined to grow in beauty from age to age, the handmaid of his work" (Pierre Teilhard de Chardin, "The Eternal Feminine," in *Writings in Time of War*, trans. René Hague [London: Collins, 1968], 193). See Susan Rakoczy, "The Tension of the Feminine in Teilhard de Chardin," *Grace & Truth* 22, no. 2 (2005): 68–82.

27. John Paul II, "Letter of Pope John Paul II to Women," in *The Pope Speaks to Women*, no. 10, p. 22.

28. Ibid., p. 21.

man and in woman these acquire different strengths, interests, and emphases."[29] This "genius" is located in woman's "particular capacity for accepting the human being in his concrete form," which "prepares her for motherhood, not only physically but also emotionally and spiritually."[30]

At the close of his apostolic letter *Mulieres Dignitatem*, he gives thanks for all women (perfect and weak) for the fruits of feminine holiness and speaks again of their feminine "genius" and their "mystery" as woman. The Spirit of Christ reveals to women "the entire meaning of their femininity," which will lead them to "a sincere gift of self to others, thus finding themselves" (MD 31). He describes Mary as "the highest expression of the 'feminine genius,'"[31] for it is she who through obedience and service lived her vocation as wife and mother.

In these statements, there is a sense of distance from women as they really are. Woman is idealized throughout the papal writings; she does not live and breathe as a real person, but rather the pope constructs an abstract anthropology of her special nature.

This is clearly apparent when John Paul II speaks of the particular value that women represent in view of their femininity. This is the "truth about woman as bride. The Bridegroom is the one who loves. The Bride is loved: it is she who receives love, in order to love in return" (MD 29).[32] This relationship extends beyond marriage to all women's interpersonal interactions with others. This interpretation of woman as first one who receives is universal and thus "shape(s) society and structure(s) the interaction between all persons—men and women" (MD 29). It extends to every woman and operates "independently of the cultural context in which she lives, and independently of her spiritual, psychological and physical characteristics, as for example, age, education, health, work and whether she is married or single" (MD 29). All women are a universal sisterhood of receptivity and self-giving. There is no room in John Paul's anthropology for initiative and self-determination.

---

29. John Paul II, *The Genius of Women* (Washington, DC: United States Catholic Conference, 1997), 28.

30. Ibid., 28.

31. John Paul II, "Letter to Women," no. 10, p. 22.

32. This echoes von Balthasar's bridal imagery for the church: "The institution guarantees the perpetual presence of Christ the Bridegroom for the Church, his Bride." The priesthood is entrusted to men alone because "their function is to embody Christ, who comes to the Church to make her fruitful." Von Balthasar, *Theo-Drama*, 3:354.

Even when he lauds a saint, Catherine of Siena, named a Doctor of the Church in 1970, his remarks are ambivalent. In his homily on the six hundredth anniversary of her death (April 29, 1980) he said, "Her feminine nature was richly endowed with fantasy, intuition, sensibility, an ability to get things done, a capacity to communicate with others, a readiness for self-giving and service."[33] The first three characteristics, especially fantasy, are not necessarily positive, since stereotypes of the female often associate women with fantasy and intuition in contrast to the male who is rational and decisive. But Catherine breaks these stereotypes, since she worked for church reform and engaged in peacemaking efforts among the warring city-states of Italy. She wrote strong letters to popes and civil authorities. She was not a passive woman lost in fantasy.

In his writings on anthropology there is no reflection on "masculine nature." Man is the norm; woman is different, idealized, and physically and psychologically passive and receptive to men and the world.

Relations between Men and Women

John Paul's interpretation of male-female relations is both positive and affirming for women but also has a number of negative connotations.

Building on his assertion of woman's inherent dignity and equality as person, he uses the language of communion to describe male-female relationships. He finds that "communion" is a broader and more accurate word than "help" or helper, one for the other. The relationship of communion of male and female is also constitutive of the image of God. He states that "we can deduce that man became the 'image and likeness' of God not only through his own humanity, but also through the communion of persons which man and woman form right from the beginning" (TB 46).

This movement from the original solitude of the "one man" to communion of male and female is also an image of the communion of the Persons of the Trinity.[34] This is a communion of equals, male and female, each reflecting the image of God.

---

33. Quoted in Peter Hebblethwaite, *Introducing John Paul II* (London: Collins, 1982), 121.

34. Catherine Mowry LaCugna describes this Communion in the Trinity: "communion is the unifying force that holds together the three coequal persons who know and love each other as peers." *God for Us: The Trinity in Christian Life* (San Francisco: Harper San Francisco, 1991), 249.

However, the pope also stresses that "devout and trusting surrender is the distinctive trait of the woman in love," while "possession [*posia-danie*] is the characteristic modality of the devotion of man to the woman he loves."[35] He further describes woman's dignity as "measured by the order of love" (MD 29). John Paul links this with the analogy of the bridegroom and the bride, in which all human beings are loved by God. And it is "precisely the woman—the bride—who manifests this truth to everyone" (MD 29). As in so many other places in his writings, he then moves to Mary as embodying "this truth": "The 'prophetic character' of women in their femininity finds its highest expression in the Virgin Mother of God" (MD 29).

The language of "domination" in Genesis 3:16—"he shall rule over you"—breaks this communion of persons into a "relationship of possession of the other as the object of one's own desire" (TB 123). John Paul II discusses this text in the context of lust, which can be experienced by both men and women, and which distorts the "nuptial meaning" of the body, which is one of gift and receptivity. Yet his reflections here are again abstract, and thus he does not take his analysis a step further to comment on how women's bodies are made the objects of lust in rape and sexual violence.[36]

But this positive interpretation of communion between men and women is not evident in other writings. He recognizes that women can take offense from the text "he shall rule over you," but this "must not under any condition lead to the 'masculinization' of women. In the name of liberation from male 'domination,' women must not appropriate to themselves male characteristics contrary to their own feminine 'originality'" (MD 10). He speaks of the fear that if women appropriate masculine characteristics, which he does not name, they "will deform and lose what constitutes their essential richness," which is their voca-

---

35. George Huntston Williams, *The Mind of John Paul II* (New York: Seabury, 1981), 161–62.

36. In *Familiaris Consortio*, John Paul II does criticize the mentality which objectifies the human and names women as the first victims: "This mentality produces very bitter fruits, such as contempt for men and for women, slavery, oppression of the weak, pornography, prostitution—especially in an organized form." John Paul II, *Familiaris Consortio* (Regarding the Role of the Christian Family in the Modern World) (Vatican: Vatican Polygot Press, 1981), no. 24, 46–47.

tion to love (MD 10, 30). But reading between the lines in light of his other writings, these unfeminine characteristics may well include initiative and leadership. In John Paul II's perspective, gender roles and characteristics are determined by "nature," and attempts to change will distort God's original intention. In the papal writings, there is no awareness at all that gender is a social construct, not an ontological category, and thus he speaks of the "special qualities proper to each" (MD 7).

The language of "complementarity" is a familiar one in his writings. Man and woman are seen to bring to the other something that is lacking. What is lacking? Since the underlying assumption is that "masculine nature" is human nature, a man cannot lack what a woman has. But a woman can somehow be completed by a man. He states that the "personal resources of femininity are certainly no less than of masculinity" (MD 10), yet in his writings there is a sense that these "personal resources" are not only different ("the feminine genius") but less than a man's.

Shortly after the release of *Mulieres Dignitatem* in 1988, the pope told a group of American bishops that "Whatever violates the complementarity of women and men offends the dignity of each."[37] Feminist scholar Sandra Schneiders has remarked that "Women have been seen to complete men the way a second coat of paint completes a house, whereas men have been seen to complete women the way a motor completes a car."[38] In the post-synod apostolic exhortation of 1988, *Christifideles Laici* (On the Vocation and Mission of the Lay Faithful in the Church and the World), signed by Pope John Paul II, the issue of complementarity is also raised:

> The condition that will assure the rightful presence of women in the Church and in society is a more penetrating and accurate consideration of the *anthropological foundation for masculinity and femininity* with the intent of clarifying woman's personal identity in relation to man, that is a diversity yet mutual complementarity, not only as it concerns roles to be held and functions to be performed, but also, and more deeply, as it concerns her make-up and meaning as a person.[39] (CL 50, emphasis in original)

---

37. Quoted in Deborah Halter, *The Papal "No": A Comprehensive Guide to the Vatican's Rejection of Women's Ordination* (New York: Crossroad, 2004), 79.

38. Sandra Schneiders, *Beyond Patching: Faith and Feminism in the Catholic Church* (New York: Paulist Press, 1991), 13.

39. John Paul II, *Christifideles Laici* (On the Vocation and Mission of the Lay Faithful in the Church and the World) (London: Catholic Truth Society, n.d.), p. 48.

John Paul's highly developed anthropology ranges wide over many areas: the creation of men and women as sexual beings, woman as person, the female body, and the relations of the men and women. But we can question whether his thought assists women in affirming their dignity as human beings. Do women recognize themselves in his interpretation of their bodies, their selves, and their relations with men? On the evidence considered thus far, his anthropology is sometimes good news, at other times bad news, and offers a mixed message indeed.

Women in Society

There are a number of references in the writings of John Paul II to women's roles in society and the world of work. While he describes the increasing presence of women in public life, his Polish context informs his argument that women should not be compelled by government or economic necessity to work outside the home.

Polish women under communism had to work outside the home. After the fall of communism, they continued to work out of economic need. Like so many women around the world, Polish married women had *two* full-time jobs—taking care of the home and family and their outside work. Husbands and wives did not divide up the household tasks equally. The conditions under which women worked within and outside the home—very cramped living quarters, doing dangerous jobs in mines, factories, etc.—made their lives extraordinarily difficult.

John Paul projects the Polish experience onto women throughout the world. "While it must be recognized that women have the same right as men to perform various public functions, society must be structured in such a way that wives and mothers are *not in practice compelled* to work outside the home, and that their families can live and prosper in a dignified way even when they themselves devote their full time to their own family" (FC 23, emphasis in original).

What will allow women to stay home and raise the children? The answer is to restructure society so that there is no economic necessity for women to work. The pope states that "society should create and develop conditions favouring work in the home" (FC 23).

This can be done by the introduction of a "family wage," which is "a single salary given to the head of the family for that person's work or other measures such as family allowances or grants to mothers devoting themselves exclusively to their families."[40] For John Paul II, the traditional roles are to continue: the head of the family is the father and the bread winner; the wife and mother stays home. In *Laborem Exercens* he writes:

> It will profit society to make it possible for a mother—without curtailing her freedom, without psychological or practical discrimination, without handicapping her in any way whatsoever in regard to other women— to dedicate herself to the care and education of her children.

> Having to abandon these tasks to take up work outside the home is wrong for society and the family when it hinders these main goals of a mother's mission. (LE 19)

Once again it appears that "biology is destiny." There is no awareness of the father's role in the family—the children are the mother's responsibility alone. There is no differentiation between women compelled to take up menial jobs for low pay and the need of professionally educated women to work as doctors, teachers, lawyers, etc., not only to contribute to society but for their own psychological and spiritual well-being as persons. The pope's warnings about mothers working outside the home must always be considered against the Polish context, which "he is reacting vigorously against."[41]

In the discussions of the 1980 synod on the family, there were many interventions that "emphasized that the time had come to take women seriously in the Church and in society."[42] But this did not appear in *Familiaris Consortio* and later in *Laborem Exercens*. *Familiaris Consortio* does recognize that women today are participating in the "public space" of society, but it emphasizes women's work should primarily take place in the home. "While it must be recognized that women have the same right as men to perform various public functions, society must be structured in such a way that wives and mothers are *not in practice compelled* to work

40. John Paul II, *Laborem Exercens* (On Human Work), in *John Paul II: The Encyclicals in Everyday Language*, ed. Joseph G. Donders (Maryknoll, NY: Orbis, 1996), no. 19, p. 61.
41. Hebblethwaite, *Introducing*, 127.
42. Ibid., 123.

outside the home . . . and that society should create and develop conditions favouring work in the home" (FC 23, emphasis in original).

The pope is not against women working, but opposes mothers working outside the home. Once she has children, she must stay home. This may be more necessary when the children are young (and many women today who are financially able choose to do this), but his view is that mothers should be home with the children. Thus we should interpret the many statements that he makes about women in society as applying only to women without family responsibilities.

In many places in his writings John Paul does laud and support women's contributions to society through their work. In his "Letter to Women" he expresses gratitude to them: "Thank you, women who work! You are present and active in every area of life—social, economic, cultural, artistic and political. In this way you make an indispensable contribution to the growth of a culture which unites reason and feeling."[43] In recognizing women's increasing contributions to society through their work, the pope continues to speak of "the proper nature of femininity":

> The Church is well aware of how much society needs *feminine genius* in all aspects of civil society and insists that *every form of discrimination of women be eliminated* from the workplace, culture and politics, while still respecting the proper nature of femininity: an inappropriate leveling of roles would not only impoverish social life, but would ultimately *deprive woman herself* of what is primarily or exclusively hers.[44] (emphasis in original)

The pope appeals for a just wage for women who work outside the home (LE 19). He recognizes that "in many societies women work in nearly every sector of life" and he stresses that "they must be able to do so without discrimination and exclusion from jobs, and also without having to give up their specific role in family and society" (LE 19), which is that of mother. Thus mothers who work outside the home by choice and/or necessity are faced with two full-time jobs. At least the pope affirms that they should receive a just wage, even though they may have to do what he does not support: work outside the home even though they have children.

43. John Paul II, "Letter to Women," no. 2, pp. 13–14.
44. John Paul II, "Feminine Genius Needed in all Aspects of Life," Angelus Homily, August 14, 1994. *L'Osservatore Romano*, 34 (August 24, 1994): 2.

John Paul evidences awareness of the double shift that women work when he points to "a widespread and distorted culture which unduly excuses man from his family responsibilities, and, in the worst cases, inclines him to look upon woman as an object of pleasure, or a mere reproductive device."[45]

In his writings John Paul II recognizes, and to a certain extent supports, women's increasing presence in society. But he also holds a romantic nostalgia for the mother at home with her children.

Women in the Church

Although the pope discusses women's contributions to many areas of society, there are relatively few references in his writings to women's ministries and experience in the life of the church. Even when consecrated women are praised, it is because they "help the Church and all mankind to experience a 'spousal' relationship to God."[46] He is best known for his total opposition to the ordination of women, but the paucity of references to women in the life of the church as a whole is troubling.

Mulieres Dignitatem is a sustained theological reflection on many aspects of women's dignity and vocation, with particular attention to anthropological issues, motherhood and virginity, and the spousal nature of the church. The section on "Jesus Christ" does present positive comments on Jesus' interaction with women in the gospels (MD 12–14), and the pope concludes that "Christ's way of acting, the Gospel of his words and deeds, is a consistent *protest* against whatever offends the dignity of women" (MD 15, emphasis in original).

Affirming the presence of women as the first witnesses to the resurrection of Christ (MD 16), John Paul II stresses that this "confirms and clarifies, in the Holy Spirit, the truth about the equality of man and woman" (MD 16). The outpouring of the Spirit is given equally to man and woman. Here there are no limits in the pope's thinking about women's roles, though later in the document he will emphasize that women cannot be priests.

In the chapter on "The Church—the Bride of Christ," John Paul speaks approvingly of "a number of women" from the earliest days of the

45. John Paul II, "Feminine Genius," 2.
46. John Paul II, "Letter to Women," no. 2, p. 14.

church who followed Christ unreservedly, from the first women disciples to Macrina, Catherine of Siena, Teresa of Avila, Mary Ward, and Rose of Lima among others, all of whom "have shared in the Church's mission" (MD 27). These women are lauded for their holiness "as an incarnation of the feminine ideal" (MD 27) and as a model for the whole church. Nowhere is there mention of women's leadership in the church.

In several of his writings the pope again uses the phrase "genius of women" to refer to women in the church. Writing on the eve of the Beijing Conference on Women in 1995, he affirmed that the "genius of women" should be "expressed more fully in the life of society as a whole, as well as in the life of the Church."[47] Once again, Mary is the model of this "genius" since she lived a life of service to others.[48] Other women throughout the history of the church—martyrs, women, and mystics—"have left an impressive and beneficial mark in history," together with "the many women, inspired by faith, who were responsible for initiatives of extraordinary social importance, especially in serving the poorest of the poor."[49]

Writing to the priests of the world on Holy Thursday in 1995, the pope urges them to read *Mulieres Dignitatem.* Following the teaching of Vatican II in *Lumen Gentium*, he situates the place of women theologically as members of the People of God and affirms that "all her members, men and women alike, share—each in his or her specific way—in the prophetic priestly and royal mission of Christ."[50] Later in the same section he reiterates that women share in the "prophetic mission of Christ,"[51] together with his priestly and royal mission. One might legitimately wonder precisely *how* he interpreted women's prophetic role in the church of the late twentieth century. Catherine of Siena spoke truth to power to the popes of her day; she is safely canonized. But today other Catherines continue to challenge the church.

There is no awareness of the burdens of sexism in the church and how it severely limits women's initiative and contributions. John Paul states: "If anyone has this task of advancing the dignity of women in

47. John Paul II, "Letter to Women," no. 10, p. 21.

48. Ibid.

49. Ibid., no. 11, p. 24.

50. John Paul II, "Excerpts from Pope John Paul II's Holy Thursday Letter to Priests," in *The Genius of Women*, 68.

51. Ibid., 70.

the Church and society, it is women themselves, who must recognize their responsibility as leading characters" (CL 49).

Women can act in the church according to the "ample room for a lay and feminine presence recognized by the Church's law," and he names "theological teaching, the forms of liturgical ministry permitted, including service at the altar,[52] pastoral and administrative councils, Diocesan Synods and Particular Councils, various ecclesial institutions, curias, and ecclesiastical tribunals, many pastoral activities, including the new forms of participation in the care of parishes when there is a shortage of clergy, except for those tasks that belong properly to the priest."[53] Nowhere is the word "leadership" used in reference to women in the church; that is reserved to men alone.

John Paul II's contacts with women were limited by the exclusively male context of the Curia and his personal staff.[54] Occasionally a woman did speak her mind and heart to him in public, and it was a very disconcerting experience.

On November 20, 1980, Barbara Engl, President of the Munich Association of Youth, was to say farewell to the pope after his visit to Munich. Peter Hebblethwaite relates that "after listening to his homily on Satan in our midst, she threw away her manuscript" and spoke from her heart "as John Paul hid his head in his hands."[55] After speaking about

---

52. Early in his pontificate he vigorously opposed girls and women as altar servers, and the 1980 "Instruction of the Sacred Liturgy for the Sacraments and Divine Worship excluded . . . . all women as altar servers" (Williams, *The Mind of John Paul II*, 351). This position was guardedly reversed in 1994 in a similar instruction to the world's bishops. Females were now allowed to be servers "by temporary deputation" for the duration of need. Local bishops were to make the decision whether women could serve, and they were to keep in mind "the noble tradition of having boys serve at the altar," which has led to a "reassuring development of priestly vocations" (Congregation for Divine Worship and the Sacraments, "Use of Female Altar Servers Allowed," *Origins* 23, no. 45 [April 28, 1994]: 777–779). The pope saw clearly that if females served Mass, they, like males, might think of a priestly vocation—which in his thinking was totally impossible. It was therefore better to limit their presence as much as possible, while implicitly acknowledging the fact that females were already serving in many parts of the world, especially North America and Europe.

53. John Paul II, *The Genius of Women*, 35–36.

54. Polish nuns cooked for him and oversaw his domestic needs. There are, of course, some women who do work in the Vatican as secretaries and in some responsible positions in the Vatican dicasteries, but because of the prohibition of the ordination of women, no woman can head any of these dicasteries.

55. Hebblethwaite, *Introducing*, 117.

young people's lack of understanding of why the church insists on priestly celibacy, she said: "Nor can young people understand why a greater sharing of women in the ministry should be ruled out. We know perfectly well that the Gospel challenges us, but we do not feel oppressed by neurosis or a lack of courage because we know that Christ has promised us the fullness of life."[56]

In the future, organizers of papal events took care to make sure that women were never able to approach the pope again and speak their hearts.

The Ordination of Women

During his pontificate, John Paul II consistently maintained that the ordination of women was a theological and ecclesial impossibility. In various documents, such as *Mulieres Dignitatem* (26–27) and the 1995 "Letter to Women," he argues that the free choice of Christ of only men "in no way detracts from the role of women"[57] in the church, nor that of anyone else who is not ordained. This is in terms of the "sacramental economy" by "which God freely chooses in order to become present in the midst of humanity,"[58] and he asserts that only men can be these sacramental signs of God's presence.

The movement for the ordination of women in the Catholic Church began in the 1960s with the formation of the St. Joan's Alliance in England. In 1974, a group of women religious in the United States sent a resolution to the National Conference of Catholic Bishops that urged them to expand the scope for women's ministries, including ordination to the priesthood.

A year later, in 1975, the first Women's Ordination Conference (WOC) was held in Detroit, Michigan. Over twelve hundred people attended and hundreds were turned away for lack of space in the meeting venue. After this meeting the WOC evolved into an organization in the United States; gradually similar bodies were founded in many countries of the world.

Also in 1975 the Papal Biblical Commission issued its report on women's ministry and the seventeen members "voted unanimously; that the

56. Quoted in Ibid.
57. John Paul II, "Letter to Women," no. 11, p. 23.
58. Ibid.

New Testament alone seemed unable to settle the question of the possibility of women priests, and the members voted 12–5 that scripture alone was not sufficient to rule out the admission of women to priesthood."[59]

Taking note of this rising tide of enthusiasm for what Rome saw as impossible, in 1976 the Congregation for the Doctrine of the Faith (CDF) published the declaration *Inter Insignores* (On the Question of the Admission of Women to the Ministerial Priesthood). This document said a decisive "no" to women's ordination and used three arguments: tradition (that the church has not ordained women), Scripture (that Christ chose only men and that not even Mary was a priest), and the need for the priest to have a physical resemblance to Christ.

It was the last argument which aroused the most controversy. The document stressed that the sacraments are based on "natural signs, on symbols imprinted on the human psychology."[60] Thus only men can represent Christ as priests:

> The same natural resemblance is required for persons as for things: when Christ's role in the eucharist is to be expressed sacramentally, there would not be this "natural resemblance" which must exist between Christ and his minister if the role were not taken by a man: in such case it would be difficult to see in the minister the image of Christ. For Christ himself was and remains a man.[61]

The theological implications of this position are very severe for women, since it implies that although they are baptized into Christ, they are unable to represent Christ. It also makes the gender of Christ as male the determining point of his identity, a position never before taught in the church.

This document was not "received" by most Catholics and did not enter into the lived experience of the faith. Three years later, in 1979, John Paul II was strongly challenged by Sister Theresa Kane, RSM, president of the Leadership Conference of Women Religious (LCWR),

59. Phyllis Zagano, *Holy Saturday: An Argument for the Restoration of the Female Diaconate in the Catholic Church* (New York: Crossroad, 2000), 54.

60. Congregation for the Doctrine of the Faith, *Inter Insignores* (Declaration on the Question of the Admission of Women to the Ministerial Priesthood), no. 44, in Halter, *The Papal "No,"* 191.

61. Ibid., no. 45, p. 191.

who greeted him at a liturgy in the National Shrine of the Immaculate Conception in Washington, DC, and spoke on behalf of the Catholic women of the United States:

> As women we have heard the powerful messages of our Church addressing the dignity and reverence for all persons. As women we have pondered upon these words. Our contemplation leads us to state that the Church in its struggle to be faithful to its call for reverence and dignity for all persons must respond to providing the possibility of women as persons being included in all ministries of our Church. I urge you, Your Holiness, to be open to and respond to the voices coming from the women of this country who are desirous of serving in and through the Church as fully participating members.[62]

The pope's demeanor during her welcome has been interpreted variously from silence to murmuring "no, no" with a pained expression on his face, which resembled his response to Barbara Engl's plea. He was responding not only to a twentieth-century woman's plea but perhaps was also thinking of his Polish context in which there is a schismatic group called the Mariavites who do ordain women.[63]

After the fall of communism in Eastern Europe in the late 1980s and early 1990s, reports began to surface of the ordination of five or six Czechoslovakian women in order to serve a local church under the threat of suppression.[64] The publicity about these women and the fact that the ordination controversy would not go away led John Paul to state his total opposition to the ordination of women in the document *Ordinatio Sacerdotalis* (On Reserving the Priesthood to Men Alone, 1994). In it he states that the church's teaching authority "has consistently held that the exclu-

---

62. Quoted in Halter, *The Papal "No,"* 32.

63. Based on the revelations of a Polish Sister of St. Clare, Felicja Kozlowska, in the late nineteenth century, which called for renewal of the Church in Poland, the followers, both men and women, of Sister Kozlowska organized themselves into an order, the Mariavites. They were excommunicated by Pope St. Pius X in 1906, but the order continued as a schismatic group with 100,000 followers. The group began to ordain women in 1928. They have a cooperative association with the Old Catholic Church. See Williams, *The Mind of John Paul II*, 36–37.

64. See the biography of one of these Czech women, Ludmila Javorova, by Miriam Therese Winter, *Out of the Depths: The Story of Ludmila Javorova Ordained Roman Catholic Priest* (New York: Crossroad, 2001).

sion of women from the priesthood is in accord with God's plan for his Church" and thus the Roman Catholic Church "has no authority whatsoever to confer priestly ordination on women" (OS 3, 13).[65]

Invoking his Marian spirituality, the pope called attention to the fact that Mary was not a priest as a sign that "the nonadmission of women to priestly ordination cannot mean that women are of lesser dignity nor can it be construed as discrimination against them. Rather, it is to be seen as the faithful observance of a plan to be ascribed to the wisdom of the Lord of the universe" (OS 9).[66]

The argument against ordination now shifted from the "physical resemblance" that a priest must have to Christ in *Inter Insigniores* to ecclesiological arguments:

> The priesthood belonged to the church's divinely mandated structure.
> It was reserved to men alone.
> The pope could not change what Christ had decreed.
> This judgment was to be "definitively held" (OS 13) by all the faithful.[67]

The reception of this document was decidedly mixed. What did it mean that this teaching was to be "definitively held" by all the baptized? A document issued in 1995, *Responsum ad Dubium* (Response to a Question), by the CDF, headed by Joseph Cardinal Ratzinger (now Pope Benedict XVI), and approved by John Paul II, invoked infallibility. It stated that "the teaching that the Church has no authority whatsoever to confer priestly ordination on women . . . requires definitive assent since, founded on the written Word of God, and from the beginning constantly preserved and applied in the tradition of the Church, it has been set forth infallibly by the ordinary and universal magisterium" (RD 3).[68]

This document unleashed a new firestorm of questions. Did the nonordination of women belong to the deposit of faith? Could a Vatican office speak infallibly? Did not only the pope, speaking *ex cathedra* on mat-

---

65. John Paul II, *Ordinatio Sacerdotalis* (On Reserving the Priesthood to Men Alone) in Halter, *The Papal "No,"* 211, 213.

66. Ibid., 212.

67. Halter, *The Papal "No,"* 98.

68. *Responsum ad Dubium* (Response to a Question Regarding *Ordinatio Sacerdotalis*), no. 3, in Halter, *The Papal "No,"* 225. On the wider implications of this seemingly new category of "definitive doctrine" see chapter 4 of the present volume.

ters of faith and morals, speak infallibly? Eminent canonists such as Ladislas Örsy disagreed with this use of infallibility: "The reason for this is theological. Infallibility cannot be delegated. It is a charism granted to the pope (as well as to the episcopal college and to the universal body of the faithful); no other office or body in the church can possess it."[69] Others pointed out that the church had not, for twenty centuries, consistently taught that women cannot be ordained. This is a new question.

But for John Paul II and Joseph Ratzinger the question was now closed for all eternity. The argument in both documents had been an argument from authority, papal authority, and the church was to accept it and end discussion. But still discussion goes on.

George Weigel, in his laudatory biography of John Paul, *Witness to Hope*, sees the arguments used in the two documents as a "strategic error." Rather than appealing to authority, Weigel maintains that the pope should have recast the argument according to his own interpretation of the spousal nature of the church. He says that the argument should have been built on the "theology of the body" that John Paul had developed, an approach that insisted that the differences between men and women "were not biological accidents but revelations of deep truths about the human condition that directly touched God's redemptive purpose for the world."[70]

Weigel states that this argument would have strengthened the pope's concepts of the "Marian" and "Petrine" churches. Mary in her obedience is the first disciple, and thus the Marian church is the church of disciples; it makes possible the Petrine church of office and authority. The Petrine church has no other purpose than "to form the Church in line with the ideal of sanctity already programmed and prefigured in Mary."[71]

Conclusion

In evaluating Pope John Paul II's teachings and writings on women, it must be emphasized that his insistence on woman's dignity as a human

---

69. Ladislas Örsy, "The Congregation's 'Response': Its Authority and Meaning," *America* 173 (December 9, 1995): 4.

70. Weigel, *Witness to Hope*, 733.

71. John Paul II, "Annual Address to the Roman Curia," *L'Osservatore Romano* (January 11, 1988), 6–8, quoted in Weigel, *Witness to Hope*, 577. Weigel describes the basis of these two "churches" in the thought of von Balthasar.

being, made in the image of God, and equal as a person to man, is a new and extremely significant teaching in the Catholic Church.

His interpretations of the relationships of men and women, of the female body, of the role of women in the family and society, are all premised upon his anthropology, which was highly influenced by the thought of Hans Urs von Balthasar. Biological differences are the basis of psychological differences. His use of "feminine genius" and "the proper nature of femininity" imply that perhaps there are two human natures, one male and one female.

While he often spoke of the growing roles of women in society, he was much more circumspect about women's ministries in the church. He never spoke about women's leadership in the church. His insistence that it is impossible for women to be ordained to the ministerial priesthood admitted of no dialogue and no change.

The pope used to remark that he was "a feminist," and his perspective is often termed the "new Catholic feminism."[72] Feminism is built on the principle of the full humanity of women and "whatever enables this to flourish is redemptive and of God; whatever damages this is nonredemptive and contrary to God's intent."[73] John Paul II's "new" feminism is decidedly mixed. It admits the principle of women's dignity and equality but draws back sharply from the implications of that equality both in society and in the church.

72. See Tina Beattie's *New Catholic Feminism: Theology and Theory* (London and New York: Routledge, 2006), in which she engages with von Balthasar. For her comments on the foundations of this new Catholic feminism, see pp. 19–26. See also, Michele A. Gonzalez, "Hans Urs von Balthasar and Contemporary Feminist Theology," *Theological Studies* 65 (2004): 566–595.

73. Elizabeth A. Johnson, *Consider Jesus: Waves of Renewal in Christology* (New York: Crossroad, 1991), 103.

11

John Paul II and Collegiality

Paul Lakeland

For all the criticisms of John Paul's practice of collegiality, there is no
doubt that he spoke often and highly of its importance. From his very
first *Urbi et Orbi* address, given the day after his election, where he spoke
of the "special bond, that is, collegiality" which "binds together the
sacred pastors" (1978), to his fine words on the "synodal dimension of
the church" as an expression of "the collegiality of the entire episcopate" (1994), to his relatively late letter on episcopal conferences, *Apostolos Suos* (1998), the collegiality of the bishops was a thread running
through his pontificate. Over and over again he wrote of the special
bond that existed among the bishops, less often perhaps of the roles that
they played together in leading the universal church. Clearly, collegiality
was important to John Paul. But what did he mean by "collegiality"?
Was his view consistent with the teaching of the council or the convictions of his brother bishops? There is a possibly apocryphal anecdote
told of him on the day of his inauguration as pope. Immediately after
the ceremony, so the story goes, he turned to Cardinal Suenens, a leading progressive voice in the church at the time, rubbed his hands together gleefully, and proclaimed, "And now for some *real* collegiality!"
But what for John Paul was the "real" in "real collegiality"?

Although John Paul spoke and wrote long and often about collegiality, his failures in this regard were probably the most frequently mentioned item in the more critical assessments of his legacy that appeared
at the time of his death. In March 2005 Hans Küng wrote of John Paul's
acceptance of Vatican II's call for collegiality, but added that "he disre-

garded the collegiality which had been agreed to there and instead cele-brated the triumph of his papacy at the cost of the bishops."[1] Tom Groome of Boston College said that "there are serious aspects of the council that it would seem as if this man did not embrace and imple-ment; for example, the call to collegiality."[2] The great Franz Cardinal König wrote at length on this topic, opining at one point that

> the Second Vatican Council, by linking its doctrine of collegiality to that of papal primacy as defined at Vatican I, gave us a precise description of the significance of the episcopal college and of its tasks in conjunction with the Petrine office. One could call it an act of divine providence, in order better to meet the new requirements for the world church. In fact, however, *de facto* and not *de jure*, intentionally or unintentionally, the curia authorities working in conjunction with the pope have appropriated the tasks of the episcopal college. It is they who now carry out almost all of them.[3]

And even the deliberately centrist Rome correspondent of the lay-run U.S. *National Catholic Reporter*, John Allen, commented that "whatever may be said publicly, John Paul II did not endear himself to some of his brother bishops . . . in the exercise of collegiality."[4]

In order to grasp John Paul II's understanding of collegiality, we have to begin with the wider historical context of Vatican II and the council, especially with the Dogmatic Constitution on the Church, *Lumen Gentium*. However, from the very first moment of the council to the last, and of course beyond, collegiality has never stopped being a controversial idea. While on the surface it sounds a clear democratizing note, drawing the bishops together into greater responsibility for the governance of the universal church, it is also susceptible to a more conservative turn. In this interpretation, the bishops' role in ecclesial governance is little more than

1. Hans Küng, "The Pope's Contradictions," *Der Spiegel*, March 25, 2005. Available most conveniently in English at http://www.spiegel.de/international/spiegel/0,1518,348471,00.html.

2. On U.S. television's public broadcasting channel, PBS, April 1, 2005. For a tran-script of the conversation, see http://www.pbs.org/newshour/bb/religion/jan-june05/pope_4-01.html.

3. Franz König, "My Vision for the Church of the Future," *The Tablet*, March 27, 1999.

4. John Allen, "He Was a Magnificent Pope Who Presided over a Controversial Pontifi-cate," *National Catholic Reporter*, April 4, 2005.

their expression of solidarity with the papal voice. Collegiality was one of the principal issues at the council in face of which the battle lines were drawn up between the majority of the bishops and the "curial party," bent on maintaining centralized control over the universal church.[5] It is an idea whose ramifications spill over into the wider notion of "coresponsibility," in which not only bishops but priests and even the laity come to share collective accountability for the shape and fate of the church.[6] It can be seen both as an important corrective to the old standoff in church history between the papalists and the conciliarists, and also as one important move in Vatican II's much-vaunted efforts to balance the papal overemphasis of Vatican I. And, of course, it has been held by the ilk of Lefebvre or other sedevacantist groups to be simply a destructive and illegitimate strike against the authority of the pope.

John XXIII and Paul VI on Collegiality

It is instructive to begin the examination of John Paul II's understanding of collegiality by briefly examining the ways in which his immediate predecessors in office fostered collegiality. John XXIII and Paul VI seem to have had discernibly different attitudes. In his masterful biography of Pope Paul VI, Peter Hebblethwaite contrasts the approaches of John XXIII and Paul VI to collegiality as "from below" and "from above."[7]

5. It is also true that further battle lines have been drawn up over whether or not this well-rehearsed drama of the council is an accurate depiction. However, those with little to gain from any distortion seem to agree that from the first moment John XXIII called the council, perhaps even to the present day, the Roman Curia have been mostly dead set against it. The most readable version of these events remains Xavier Rynne's articles for *The New Yorker*, subsequently published in book form and now available in a one-volume edition, *Vatican Council II* (Maryknoll, NY: Orbis, 1999). The most authoritative source is the magisterial five-volume *History of Vatican II* (Maryknoll, NY: Orbis, 2000–2006), eds. Giuseppe Alberigo and Joseph A. Komonchak. Alberigo has also written *A Brief History of Vatican II* (Maryknoll, NY: Orbis, 2006) for those with less stamina. The most interesting account may well be Yves Congar's *Mon Journal du Concile* (Paris: Cerf, 2002). For a sample of the opposite point of view, albeit a rather extreme and intemperate version, see Ralph M. McInerney, *What Went Wrong with Vatican II: The Catholic Crisis Explained* (Manchester, NH: Sophia Institute Press, 1998).

6. The locus classicus here is Léon Joseph Suenens, *Coresponsibility in the Church*, trans. Francis Martin (New York: Herder and Herder, 1968). Suenens's autobiography is also instructive here: *Memories and Hopes* (Dublin: Veritas, 1992).

7. Peter Hebblethwaite, *Paul VI: The First Modern Pope* (New York: Paulist Press, 1993), 352.

John XXIII, the architect of Vatican II, died in May 1963, before the notion of collegiality had come to occupy center stage in the deliberations of the council fathers, but several hints suggest a more generous understanding of episcopal coresponsibility than was later demonstrated in the increasingly cautious reign of his successor, Paul VI. In their two approaches we can see the battle lines drawn up long before there even seemed to be a battle to fight. Both by temperament and conviction, the two pontiffs held differing views of the church and so of the place of the bishops in church governance.

When John XXIII convoked the Second Vatican Council, he did not see it as the completion of its 1870 predecessor, but as a fundamentally new council, indeed a "new Pentecost."[8] While he was responsible for giving the Roman Curia a major role in preparations for the council, he may have been surprised and dismayed by their efforts to subvert and control the assembly. During the first session and after, he allowed and even encouraged the insistence of the great body of the bishops that they have a more decisive role in setting both the agenda and the outcomes of the council. Numerous small but decisive steps, including the increasing prominence the pope gave to more progressive figures like the Belgian Cardinal Suenens and the Italian Lercaro testify to his awareness of the dynamics,[9] as also did his decision not to be present in the council assemblies for fear that he would inhibit freedom of speech. It was with his encouragement and under his watch that toward the end of the first session the bishops began to discuss the questions of ecclesiology that would rapidly come to be accepted as *the* focus of the council. It seems likely, though it can never be proven conclusively, that Pope John hoped for a much more proactive role on the part of the world's bishops in decision making in the church.

When Paul VI was elected to succeed John XXIII in June 1963, he moved rapidly to confirm his commitment to the continuation and completion of Vatican II, sentiments not really surprising in a man who had as Cardinal Montini of Milan sided pretty clearly with the more progressive majority during the first session. John XXIII evidently had confi-

8. On John XXIII's intentions for a new council and not a continuation of Vatican I, see Alberigo, *A Brief History of Vatican II*, 1–20, esp. 19.

9. See, for example, Hebblethwaite, *Paul VI: The First Modern Pope*, 300.

dence in Montini. It is said that he prayed that Montini would be his successor. In any case, Paul VI supported the bishops in their commitment to collegiality and enthusiastically promoted the idea of the Roman synod of bishops as a place for collegiality to continue to be expressed after the council had ended. He even planned to build a new building to house the bishops, perhaps initially imagining a more permanent presence than the form of synod that eventually emerged. He also promised a thorough reform of the Roman Curia, a reform clearly needed if the Curia was to stop thinking of itself as governing the universal church under papal instruction and begin to see itself as the servant of the entire church. This promise, sincerely meant, was never fulfilled, though he certainly took important steps to internationalize its membership.

While Paul VI was indeed a man of the council, he was also a nervous and cautious individual who sought desperately to win overwhelming "yes" votes for the confirmation of council documents. As anyone knows who works on such matters, compromise is the only way to achieve this kind of result, and the texts on collegiality in *Lumen Gentium*, the Vatican council's Dogmatic Constitution on the Church, were no exception. Like the bishops themselves, Paul agonized over just what collegiality might mean, supported the decision to ask the council fathers to respond to five specific questions to clarify their concerns, and—most notoriously—issued on his own authority a *nota praevia* explaining and, some said, undercutting the intentions of *Lumen Gentium*. However, the explanatory note—which stressed and repeated the words of the council fathers themselves that episcopal collegiality was always exercised *cum Petro et sub Petro*—was neither included in the final text nor voted on by the bishops, which gives support to those who consider it simply a political sop to the Curia in search of that overwhelmingly positive vote. Of course, this kind of maneuvering provided ammunition for later efforts to paint Paul VI as a weak and vacillating pontiff who did not really support the conciliar expression of collegiality, just as it could be used to support minimalist interpretations of collegiality adduced on other grounds.

Collegiality in *Lumen Gentium*

During the second session of the council, the commission drafting the text of *Lumen Gentium* came directly to the bishops with five questions for clarification. The structure of council debates, with none of the to and fro of the parliamentary system, made it very difficult to determine who spoke for whom and thus what the true feelings of the majority were. Four of the five questions dealt directly with collegiality, and in their responses the bishops overwhelmingly agreed that episcopal consecration is the highest degree of sacred orders, that each bishop becomes a member of the sacred college by virtue of his consecration, that together with the pope and never without him the college of bishops exercises "full and supreme authority in the church," and that the bishops enjoy this power by divine right. Voting as they did, the conciliar majority clearly scotched more conservative efforts to insist that episcopal authority and thus membership of the college is by delegation from the pope. That same month, October 1963, the bishops sent the text of *Lumen Gentium* back to the commission with instructions to reverse the order of chapters two and three, thus placing the discussion of the people of God ahead of that of the hierarchy. These decisive acts set fast the council's ruling vision of the church as the baptized, priestly people of God.

A complex and nuanced understanding of collegiality is laid out in *Lumen Gentium*, evidently influenced by the results of the direct questionnaire to which the bishops had responded so clearly.[10] The bishops, successors of the apostles (LG 21), form an episcopal order with a "collegiate character and structure," and into which they enter "in virtue of the sacramental consecration." "Together with its head, the Supreme Pontiff, and never apart from him, it is the subject of supreme and full authority over the universal church" (LG 22). Bishops exercise pastoral care over their own dioceses but should also have concern for the universal church. "Each bishop represents his own church" and together with the pope they "represent the whole church in a bond of peace, love and unity" (LG 23). They have the responsibility to teach (LG 24), to preach (LG 25), to be stewards of the Eucharist (LG 26), and to govern their particular church (LG 27). As teachers, they "proclaim infallibly the doctrine of Christ" when acting in communion with one another and with the pope; "even though dispersed throughout the world," they "are in agreement that a particular teaching is to be held definitively" (LG 25).

10. Quotations from *Lumen Gentium* taken from Austin Flannery, OP, *Vatican Council II: The Basic Sixteen Documents* (Costello Publishing Company, 1996).

The understanding of collegiality spelled out in *Lumen Gentium* is complex and subtle but not always crystal clear. This much is evident, that the bishops exercise the fullness of collegiality in acting, in concert and together with the pope, either in an ecumenical council or when all speak with one voice, at the wish of the pope or at least in a way that the pope can "receive." Well and good. But there are other ways in which collegiality is also somehow expressed, as when they assist one another or somehow show their concern for the whole church, or indeed when they speak in forums such as episcopal conferences. In all these cases they are not of course acting with one voice, nor necessarily at the behest of the pope. These forms of collegiality are real but, to borrow the words of the *Nota Praevia* which Paul VI attached to the text of *Lumen Gentium*, they are not "in full act," that is, somehow not representative of the fullness of collegiality.[11] This distinction will be important in examining John Paul II's particular understanding of collegiality. This indeed is the crux of the issue. No one would wish to deny that the fullest expression of collegiality lies in just such collective acts of judgment, in council or not. But the question is whether there is something more, perhaps something less formal, but something which nevertheless gives greater voice to the bishops than they previously had.

While it is evident that episcopal collegiality is deemed an important characteristic of the church, *Lumen Gentium* never makes it entirely clear whether collegiality is in service of primacy or primacy in service of collegiality. Is the collegial action of the bishops envisaged as a support to the work of the Supreme Pontiff, bringing solidarity and affirmation of unity to his pronouncements, or is it that the pope is the symbol and focus of the unity of the bishops scattered around the world? Is episcopal collegiality simply a powerful symbol of the unity of the worldwide church, or is it a mechanism through which the bishops can exercise some element of shared governance? It is hard to avoid the impression that John XXIII would have welcomed assistance in governance, that

11. On the general issue of collegiality in relation to the authority of episcopal conferences, see the excellent discussion by Joseph A. Komonchak, "The Roman Working Paper on Episcopal Conferences," chapter 6 of *Episcopal Conferences: Historical, Canonical and Theological Studies*, ed. Thomas J. Reese, SJ (Washington, DC: Georgetown, 1989). The entire text of this book is available electronically at http://woodstock.georgetown.edu/church_studies/reese/ec/index.htm.

some at least of the council fathers would have favored it (Suenens, König, and others), but that Paul VI was extremely wary of any real power sharing at the level of the universal church. And while John Paul I had so little time, there are interesting words in his *Urbi et Orbi* address in August 1978, where he calls on the college of bishops, seeking their "collaboration in the government of the universal Church."[12] It is exactly this emphasis on shared governance that is notable by its absence in the words and especially the deeds of his successor.

John Paul II on Collegiality

Just a few weeks after his short-lived predecessor, it was John Paul II's turn to present his *Urbi et Orbi* address. The theme of his message was fidelity to the Second Vatican Council, in which he singled out ecclesiological issues for special focus. In particular, "the special bond, that is, collegiality, which 'with Peter and under Peter' binds together the sacred Pastors."

> In order that we may become better informed and more vigilant in undertaking our duty, we particularly urge a deeper reflection on the implications of the collegial bond. By collegiality the bishops are closely linked with the successor of the blessed Peter, and all collaborate in order to fulfill the high offices committed to them: offices of enlightening the whole People of God with the light of the Gospel, of sanctifying them with the means of grace, of guiding them with pastoral skill.[13]

With hindsight, this programmatic statement is both ironic and informative. Ironic, because the failure to implement "the collegial bond" is one of the most frequent criticisms of John Paul's pontificate. Informative, because the collaboration to which the pope refers specifies only those roles that the bishops fulfill within the boundaries of their own dioceses—teaching, sanctification, and pastoral care. The plea for the assistance of shared governance that his predecessor had made is not present.

---

12. See http://www.vatican.va/holy_father/john_paul_i/messages/documents/hf_jp-i_mes_urbi-et-orbi_27081978_sp.html (my translation from the Spanish text).

13. Unfortunately, the Vatican web site offers this message only in Italian or Portuguese. The English text is available at http://www.catholicculture.org/library/view.cfm?recnum=1139.

Throughout his lengthy pontificate, John Paul II returned frequently to the topic of collegiality. Nowhere was this more illuminating than in his Holy Thursday 1979 letter to the bishops, so early in his pontificate, where he makes a distinction that will come to mark his thinking on the topic:

> We must express the wish, today especially, that everything that the Second Vatican Council so wonderfully renewed in our awareness should take on an ever more mature character of collegiality, both as the principle of our collaboration [*collegialitas effectiva*] and as the character of a cordial fraternal bond [*collegialitas affectiva*], in order to build up the Mystical Body of Christ and to deepen the unity of the whole People of God.[14]

Effective collegiality refers to the principle in virtue of which the bishops can speak collectively in council or with the pope, sharing indeed in a certain infallibility. They always act with Peter and under Peter. And "Peter" could always do alone, it would seem, what they in fact are doing together. (So is there a difference, is there some addendum or improvement provided by the act of episcopal solidarity? Is the statement somehow more effective or more acceptable than it would be as the word of the pope alone? If not, what does collegial action add, and what in addition does it mean to the bishop's sense of his role in the universal church?) But *affective* collegiality is the bond of solidarity within the episcopal college. Much later, toward the end of his pontificate, John Paul attempted to clarify the meaning of affective collegiality, referring to it as "the spirit of collegiality . . . which is the basis of the Bishops' concern for the other particular Churches and for the universal Church." "Consequently," he continued, "if we must say that a Bishop is never alone, inasmuch as he is always united to the Father through the Son in the Holy Spirit, we must also add that he is also never alone because he is always and continuously united with his brothers in the episcopate and with the one whom the Lord has chosen as the successor of Peter."[15]

While the distinction between affective and effective collegiality has become common currency in Vatican documents and in the writings of

14. http://www.ewtn.com/library/papaldoc/jp2bps79.htm.
15. *Pastores Gregis* 8.

John Paul II in particular, its origins and, indeed, its precise meaning, are somewhat mysterious. It seems that it first emerged in the course of the 1969 extraordinary Rome synod, though it does not appear in any documentation from that time. It derives, in all probability, from efforts to clarify the distinction we referred to above between the full exercise of collegiality in formal united pronouncements of the bishops together with the pope and all other "lesser" exercises of collegiality in mutual support, episcopal conferences, and so on. "The spirit of collegiality, or affective collegiality," writes the pope in *Pastores Gregis*, "is always present among the Bishops as *communio episcoporum*, but only in certain acts does it find expression as effective collegiality." He continues, "The various ways in which affective collegiality comes to be realized in effective collegiality belong to the human order, but in varying degrees they concretize the divine requirement that the episcopate should express itself in a collegial manner."[16]

There is, of course, a value beyond the sheer affectivity of affective collegiality, in that solidarity can be helpful in times of confusion. This is what, in his 1979 encyclical *Redemptor Hominis* (RH), John Paul seemed to be saying when he commented that affective collegiality "showed itself particularly relevant in the difficult postconciliar period, when the shared unanimous position of the College of the Bishops—which displayed, chiefly through the synod, its union with Peter's successor—helped to dissipate doubts and at the same time indicated the correct ways for renewing the Church in her universal dimension" (RH 5).[17] At this point in the letter John Paul makes supportive references to national episcopal conferences, councils of priests, and diocesan, provincial, and national synods, writing approvingly of lay involvement in synods and pastoral councils. He is clearly placing all such participatory structures in the context of the solidarity and unanimity that should mark the exercise of affective collegiality, an association that should be suggestive about the dearth of effective roles. For if the role of all these groups is in their different ways an exercise of coresponsibility on the part of the whole church, where is the place for the creative contributions that some

16. Ibid.

17. Available at http://www.vatican.va/holy_father/john_paul_ii/encyclicals/documents/hf_jp-ii_enc_04031979_redemptor-hominis_en.html.

might think would emerge from different experiences, different roles, the different genders, and different geographical locations? It would seem that difference of opinion and honest debate or disagreement with papal directives could never be classified as an act of effective collegiality. But might it not be that just such a to and fro of public debate is one important way in which affective collegiality could and should be exercised? The bond of unity among the bishops in their concern for the universal church should surely be expected to show itself at times in healthy disagreement about its future direction. Furthermore and, logically speaking, if effective collegiality is only fully exercised in speaking with one voice under the leadership of the pope, it is quite difficult to see what is so "effective" about it.

John Paul II's consistent reliance on the distinction and relationship between affective and effective collegiality is all of a piece with his concern to reassert the importance of centralized ecclesiastical authority. In *Pastores Gregis*, for example, the pope seeks to clarify the meaning of collegiality by drawing an ecclesiological analogy. "A parallelism can thus be established," he writes, "between the Church as one and universal, and therefore indivisible, and the episcopacy as one and indivisible, and therefore universal." The true nature of the parallelism, in John Paul's mind, is that "the principle and foundation" of the unity of the church or of the body of bishops "is the Roman Pontiff." The universal church "is not the sum of the particular churches or a federation of the latter," but "precedes creation itself." Just so, the college of bishops "is a reality which precedes the office of being the head of a particular church."[18] Hence, "just as the universal Church is one and indivisible, so too the College of Bishops is one 'indivisible theological subject,' and hence the supreme, full and universal power possessed by the College, and by the Roman Pontiff personally, is one and indivisible."[19]

The practical significance of this abstruse set of arguments is worth thinking about. In the first instance, it reintroduces the pattern of deductive and ahistorical thinking in and about the church which the council fathers seem to have wanted to eliminate. A putative theological truth (the preexistence of the church, presumably from all eternity) rec-

18. *Pastores Gregis* 8, quoting himself in *Apostolos Suos* 12.
19. Ibid.

ognized only much later in history is given hermeneutical privilege over the actual events of history. A more inductive and historically sensitive approach would recognize that the early church stumbled its way into a pattern of ecclesiastical arrangements over many centuries. While it is perfectly legitimate to reflect theologically on the value of these historical developments, the effort to canonize them by locating them in the mind of Christ flies in the face of sound historical scholarship.

It can also lead to some conclusions that are conveniently supportive of the ecclesial outlook bent on "restoring" what, it is sometimes claimed, was lost at Vatican II. For example, John Paul immediately draws the conclusion from his words quoted above that there are many ways to be bishop, and the connection to a geographical area as leader of a local church is only one of them. There are auxiliary bishops and there are others who act as representatives "of the Roman Pontiff in the offices of the Holy See or in Papal Legations." It would seem that we have come a long way from the ancient church's belief that a bishop was married to his diocese, and while this might well be a legitimate historical development, to justify that development on the grounds that it follows directly from the preexistent church evident in Jesus' establishment of the apostolic college is deeply misleading.

In recognizing the relationship between collegiality and ecclesiology, we may be at the heart of John Paul II's seizing upon the obscurity of the affective/effective distinction.[20] That we may also be at the end of the line for any resolution of the argument is one clear lesson of the famed "Ratzinger/Kasper" debate over the priority of the universal or the local church.[21] This began when Cardinal Walter Kasper, then bishop

20. At the end of Joseph Komonchak's extraordinarily careful analysis of the distinction (see note 11, above), he concludes that "the distinction between affective and effective collegiality should be abandoned." Of course it is important to note that Komonchak drew his conclusions from an examination of the *instrumentum laboris* or preparatory working text that provided the basis for the papal *Apostolos Suos*, and he might conceivably have found the pope's own version of the distinction more persuasive.

21. Kasper takes on the CDF initially in a book chapter, "*Zur theologie und Praxis des bischöflichen Amtes*," in *Auf neue Art Kirche Sein: Wirklichkeiten—Herausforderungen—Wandlungen* (Munich: Bernward bei Don Bosco, 1999), pp. 32–48. Ratzinger responded in an article in the *Frankfurter Allgemeine Zeitung* for December 22, 2000, 46. Kasper argued further in "On the Church: A Friendly Response to Cardinal Ratzinger," *America* 184 (April 21–30, 2001), and was answered yet again by Cardinal Ratzinger in *America* 185 (November 19, 2001). The easiest approach to this complicated set of exchanges is provided by an excellent overview

of Rottenburg, took exception to the statement in a 1992 document from the Congregation for the Doctrine of the Faith (CDF) that the universal church "is not the result of the communion of the churches, but in its essential mystery it is a reality ontologically and temporally prior to every individual particular church."[22] While the argument is a complex one, especially as it is further developed in the public exchange between Kasper and then Cardinal Joseph Ratzinger, Kasper's principal point is that Vatican II had expressed the relationship between the local and universal church in a way that saw the local church as an expression of the universal church, indeed the only concrete expression of the universal church, while the language of "ontological priority" employed by the CDF made the universal church an abstraction and failed to recognize that it is only real in and through the local churches out of which it was first formed.[23] The core of Ratzinger's response is that the preexistence of the church is attested to by early church fathers (Clement of Rome and the Shepherd of Hermas), and that the preexistent church, like the preexistent Israel of Jewish teaching, is all that preserves ecclesiology from simply seeing the church as a human organization. Kasper finds the same problem in *Apostolos Suos*, and also links it to collegiality, believing that the relationship between the college of bishops together with the pope, and the pope alone, is inadequately expressed. The result is that the authority of the college of bishops may in practice be little more than a "naked fiction," in Cardinal Kasper's words, since the pope can always act without formally involving the college.

The larger problem with John Paul's understanding of episcopal collegiality is that it does not seem to be faithful to the conciliar intent. The council clearly wished to stress the joint responsibility of all the bishops for the governance of the universal church, and used the term collegiality to emphasize the collective authority of the world's bishops, together with the pope as the symbol of their unity and the unity of the church. Collegiality was expressed as a Spirit-filled joint responsibility

---

from Kilian McDonnell, "The Ratzinger/Kasper Debate: The Universal Church and Local Churches," *Theological Studies* 63 (2002): 227–50.

22. John Paul II, "Letter to the Bishops of the Catholic Church on the Church Understood as Communion," *Origins* 22 (June 25, 1992): 108–12. The quotation is from par. 9.

23. This point had been made earlier by Joseph A. Komonchak, "On the Authority of Bishops' Conferences," *America* (September 12, 1998): 7–10.

for the good of the universal church. The only "effective" role the bishops assigned themselves was in the solemn arena of an ecumenical council. Beyond that, they were content to leave in a healthily fuzzy condition the juridical dimensions of collegiality. However, the curial mentality that was always at war with the pastoral intentions of the council could not be happy with such ambiguity, and thus was born the contorted relationship between affective and effective collegiality. John Paul's restorationism seized on the distinction and assured the triumph of that stratagem.

One of the most thoughtful discussions of the meaning of collegiality was provided by John R. Quinn, retired archbishop of San Francisco, responding to John Paul II's encyclical letter on Commitment to Ecumenism, *Ut Unum Sint*.[24] John Paul famously raised the question of how the papacy might be reformed to become more clearly "a service of love recognized by all concerned" (UUS 95), and Quinn's book-length answer includes a substantial chapter on collegiality and the papacy. Quinn writes that the central issue is to "enshrine the convergence of primacy and collegiality affirmed in balanced tension."[25] Interestingly enough he finds the source for this in the support Pius IX gave to the German bishops when they insisted against Bismarck that Vatican I had not made the pope an absolute sovereign. They were clear that they could "decisively refute the statement that the bishops have become by reason of the Vatican decrees mere papal functionaries with no personal responsibility."[26] In contrast to this healthy understanding of their reciprocal relations, an understanding with which Vatican II is fully consistent, Quinn is distressed by the poor practice of collegiality since the council, specifically in the attacks mounted by Ratzinger and Jerome Hamer on the status of episcopal conferences, and on the synods of bishops, which he considers to have been "a great disappointment."[27]

The establishment of the Rome synod of bishops by Paul VI during the final sessions of the council was understood at the time to be a prime instrument of episcopal collegiality. Paul spoke of it that way. However,

---

24. John R. Quinn, *The Reform of the Papacy: The Costly Call to Christian Unity* (New York: Crossroad, 1999).

25. Ibid., 83.

26. Quoted in Quinn, *The Reform of the Papacy*, 79.

27. Ibid., 110.

even during Paul VI's reign it became clear that it would be no such thing. John Paul II continued in the fiction that real collegiality was enacted there, though the synod is called by the pope, the topic of discussion is determined by the pope, items that may not be discussed are indicated by the pope, and the conversations and deliberations of the bishops are not made public, at least in theory, but rather handed over to the pope for his personal use as he prepares a document on the synod's theme. The post-synodal document is published in the pope's name, ostensibly owing much to the bishops' work, but it is impossible to tell how much this is true, since their final "propositions" are never made public. Archbishop Quinn adds three further problems with the synods: they include members of the Roman Curia, they all take place in Rome, and the form of the meetings means that for the first two weeks bishops make formal presentations without the opportunity of responding to one another after the manner of a healthy debate.

The Rome synod of bishops under the papacy of John Paul II was, as an exhibition of collegiality, pretty much a sham. It was neither effective collegiality, since the bishops simply advised in private, nor was it a particularly good example of affective collegiality, since its structure belies the trust that is supposed to reside in the affective bond. Collegiality in this way becomes an instrument of centralization, just as it is profoundly alienating to the bishops' sense of themselves as a college, engaged collectively in responsible leadership of the universal church. Collegiality becomes hegemonic, and a bishop exercising his collegial responsibilities at the Rome synod is trapped in that classic hegemonic snare of embracing his own oppression. Sometimes bishops say they are powerless, and our response might be to smile. But in many ways they are, and not a little of this is attributable to the way that the conciliar understanding of collegiality has been converted to the service of curial centralization. In this denial of the meaning of Vatican II, enwrapped as it is in theological abstractions about the preexistence of the universal church, John Paul II is not innocent. Much of the theoretical justification for this particular reading of collegiality may have been the work of Cardinal Ratzinger as prefect of the CDF. But most of it happened on John Paul's watch, and much of it is published in documents that bear his signature. Given the evidence, it is, moreover, exactly what one could expect of a man of John Paul's temperament, impatient with the democratic process and strongly convinced of being personally guided by the Spirit and protected by the Virgin. One might ask what possible need he could have had for shared governance?

In the end, perhaps, John Paul II's version of collegiality is guided by and explicable partially in terms of his personality, partially through his personal history. Even those least impressed by his teaching are in no doubt that he was a profoundly charismatic leader. Why else would young people completely uninterested in his conservative ethical and doctrinal positions travel halfway across the world to glory in his presence? In his prime as pope, John Paul was obviously warm and welcoming, seemingly sometimes verging on the sentimental, always ready with the expressive smile and the warm hug. He genuinely seemed to love the crowds, the people of God—especially those who were "poor or afflicted in any way"—and his brother bishops. But it must be stated that he never gave an inch on any of the profoundly centralizing governance style nor in the traditional cast of his theological opinions. His vision of the church was of a deeply *affective* community under strong, centralized *effective* leadership. This leadership was strengthened, he seemed to say, through the affective bond of unity of the bishops, teaching and believing in solidarity with the Bishop of Rome. And here is where the personal history combines with the personality to render him inflexible. The role of the papacy in John Paul's understanding is deeply influenced by the role of the Polish church under communism. Strong centralized leadership was essential in protecting the church in Poland, which was pretty much identical to saying protecting the people. Open exchanges and difference of opinion would have been interpreted as weakness, and would have weakened the church. Sadly, John Paul II had absolutely no personal experience of life in a democratic political environment where frank and open public exchange of views is reasonably accounted a sign of the health of the community. Had he been the product of a different world, he might have found more of a place for truly effective collegiality.

12

John Paul II
and the Consecrated Life

Gemma Simmonds, CJ

Approximately one million people live under religious vows in the Catholic Church, numbering 0.12 percent of its membership. Of these, 72.5 percent are women and 27.5 percent men, over 80 percent being lay religious, brothers, and sisters. Some belong to historic orders while others belong to the new orders that have emerged since Vatican II, including some deriving from the "new movements" for the laity, such as Focolare.[1] In October 1994 a synod of bishops met to discuss the consecrated life, and in March 1996 John Paul II issued *Vita Consecrata* (VC), the final of his post-synodal exhortations on the three "states of life" in the church.[2] Like *Christifideles Laici*, on the mission of the laity in the world, and *Pastores Dabo Vobis*, on the priesthood and priestly formation, this exhortation was written with the aim of interpreting Vatican II and implementing its documents "authentically."[3]

The *Lineamenta*, published in preparation for the discussions, were described by one female general superior as prosaic at best and patronizing at worst. Male superiors general were elected members, but no provision was made for the participation of laity or of women religious. Hope was restored when in May 1993 John Paul announced that twenty

---

1. James Sweeney, "Prophets and Parables: a Future for Religious Orders" in *Informationes Theologiae Europae* (Frankfurt: Peter Lang, 2001), 273–292, 274.

2. See http://www.vatican.va/holy_father/john_paul_ii/apost_exhortations/documents/hf_jp-ii_exh_25031996_vita-consecrata_en.html.

3. In the sense that *authenticum*, when applied to magisterium, means "authoritative."

representatives could be elected from among the sisters of the world-wide Union of International Superiors General and another twenty female and ten male religious nominated as nonvoting auditors.

The *Instrumentum Laboris*, published in June 1994, was a considerable improvement, based more on the responses and experience of religious themselves than on a picture of their reality and aspirations built up in Rome. The synod was more problematical, as some bishops made clear their hostility to the reforms religious had undertaken since Vatican II.[4] To the surprise and dismay of many religious, the English translation of *Vita Consecrata* refers to the consecrated life as having an "objective superiority" over other forms of Christian life (VC 32). This notion is at variance with Vatican II's dogmatic constitution on the church, *Lumen Gentium*, and was the basis of the main controversy that arose within the synod around the precise role of consecrated life within the church. While *Lumen Gentium* states that it is a charismatic gift of the Spirit, and belongs to the life and holiness of the church, not its hierarchical structure, it nevertheless also makes clear that the call to holiness is universal.[5] What emerged in debates were two different paradigms, a consecration paradigm, reflecting the concern of the magisterium to define consecrated life within the structure of the church, and the charism paradigm, reflecting the lived experience of religious and their interpretation of their place in the church. While not mutually exclusive, these paradigms pointed to tensions and sensitivities between charism and hierarchy.[6]

Overall, however, the synod was judged a success, the pope attributing this to the contribution of religious themselves, and confirming that women would participate in the drafting of the post-synodal exhortation. The final version pledges to open up spaces for women to participate more fully in the decision making processes of the church. Thirteen years after the synod the dream remains unrealized. One female general

4. *Vita Consecrata* and subsequent texts would prove more positive and supportive, see James Sweeney, "Religious Life after Vatican II," in *Catholics in England 1950–2000: Historical and Sociological Perspectives*, ed. Michael P. Hornsby-Smith (London: Cassell, 1999), 283.

5. George Weigel, *Witness to Hope: The Biography of Pope John Paul II* (New York: HarperCollins, 1999), 783–84; Sweeney, "Prophets and Parables," 281–82. There is some inconsistency in *Lumen Gentium* 31, 40–44 on this matter.

6. The theological questions and distinctions are summed up with masterly clarity by James Sweeney in "The Synod and Theology," *Religious Life Review* 34 (1995): 75–85.

superior points to the unreconstructed starting point of its suggestion that women's new self-awareness will help "men to reconsider the way they organize social, political, economic, religious and ecclesial life," as if the organization of these aspects of life were the prerogative of the male sex in the first place.[7]

Vita Consecrata emphasizes "ordered ecclesial communion" between religious and bishops in which religious offer allegiance of mind and heart to the magisterium of the bishops and bind themselves to the pope in his ministry of unity and missionary universality (VC 46–49). John Paul's exhortation uses rich and beautiful biblical imagery to describe a way of life he considers to be "at the very heart of the church." Nevertheless, anecdotal evidence among many religious suggests that he had little sympathy for or understanding of the particularity of consecrated life.

As Karol Wojtyla, he is said to have been one of the council fathers who most strenuously objected to the canonical exemptions enjoyed by religious orders and who, then and later, urged for them to be brought more closely under diocesan jurisdiction.[8] His direct interventions as pope in the internal affairs and governance of the Jesuits, Carmelites, and Franciscans appear to confirm this stance. His attitude toward women religious spoke of an understanding of their role at odds with that of many sisters themselves. Whereas throughout his pontificate he made clear his admiration for Mother Teresa of Calcutta, as well as for her style of consecrated life and her governance of it, a number of female religious in another style found themselves the focus of critical attention. The liberation social movement within Catholicism, whether encompassing racial or feminist liberation or the "option for the poor" on different continents, was enthusiastically espoused and often spearheaded by members of religious orders. The sustained resistance to these move-

---

7. *Vita Consecrata* 57–58 and Doris Gottmoeller, "*Vita Consecrata*: the Exhortation on Consecrated Life" in *Religious Life Review* 36 (1997): 214–26, at 214–15. Elizabeth Starken, another *auditrice*, speaks of John Paul's particular appreciation of the female presence at the synod in "Reflections on the Synod, 1," in *Religious Life Review* 34 (1995): 86–89. Cf. also, chapter 4 of the present volume on the teaching office of the church.

8. Michael Walsh, *John Paul II: a Biography* (London: Harper Collins, 1994), 98 and Avery Dulles, *The Splendor of Faith: the Theological Vision of Pope John Paul II* (New York: Crossroad, 1999), 5.

ments of John Paul II's pontificate coincided with an enthusiastic support for restorationist versions of consecrated life and new ecclesial movements, such as Opus Dei, Communione e Liberazione, or the Neo-Catechumenate, which tended to favor a more conservative ecclesiology and interpretation of conciliar reforms.[9] To understand these events we must explore his attitude toward consecrated life in the light both of ecclesiological developments emanating from Vatican II and of specific crises that arose within the church in which religious took a prominent part.

Charism and Authority: The Context

Whereas priesthood and marriage are sacraments of the church, consecration to the religious life is not. Religious orders derive from specific needs or spiritual movements within the history of the church to which charismatic individuals or groups responded, believing themselves called to minister in distinctive ways. The delicate and often difficult genesis of given orders frequently involved tension with established structures of ecclesial authority, alongside which they have grown as parallel, inter-related traditions.[10]

The ecclesiology of Vatican II, with its stress on church as *communio* and the holiness of the lay state, favored the diocese and the parish as the *locus* of the life of the church and strengthened the authority of the bishop. Religious orders, many of which are traditionally exempt from episcopal control, were urged to reform by a return to the original charism or inspiration of their founder and an adaptation of this charism to contemporary conditions in the world.[11] Through this return *ad fontes*, many found that they had strayed from their founding vision in response to the institutional needs of the church and society. Social and economic changes also meant that, in many countries, it was no longer felt necessary for religious orders

9. Sweeney, "Prophets and Parables," 288–90.

10. Where the apostolic exhortation *Redemptionis Donum* of 1984 speaks of the consecrated life as being a "fuller expression" of baptism (7), *Vita Consecrata*, written ten years later, would refer to it as an "essential and characteristic" element of baptism, expressing the church's very nature (29).

11. Walter M. Abbott, ed., "Decree on the Appropriate Renewal of the Religious Life" (*Perfectae Caritatis*) in *The Documents of Vatican II* (London: Chapman, 1967). See also, *Vita Consecrata* 36–37.

to provide the educational and welfare services which were increasingly run by the state. Vocations to such orders fell as rising numbers of professionally trained young Catholics committed themselves to pastoral ministries without feeling the need to do so under religious vows.

The drive to institutionalization in the nineteenth century and the imposition of uniform models under the 1917 Code of Canon Law had ironed out many of the individual charismatic features of religious life.[12] The impact of their rediscovery in the developed world (and, increasingly, in Asia and Latin America), cannot be underestimated. Few constituencies within the Catholic Church responded to Vatican II's call for reform as radically as the religious orders. In particular many embraced with enthusiasm the invitation in the Pastoral Constitution on the Church in the Modern World, *Gaudium et Spes*, to participate in full solidarity with the joys and hopes, griefs and anxieties of the world (GS 1). The seeds of reform of religious life were sown some years before the council, but few could have predicted the fruits that would emerge.[13] The results of post-conciliar reform in religious life were neither peaceful nor always successful, causing pain and alarm both outside and within orders, as challenges to structures of ecclesial and secular power emerged from them.

In some instances, restorationist countermovements to these reforms had already begun by the time John Paul II became pope. They would find support and sympathy in many of his pronouncements. In the 1984 exhortation to religious, *Redemptionis Donum* (RD), which marked the Jubilee year, John Paul described the recently revised Code of Canon Law as the "final conciliar document," which would be "a valuable aid and a sure guide in concretely stating the means for faithfully and generously living your magnificent vocation in the Church" (RD 2, 14). Not many religious drew inspiration from Canon Law in the same way that they did from the great dogmatic constitutions, and the word "faithfully" there seems to hint at some unease on the pope's part at interpretations of the council that were less than legitimate. The exhortation contains a beautiful and appreciative meditation on the "treasure" of consecrated life within the church, but there is an undertone of admonition.

---

12. Sweeney, "Prophets and Parables," 276–77.
13. Sweeney, "Religious Life," 267–72. See also, Amy Koehlinger, *The New Nuns: Racial Justice and Religious Reform in the 1960s* (Cambridge MA: Harvard University Press, 2007).

The emphasis in the exhortation on what John Paul calls "submission-obedience" refers both to Christ's obedience unto death and to that "which in a spirit of faith consecrated persons show to their legitimate superiors, who hold the place of God." This same submission is, however, viewed as "a particular expression of interior freedom" (RD 13). Religious are urged to "'think with the Church' and always act in union with her, in conformity with the teachings and directives of the Magisterium of Peter and of the pastors in communion with him, fostering, at the personal and community level, a renewed ecclesial awareness" (RD 14). Obedience is once again stressed, this time to the renewed constitutions that emerged after the special period of experimentation and renewal, "may this gift of the Church encourage you to . . . live them in generosity and fidelity, remembering that obedience is an unambiguous manifestation of love" (RD 14). These words would come to sound questionable to Discalced Carmelite ears when their renewed constitutions were rejected by the author himself.

In the aftermath of the council, many of the more outlandish external manifestations of the otherness of religious disappeared, along with cloistered lifestyles imposed inappropriately by Canon Law on a number of congregations in defiance of their original charism. In other cases the insertion of religious into extreme situations of socioeconomic poverty also led to their abandoning signs of separateness or difference. For the significant number of religious who lived and sometimes died as martyrs for justice during John Paul's pontificate, this radical option for the poor was a more genuine form of asceticism than the manufactured rigors of institutional religious life. He and many others felt, however, that these were negative moves, leading to a high degree of assimilation into mainstream secular culture and the "disappearance" of consecrated life from society.

His strong appreciation of the effect and value of religious symbols lies behind his repeated calls for religious to wear distinctive dress, to "faithful observance of the Church's norms regarding also the outward manifestation of your consecration and of your commitment to poverty." He saw this not as a matter of discipline but of mission: "Your mission must be seen! Deep, very deep must be the bond which links it to the Church!" (RD 14–15; VC 25, 38). When visiting the United States in 1979, he had reacted with apparent displeasure when Sister Theresa Kane, president of the Leadership Conference of Women Religious, spoke of the need to open all ministries of the church to women. Seeing many religious gathered who were wearing secular dress, he directed them to return to wearing a "permanent, exterior sign" of their consecration in response not only to his personal conviction but to the desire of the church expressed by the faithful.[14] A commission of inquiry into female religious life in the United States was appointed in 1983 under Archbishop Quinn of San Francisco. In 1991 John Paul challenged the Conference of Latin American Religious (CLAR), placing Vatican appointees above duly elected officials. Both instances clearly signified a disquiet at some of their choices and policies that became explicit in *Vita Consecrata*.

This would not be the last time John Paul II came into conflict with religious in the United States. Individual religious such as Sister Jeanine Gramick and Father Robert Nugent, whose national reconciliation ministry for the church and lesbian and gay people would be prohibited, or Mother Angelica, founder of the Eternal Word Television Network, came to represent and symbolize conflicting liberal and conservative camps within American Catholicism. The condemnation of Gramick and Nugent's published work reflects how many of the controversies concerning religious during John Paul II's pontificate were symbolic or representative of wider ideological or moral issues within the church, and the pope's anxiety to rein in those who were spearheading "disordered" responses to them.[15]

White Pope and Black

Accounts of the dramatic conflict between John Paul II and the Jesuits differ according to sympathy with both parties and the interpretation of what lay behind it. Pedro Arrupe, one of the most remarkable and charismatic Jesuit general superiors since Ignatius himself, had witnessed the

14. Walsh, *John Paul II*, 66, 73, n. 26. The leadership conference of women religious in the United States would split into two different bodies over such issues, one seeing itself as supporting papal and traditional teaching and values, the other representing a more reformist stance. See Weigel, *Witness to Hope*, 352–53 and Sweeney, "Religious Life," 279.

15. "Erroneous and Dangerous Propositions in the Publications *Building Bridges* and *Voices of Hope* by Sister Jeannine Gramick, SSND, and Father Robert Nugent, SDS," *National Catholic Reporter Online* (October 24, 1997). See http://ncronline.org/NCR_Online/documents/gn06.htm.

horrors of Hiroshima as a young priest.[16] Elected general in 1965, he spearheaded the Jesuit response to the Second Vatican Council and to a rapidly changing global situation. The decrees of the order's thirty-second General Congregation (December 1974–March 1975) define as the fundamental priorities for Jesuit action "the service of faith and the promotion of justice" through the option for the poor and resistance to all forms of structural oppression. Jesuit missionaries were to be sensitive to the need for inculturation, breaking with the European cultural imperialism that had characterized the church's missionary endeavor for so long, resulting in a presentation of the Catholic faith that Arrupe described as "over-Westernized, paternalistic and complacent."[17]

Both outside and within the Society, responses were not neutral. Some leaped to the challenge, while others feared that Arrupe and his assistants were leading the Jesuits in a Gadarene rush over a cliff, abandoning the Society's true ecclesial and theological mission in favor of ill-advised political engagement.[18] John Paul II was not the first postconciliar pope to have expressed disquiet at Jesuit reforms. In 1974 Paul VI had notified the Jesuits of his uneasiness at their proposal to abolish historical distinctions within their membership, and refused to accept their subsequent vote to that effect.[19] Following his death, an address by John Paul I intended for the Jesuits was released with John Paul II's agreement. Fuelled by negative reports from disaffected Jesuits, bishops, and apostolic nuncios around the world, it reproached the Society for turning its publications and its teaching into a "source of confusion and disorientation." John Paul II's opinion was even more robust and spoke of "deplorable deficiencies" in Jesuit government. Arrupe decided to resign as general superior and convene a new General Congregation to elect his successor. He was felled by a paralyzing stroke in August 1981. Two months later the pope overrode the Constitutions of the Society by ordering a delay in proceedings and appointing Father Paolo Dezza, an eighty-year-old conservative in his confidence, as his personal delegate, with Giuseppe Pittau as his assistant. It

---

16. Alain Woodrow, *The Jesuits: A Story of Power* (London: Chapman, 1995), 214–18.

17. Ibid., 222–26.

18. Jesuit anecdote attributes this most strongly to conservative forces within the Spanish province, who went as far as wishing to secede from the rest of the Society.

19. See *Documents of the 31st and 32nd General Congregations of the Society of Jesus* (St. Louis, MO: Institute of Jesuit Sources, 1977), 519–36.

was a decision widely interpreted as a repudiation of Arrupe's policies and of the thirty-second General Congregation.[20]

Weigel describes this intervention as "shock therapy . . . creating conditions for a new relationship of greater trust."[21] This is not how most Jesuits saw it, but whatever their private feelings, they responded to this humiliating reproof with impressive obedience. At a gathering of all the Jesuit provincial superiors, the pope was able to commend their acqui-escence while making clear that in future he expected closer collabora-tion with all the church's hierarchical and institutional authorities and a return to traditional apostolates and "sound, pure doctrine."[22] In a letter sent out by Father Dezza to the whole Society in 1982, obedience to authority and the renunciation of "individualism" were once again em-phasized: "The Supreme Pontiff and the bishops are the visible signs of the love and presence of Christ among his people . . . The Ignatian charism incites us to show them total loyalty . . . It is certainly not in keeping with the Society's spirit to oppose the church's authority as though we were placed above it."[23]

The famous Jesuit "fourth vow" is often interpreted by those outside the Society as one of blind obedience to the pontiff. It is, in fact, a vow whose object is universal mission, binding those who take it to the service of the church, under the pope, in a way that is not restricted to the more local concerns of individual dioceses. The drama of John Paul II's inter-vention would indicate a difference in interpretation and understanding of what "universal mission" and the obedience it entails might mean.[24]

Opus Dei and Other Movements

If John Paul's tense relations with the Jesuits and his intervention in their governance had at its root his wish to bring them under the greater control of diocesan bishops, this is contrasted by his warmth toward Opus Dei, culminating in the establishment of a "personal prelature."

20. Woodrow, *The Jesuits*, 230.
21. Weigel, *Witness to Hope*, 430.
22. Woodrow, *The Jesuits*, 234–42.
23. Ibid., 244.
24. Ibid., 230–31, 250–52. By 1990 a reconciliation had been sufficiently established for a friendly and positive letter to arrive from the pope in celebration of the Society's 450th an-niversary, see Walsh, *John Paul II*, 228–29.

This effectively recognized it as a diocese without geographical borders, enabling the deployment of its priests across national and diocesan boundaries. Ironically, this bears a strong similarity to the desire for apostolic autonomy and mobility inherent in the Jesuit fourth vow. Opus Dei is no religious order, however, but a movement which radically interprets Vatican II's emphasis on the lay vocation in the world. Perhaps this lay behind John Paul's sympathy for a movement that so closely echoed his own understanding of *Gaudium et Spes.* It is notable, nevertheless, that if he wished religious orders to come under closer diocesan control, he had no scruples about releasing Opus Dei from that same control, to the consternation of bishops and Roman Curia alike.[25]

Weigel draws another contrast between John Paul's treatment of the Jesuits and of the Legionaries of Christ, a conservative priestly renewal movement, described as "self-consciously orthodox and loyal to the church's teaching." He deplores "Jesuit involvement in partisan political activity in various Latin American venues," while keeping notably silent on similar partisan stances (at the opposite end of the political spectrum) on the part of the Legionaries and various other new ecclesial movements around the world. Weigel sees the Jesuit controversy and its contrast with the support of new ecclesial movements as a conflict between authentic and false interpretations of Vatican II. He understands it as an expression both of John Paul's "respect for the freedom of others" and his desire to nurture and encourage what he saw as true expressions of the spirit of the council.[26]

Pope John Paul gave many signs of approval of the "new movements," including appointing a member of Opus Dei, Dr. Joaquín Navarro-Vals as the Vatican's press officer. As half a million representatives of the new ecclesial movements stood before him in St. Peter's Square and beyond in May 1998, John Paul affirmed the presence of the Holy Spirit among them and likened it to the spirit of Pentecost. He reassured them that the tensions experienced between the movements and the mainstream church within the past few decades were a normal part

---

25. See Weigel, *Witness to Hope*, 449–50 and Woodrow, *The Jesuits*, 248.

26. Weigel, *Witness to Hope*, 470. For another point of view, see Walsh, *John Paul II*, 170, 222. It would be left to John Paul's successor to take a more critical look at the Legionaries and their founder, Father Marcial Maciel. See Gerald Renner, "Scandal: The Story of Fr. Maciel," *The Tablet*, May 27, 2006.

of their growth and of the testing of spirits.[27] For many religious, the extended period of experimentation after Vatican II was part of the same tension.

Franciscans, Dominicans, Carmelites, and Questions of Authority

Conflict sometimes arose between John Paul and individual members of particular orders when they came to symbolize wider problems with the postconciliar reinterpretation of an order's charism. The appointment of the former secretary to the Congregation for the Doctrine of the Faith (CDF), Dominican Archbishop Jerome Hamer, as prefect for the Congregation for Religious and Secular Institutes in 1984 appeared, for some, to herald a new tightening of discipline when it came to dealing with religious orders and those of their members considered to be out of line.[28] This is illustrated most vividly in the case of Leonardo Boff and the Franciscans.

In 1984 Boff, a noted Brazilian exponent of liberation theology, was summoned to Rome for a meeting with his former doctoral supervisor, Cardinal Ratzinger. While John Paul defended the CDF's proceedings as rigorously respectful of the persons with whom it entered into contact, such summonses were not always experienced in this way by those who received them. Now prefect of the CDF, the future Pope Benedict XVI had expressed the view that liberation theology was "in the final analysis unacceptable."[29] Boff came as required, not only with the stated support of his order but accompanied by two Franciscan cardinals, Aloisio Lorscheider, president of the Brazilian bishops' theology commission and Evaristo Arns, Archbishop of São Paulo and champion of the poor. It was a show of brotherly solidarity in a style of theology and ministry not lost on the Vatican.[30]

---

27. Weigel, *Witness to Hope*, 838. The need to "test the spirits" is expressed again to new communities of consecrated life in *Vita Consecrata* 56, 62.

28. Walsh, *John Paul II*, 135, describes Hamer as an archconservative, in contrast to his Argentinian predecessor.

29. Ibid., 139–40, 144.

30. Similar solidarity was shown within the Order of Preachers when the master general accompanied the Flemish theologian Edward Schillebeeckx to an interview of the same kind. See Walsh, *John Paul II*, 156, n. 7.

In August of that same year the CDF had issued its Instruction on Certain Aspects of the "Theology of Liberation," in which it appeared to state that those using Marxist analysis to interpret society and the Christian tradition were effectively Marxist themselves, and that no application of Marxist thought could be accepted. While this document did not come under John Paul's own name, there is little doubt that it expressed both his anxiety at what was emerging from within the Latin American church and his repudiation of what he perceived to be communist ideology. In his response to the 1983 synod on penance and reconciliation, John Paul made clear that he rejected both the outmoded content and the non-Christian derivation of any notion of anonymous collectivity behind the term "social sin," so prevalent in liberation theology.[31] He nevertheless acknowledged that "private" sin affects human solidarity and is "social" insofar as it is an offense against other human beings or represents confrontation between groups, including class struggle.

Despite his undoubted sympathy for the struggle for social justice on behalf of the poor, his tour of South and Central America in January 1985 found John Paul attacking as illusory the placing of the Gospel at the service of politics and doctrines or ideologies "contrary to Catholic dogmas" and "of materialistic inspiration or dubious religious content." The inference was clear.[32] In May the CDF imposed a period of penitential silence on Boff, to which he responded with a denial that he was a Marxist and an affirmation of his faith as a Christian and a Franciscan. When the Franciscans began their general chapter in Assisi in the same month, they received a strongly worded letter from the pope in which he expressed fears of a "ruinous crisis of authority" within the order. His lack of faith in their ability to curb "theories and practices which have shown themselves to be an obstacle" to their primary evangelical witness was demonstrated by his imposition of the secretary of the Congregation for Religious as president over their chapter, contrary to their rule and custom. The Franciscans responded by electing their current minister general, implicitly criticized in these moves, to a further term of office.[33]

---

31. Gustavo Gutiérrez, *A Theology of Liberation: History, Politics and Salvation* (London: SCM, 1974), 102–3.

32. Ibid., 145.

33. Ibid., 148–49. On Boff and liberation theology in general, cf. chapter 9 of the present volume.

In April 1986 a more positive-sounding Instruction on Liberation Theology was published. While once again highlighting the dangers of Marxism and insisting that the church's essential mission was the liberation from sin and death that could only be achieved through individual conversion through faith in Christ, it acknowledged the sinfulness of some social and political structures and called for justice on behalf of the oppressed. Hailed by the pioneer of liberation theology, Peruvian Gustavo Gutiérrez, and the Brazilian bishops as a welcome end to painful tensions, the Instruction did not entirely convince Leonardo Boff. After a further period of penitential silence in 1990, Boff left the Franciscan order and the priesthood.[34] For many years a diocesan priest, Gutiérrez himself applied to join the Order of Preachers. The reasons he has given for this decision late in life are his admiration for Dominican commitment to preaching and theology and his devotion to the prophetic figure of Bartolomé de Las Casas. Among other religious it is widely assumed to have been a move aimed at operating theologically in the relatively greater freedom of a religious order than of a diocese.

The matter of the "proper" and "faithful" interpretation of Vatican II reared its head once more in the controversy between John Paul and cloistered members of the Discalced Carmelite order. Emerging from the reform of St. Teresa of Avila, their rule of 1581 underwent the same process of revision as other religious rules of life in the aftermath of the Second Vatican Council. The Carmelite spiritual tradition was particularly precious to the pope. Initiated as a young man into Carmelite mysticism by a spiritual mentor, the devout tailor Jan Tyranowski, Karol Wojtyla considered a Carmelite vocation and would later write a doctoral thesis on John of the Cross.[35] Although the revised Carmelite rule had been approved by Paul VI, a minority of mostly Spanish nuns held out against it in favor of the original rule. Instead of leaving it to the Carmelites themselves to sort out this conflict, John Paul intervened personally, instructing the Congregation of Religious and Secular Institutes to draw up a new constitution. His intervention was no minor matter. To religious not only the content of their rule but also the structures of governance laid down by their founding members and historically ap-

---

34. Cf. Weigel, *Witness to Hope*, 457–59, 496.
35. Ibid., 58–62 and Avery Dulles, *The Splendor of Faith*, 3.

proved by the church, touch into the very heart of their charism and identity. The general superior of the Carmelites received "with disgust" a letter from the Vatican Secretary of State which he described as hard and polemical in content.[36] Fences were later mended and the whole Carmelite family would rejoice when, in 1997, the pope named Carmelite saint Thérèse of Lisieux a Doctor of the Church.

In a short space it is not possible to do justice to the situation of religious all over the world at the end of John Paul's pontificate. The downfall of Soviet communism, in which he is widely regarded to have played so significant a role, opened up the persecuted churches of the former communist bloc to a new wave of religious vocations. Where there are significant numbers of younger religious in the world is now largely Eastern Europe, Africa, and Asia. Within the next ten to twenty years there will be a massive demographic shift among religious that will undoubtedly have an impact on styles of life and leadership. In churches where the ecclesiology has not been notably marked by postconciliar reforms, or where the role of women religious and lay brothers has not greatly evolved, the contrasts with the West are stark.

In 1992 David Nygren and Miriam Ukeritis, both religious and psychologists, published the results of their major Religious Life Futures Project surveying the opinions and experience of over ten thousand religious in the United States. A generally hopeful document, it illustrates the generosity and commitment of American religious, often in challenging circumstances. It makes clear, however, that "a significant percentage of religious no longer understand their role and function in the church," this being a greater problem for female than for male religious. "Vatican II substantially reinforced the role of laity in the church, but did not clarify for religious the unique contribution of their vocation."[37] John Paul II's vigorous attempts to provide this clarification were not always welcomed by religious themselves.

It is not necessarily the fault of religious that the socially transformative religious impulse to which so many of them committed themselves in the aftermath of Vatican II has faltered. Religion itself in the West is becoming

36. Walsh, *John Paul II*, 146–47.
37. David J. Nygren and Miriam D. Ukeritis, *The Future of Religious Orders in the United States: Transformation and Commitment* (Westport, CT: Praeger, 1993), 249.

on the one hand increasingly individualized and on the other relentlessly squeezed out of the current social order so that the critique it offers to society in the name of the Gospel goes largely unheeded. The apocalyptic and ultimately pessimistic "culture of death" against which John Paul II promoted "life issues" is not the viewpoint from which many religious, inspired by the optimism of *Gaudium et Spes*, see the world.[38] But nor can all that he said about religious life be put down solely to a restorationist project whose aim is to reassert the power of a dwindling institution.

Political, social, and ecological engagement cannot of themselves mediate the transformative grace of the incarnate Christ. John Paul was open to further changes in the historical forms of consecrated life, but insisted that it could only flourish in the "radical gift of self for love of the Lord Jesus and, in him, of every member of the human family" (VC 3). Whereas he advocated "creative fidelity" to original rules and charisms, opening up possibilities of new responses to changed world situations, he reacted negatively when this love was translated into challenging political or ecclesial structures (VC 36–38, 43, 82–85). There is honesty in *Vita Consecrata*'s acknowledgment that tensions over authority between religious orders and the hierarchical structure are nothing new. But the repeated calls to conformity with the church's structures of power and avoidance of the "strong centrifugal and disruptive forces at work today" do not give the impression of an instinctive understanding or appreciation of the prophetic role religious claim for themselves (VC 46–47).[39]

In 2004 the Union of International Superiors General organized a World Congress on the Consecrated Life in Rome, attended by 850 participants of whom over 300 were female general superiors. There was considerable disappointment when John Paul declined to attend, sending a message instead. Nevertheless his teaching strongly expresses his appreciation of the power of religious vows as a counterbalance to the idolatries of the modern world. In his tireless insistence on the beauty and holiness of the consecrated life, at least, John Paul's challenge to religious throughout his papacy paradoxically remains one of his strongest legacies.

---

38. Sweeney, "Religious Life," 280.

39. One has only to recall the struggles of Mary Ward, Mary McKillop, or Ignatius Loyola in their efforts to bring about something new in the church.

13

John Paul II and Ecumenism

Raymond G. Helmick, SJ

The ecumenical urge among Catholics had already struck upon a period of recession by the time Pope John Paul II was elected. It had constituted one of the major interests of the Second Vatican Council, but had since then been dampened by the atmosphere of anxiety that prevailed in the church and by a new sense of estrangement that had arisen as various Christian denominations moved in a different direction than Catholics on sociosexual questions. That many other churches were not with the Catholic Church on the important matter of abortion was particularly disappointing to those who had looked, at the time of the council, for growing consensus among Christians.

We might usefully look back at the ways the ecumenical imperative had taken root in Catholic consciousness as a means of discovering and fostering unity among Christians, in belated responsiveness to the prayer of Christ that all may be one.

As a Protestant and Orthodox interest, ecumenical concerns had standing from early in the twentieth century. For Protestants it was a gradual outgrowth of the great mission conference of 1910 in Edinburgh, though it took them some time to conclude that Catholics too belonged within the unity of Christians. Catholic hierarchy and popular sentiment resisted and rather resented it. Catholics and Protestants had spent more than four centuries denouncing one another and presupposing, from either side, that the other acted in bad faith. The standard Catholic formula for unity of Christians was the "Return," that all others—"heretics" and "schismatics"—should admit their errors and return to one fold.

In many ways for Roman Catholics, it was the Resistance during World War II that broke through these attitudes, and to this Karol Wojtyla would be especially sensitive. None of the churches had done well in the face of the Nazi onslaught, though the future pope was remarkably fortunate in the protection he had from his own Archbishop Adam Stefan Sapieha in Krakow. In most cases courageous individuals, often mavericks, joined their slender forces against the Nazis at grave risk to themselves. For lack of real support within their institutional structures, they had to look outward to find those they could trust. Their allies turned out to be Catholics and Protestants, atheists and agnostics, communists and others of such personal integrity that one could trust one's life with them. By war's end these individuals had amassed credit that no others had, and the mutual respect among them proved formative for the relation among churches in Europe. It took some fifteen years for their insights to cross the ocean in books to the Americas, but by Vatican II the Catholic Church was ready for the ecumenical advance we then witnessed.

Critical too was "the Boston heresy," the episode in which Jesuit Father Leonard Feeney, leading a phalanx of Catholic students at his St. Benedict Center near Harvard University, adopted an extreme view of the *Nulla salus extra ecclesiam* tradition, denying salvation to any outside the papal Catholic fold.[1] The necessary condemnation of that teaching in 1949, in a document meticulously edited by Pope Pius XII himself, opened the way to the ecumenical and interreligious breakthroughs of the council: *Lumen Gentium*, the Dogmatic Constitution on the Church; *Nostra Aetate*, the Declaration on the Relation of the Church to Non-Christian Religions; *Dignitatis Humanae*, recognizing the right to religious freedom; and the decree *Unitatis Redintegratio* on the ecumenical task of the church. As theologians went back to the great controversial questions of the sixteenth century, typically the impasse over justification, it became evident that these were not the problems of the twentieth century. The fine nuances had to be worked over carefully on these doctrinal matters, but the new discovery was that they could be resolved and agreement reached, at least among those who wanted to find it.

---

1. This critically important event in the experience of the Roman Catholic Church has received little serious study. I have been privileged to see the manuscript of a meticulously researched book by Reverend Richard Shmaruk of the Boston Archdiocese which, when published, will do much to fill this gap.

Yet the ecumenical fervor waned. New problem areas arose, generally not so much between the different Christian faith communities as within each of them. The sociosexual issues especially divided the churches: birth control, the place of women. These tended to take precedence over issues of war and peace, poverty or oppression. In the Catholic Church, they were taken off the table from Vatican II's deliberations and reserved to the Holy See and its curial offices, while in the Protestant churches they tended to fall subject to shifting popular opinion, to the scandal of Catholic and Orthodox leadership. The ecclesiological and sacramental questions were put to bilateral commissions, the Catholic members appointed by the Holy See, but when they came back with conclusions, agreed to whatever extent among the churches, they generally languished in the curial offices of the Vatican unconfirmed. On the great life issues, abortion and the end of life, the Catholic Church felt abandoned by many of its fellow Christians. And the general acceptance among Protestant churches of women ministers, especially when it was done within the Anglican Communion, to which the Catholic Church felt closest, became increasingly a wall between the churches.

The new pope's life experience in Poland had not so much equipped him to deal with Protestants as it had with Jews. But as the solid commitment of the Catholic Church to the ecumenical pursuit required his attention, he would take strong positions that often astounded those who were uneasy with the new direction. His restorationist bent toward a reassertion of central authority might have inclined him to empathize more with the Orthodox than with the more loosely governed churches of the Reformation, but his view was consistently of an underlying real unity of the church.

A first major ecumenical initiative came in 1979, when Pope John Paul visited the ecumenical patriarch of the Orthodox, Demetrios I, in Istanbul. It had become custom since Vatican II that the two sister churches, Rome and Constantinople, would send representatives to each other's major feasts, Peter and Paul on June 29th, Andrew on November 30th. The pope determined to make this visit himself on the first occasion he could. On the eve of the feast, in St. George's Cathedral in the Phanar, he referred to one of the great ambitions of his pontificate.

Despite all the great historical controversies, he told his listeners, "these two sister-Churches had maintained full communion in the first millennium of Christian history." They had "developed their great vital traditions" within the bond of unity. Now they were meeting in "this common apostolic faith . . . to walk toward this full unity which historical circumstances have wounded." The patriarch's response described their meeting as "intended for God's future—a future which will again see live unity, again common confession, again full communion in the divine Eucharist."[2]

In the liturgy of St. Andrew the following day, the pope exchanged the kiss of peace with Demetrios, joined him in giving the final blessing of the Mass, and asked if, at the end of the second millennium, "is it not time to hasten towards perfect brotherly reconciliation" for the sake of evangelization? This was thematic for John Paul's entire pontificate. The visit brought about the opening of a formal dialogue between the Roman Catholic Church and Orthodoxy at an international level.[3]

Churches of the Reformation

For 1983, the 1950th anniversary of the redeeming death of Jesus Christ, the pope declared a Holy Year, following the precedent set by Pope Pius XI for the 1900th anniversary in 1933. The year 1983 also marked the 500th anniversary of the birth of Martin Luther. On October 31st the pope addressed a letter to Cardinal Johannes Willebrands, president of the Secretariat for Promoting Christian Unity, praising the "deep religious feeling manifested by Luther," whom he described as "driven with burning passion by the question of eternal salvation." It was time, the pope wrote, to heal the Reformation breach, relying on continued historical scholarship "without preconceived ideas," in order to "arrive at a true image of the reformer, of the whole period of the Reformation, and of the persons involved in it. Fault, where it exists, must be recognized, wherever it may be."

This was a far cry from the familiar blaming of Protestants for abandoning the church, and the use of such terms as "the reformer" in a papal document about Luther had no precedent. Lutherans and Catholics, the letter continued, would have a "new point of departure" for

2. The whole event is described in a volume by John Paul II himself, *Turkey: Ecumenical Pilgrimage* (Boston: St. Paul Editions, 1980), at 27.

3. Ibid., 39–48.

theological dialogue, beginning with what they have in common: "in the Word of Scripture, in the Confessions of Faith, and in the Councils of the ancient Church." This dialogue should proceed in a spirit of "penitence and readiness to learn from listening."[4]

On the Third Sunday of Advent, following up on this letter about Luther, the pope visited the Lutheran Christuskirche in Rome, participated in an Ecumenical Service of the Word, and preached. The Luther quincentenary, he proclaimed, should be "the daybreak of the advent of the rebuilding of our unity and community." Such an undertaking "is also the best preparation for the advent of God in our time."[5]

The Holy Year, 1983, had seen a procession of Orthodox figures coming to be received by the pope: on April 16th Karekin Sarkissian, the Armenian Catholicos of Cilicia; on May 13th Ignatius IV Hakim, the Greek Orthodox Patriarch of Antioch; on June 6th Moran Mar Basileius Marthopma Matheos I, Catholicos of the Syrian Orthodox Church of India; on June 30th Metropolitan Melitos of Chalcedon, representing the Ecumenical Patriarch Demetrios for the Roman celebration of Peter and Paul.[6]

On April 22–27, 1985, the pope summoned to Rome the ecumenical commissions of sixty-three national bishops' conferences to review the progress of ecumenism twenty years after the conclusion of the council. John Paul addressed them on April 27th.

The goal of ecumenism, he declared, was no less than "the full communion of Christians in one apostolic faith and in one eucharistic fellowship at the service of a truly common witness." This would reflect the communion of the persons of the Trinity.[7]

Two months later, on June 28, 1985, the pope addressed the Roman Curia. It was the twenty-fifth anniversary of the creation of the Secretariat for Promoting Christian Unity (CU).

4. The letter to Cardinal Willebrands, "Martin Luther, Witness to Jesus Christ," is printed in the Secretariat for Promoting Christian Unity's *Information Service* 52 (1983/II): 83–92.

5. An account of this visit can be found in E. M. Jung-Inglessis, *The Holy Year in Rome: Past and Present* (Vatican City: Libreria Editrice Vaticana, 1997), 297–99.

6. Listed in George Weigel, *Witness to Hope: The Biography of Pope John Paul II* (New York: HarperCollins, 1999), 472.

7. John Paul II, "Address to the Meeting of Delegates of the National Ecumenical Commissions," Secretariat for Promoting Christian Unity, *Information Service* 58 (1985/II): 71f.

There had been tension within the Curia, between the Congregation for the Doctrine of the Faith (CDF) and the CU over ecumenical matters. Particularly when the final report of the Anglican/Roman Catholic International Commission (the ARCIC I Commission's study of the Eucharist) had been prepared in 1981, there was long delay before the necessary permission was granted by the CDF for its publication. One of the first acts of Pope John Paul after his election had been to appoint the then archbishop of Munich-Freising, Joseph Cardinal Ratzinger, prefect of the CDF, and the two met constantly and conferred together. Cardinal Ratzinger's concern was always for clear definition of the faith, which the pope shared, but Pope John Paul had also an urgency about him for progress toward the unity of Christians. When finally permission was given for publication of the ARCIC I report, the CDF gave no assent to the agreed terms but added a list of its own "Observations" and required that the Commission publish its report and the observations together.[8]

Officials in the Curia and in the CDF had been expressing concern about a 1983 book by Karl Rahner and Heinrich Fries, *Unity of the Churches: An Actual Possibility*[9] (in German, *Einigung der Kirchen: reale Möglichkeit*), in which the authors proposed to break the ecumenical logjam by bracketing certain theological issues for later consideration. For the CDF this crossed a red line and seemed to reduce ecumenism to a matter of negotiation of doctrine between what would be regarded as merely voluntary organizations.

The pope's anniversary address to the Curia gave an unambiguous affirmation that "*the Catholic Church is committed to the ecumenical movement with an irrevocable decision.*" This was "one of the pastoral priorities of the bishop of Rome."[10] He proceeded then to a theological clarification,

---

8. "Observations on the Final Report of ARCIC," *L'Osservatore Romano*, July 28, 1986, 3. The "Observations" appeared here, rather than in a joint publication with the ARCIC I report itself, because Bishop Butler, Roman Catholic Chair of the Consultation, declined to publish them himself, saying that it was a document of the CDF, which that office could publish on its own. For this action, he was removed from the chairmanship of ARCIC. (Private communication from Father Francis A. Sullivan, SJ)

9. Karl Rahner and Heinrich Fries, *Unity of the Churches: An Actual Possibility* (New York: Paulist Press, 1985).

10. John Paul II, "The Twenty-fifth Anniversary of the Secretariat for Promoting Christian Unity: Address to the Roman Curia," Secretariat for Promoting Christian Unity, *Information Service* 59 (1985/III): 10 (emphasis in original).

giving what is his most central teaching on the unity of the church. God the Holy Spirit, and no human endeavor, is the source of Christian unity. Although that Spirit-given unity has never been revoked by God, it has been damaged by human error and willfulness. Hence ecumenism is not at all like the negotiation of a treaty or contract. The unity of the church has been given, once for all, at Pentecost, and the ecumenical task is to "recompose" that already-given unity in visible form.[11]

The common confession of the truths of Christian faith, the pope continued, "has to be sought in love: Christian truth cannot be assimilated without charity."[12] This in turn required "reciprocal humility, inspired by love and the cultivation of truth" to overcome the wounds of centuries. The goal was full, deep unity, recomposed in doctrine, worship, and service to the world. Every Catholic had a responsibility to help bring about this unity, which was willed by Christ and given to the church by the Holy Spirit.[13]

The pope had thus laid down firm principles for the pursuit of Christian unity as a full commitment on the part of the Catholic Church, reconfirming the declaration by Pope John XXIII that had stunned the world twenty-five years before. More was to come, as John Paul would continue to press this cause in unexpected, even radical ways.

At the tangible level of curial relations, of course, the problem of differing approaches and attitudes did not go away. The CDF complained that it was brought into doctrinal discussions too late in the various bilateral commissions between the Catholic and other churches. The CU felt that the kinds of criteria the CDF made the center of its focus were too narrow to afford serious attention to the other Christians' concerns. Behind this there remained the CDF's suspicion that ecumenical discussion had become a negotiating process.

To meet this impasse, the pope called a joint plenary of the two offices, which was held January 30–February 1, 1989.[14] Somewhat in the fashion of Franklin Roosevelt's presidential style of the New Deal years, John Paul seems to have regarded it as a benefit that the CDF and the

11. Ibid., 2.
12. Ibid., 7.
13. Ibid., 9.
14. Weigel, *Witness to Hope*, 588f., gives an account of this plenary meeting based on his own interview with Cardinal Edward Cassidy, January 14, 1997.

CU should push and shove a bit, the CU always probing for possible agreement with other traditions, the CDF always checking to see if red lines had been breached or premature agreement reached. The joint plenary seems to have been the pope's way to let the two offices see their relation in that light.[15] An unpublished set of internal best practices came from this three-day meeting to see that the CDF came into doctrinal discussions led by the CU in good time. Not until March 25, 1993, did this result in a formal manual, the *Directory for the Applications of Principles and Norms on Ecumenism*, which the CU had developed in close consultation with the CDF. But the relation remained one of tension, at times constructive, at times resulting in a backlog of bilateral agreements to which other Christians had given their assent while they remained tabled by the Catholic Church.

On the key Reformation quarrel about the doctrine of justification, Reformed theologian Karl Barth had come to a recognition as far back as the 1950s, well before Vatican II, that the Council of Trent's Decree on Justification, long assumed to be the definitive sixteenth-century condemnation of Protestant teaching, gave evidence instead of substantial agreement between the Catholic and Protestant positions. The celebrated Catholic theologian Hans Küng, writing his doctoral dissertation under Barth's direction, confirmed this agreement, which Barth celebrated in his January 31, 1957, letter of introduction to Küng's published book *Justification*.[16]

Through the 1990s this question gripped the attention of Lutherans and Catholics, until a *Joint Declaration on the Doctrine of Justification* was released on June 25, 1998, by the Lutheran World Federation and the Pontifical Council for Promoting Christian Unity (as the former Secretariat was now known). Cardinal Edward Cassidy, president of the Pontifical Council, announced in a press conference that the declaration represented "a consensus on basic truths concerning the doctrine of justification" and the relation of faith to good works in the scheme of salvation. The declaration had resulted from nearly as much consultation between

---

15. A communiqué summarizing the joint *plenarium* and Pope John Paul's address to the closing session appears in Pontifical Council for Promoting Christian Unity, *Information Service* 70 (1989/II): 56–58.

16. In the English translation, Hans Küng, *Justification: The Doctrine of Karl Barth and a Catholic Reflection* (New York: Thomas Nelson and Sons, 1964), xix–xxii.

the CU and the CDF as between the Catholic and Lutheran members of the joint commission, but on the same day the Holy See published a *Response of the Catholic Church to the Joint Declaration of the Catholic Church and the Lutheran World Federation on the Doctrine of Justification* that called for new clarifications. This document had been jointly prepared by the CDF and the CU.[17] Lutherans expressed an acute sense of betrayal, suggesting that the Catholic Church had reneged on both its own and the Lutheran theologians. Cardinal Cassidy wrote a personal letter on June 30th to Dr. Ismael Noko, secretary-general of the Lutheran World Federation, reiterating, and even underlining in his letter, that "there is a consensus in basic truths on the doctrine of justification," and that "very few" further clarifications were required. He wrote that these clarifications "do not negate" the consensus and that the church was prepared to "affirm and sign the Joint Declaration." No "major problems" impeded "further study and a more complete presentation."

The outcome thus far, in sum, was damaging to trust. Dr. Noko wrote on August 20th to the executive committee of the LWF, enclosing Cassidy's letter which, he said, "introduces a new perspective on how to read, understand and interpret" the *Response*.[18] After renewed discussion between the two cardinals, Ratzinger and Cassidy, and some Lutheran theologians and officials, the Holy See suggested that an agreed "Annex" be appended to the *Joint Declaration*, clarifying the concerns that had been raised but emphasizing that those concerns did not invalidate the consensus on "the basic truths of justification." This annex, an "Official Common Statement" that clarified the two partners' variant understandings of the enduring human propensity to sin, of human cooperation with God's grace, and the necessity of locating the doctrine of justification within the broader scheme of Christian belief, concluded: "The teaching of the Lutheran Churches presented in this *Declaration*

---

17. Texts of both the *Joint Declaration* and the *Response*, and of a press conference statement by Cardinal Cassidy of June 25, 1998, are in *Origins* 28, no. 17 (July 16, 1998): 120–32. Weigel, *Witness to Hope*, 826–28, gives an account of the whole episode based on interviews with Cardinal Edward Cassidy on October 10, 1998 and June 7, 1999, and with Cardinal Joseph Ratzinger on December 16, 1998.

18. Cardinal Cassidy provided George Weigel (*Witness to Hope*, n. 58, 943f.) with a copy of his letter of June 30, 1998, to Dr. Noko. For Dr. Noko's letter, see *Origins* 28, no. 17 (October 8, 1998): 228–90.

does not fall under the condemnations of the Council of Trent. The condemnations in the Lutheran Confessions do not apply to the teachings of the Roman Catholic Church presented in this *Declaration*."

Pope John Paul now gave his personal agreement to the clarifications, and the amended document was signed by Lutheran and Roman Catholic representatives in Augsburg on October 31st, Reformation Sunday, 1999. The course had been rocky, but a major ecumenical accomplishment was achieved.

Churches of the East

Ecumenical effort with the churches of the East took a different course. An early result was agreement with the small Iraq-based Assyrian Church of the East, which for fifteen hundred years had been separated from the rest of Christianity, both East and West, over the issues of the Council of Ephesus (AD 431). A Common Christological Declaration accepted that the same faith in Christ could be expressed in different formulas and hence affirmed that Catholics and Assyrians are "united today in the confession of the same faith in the Son of God."[19] This had been entirely John Paul's initiative. Other approaches resolved centuries-old differences with the "monophysite" churches, which had not accepted the doctrine of the two natures of Christ proclaimed by the Council of Chalcedon (AD 451), which is the touchstone of Orthodoxy. Even as the pope's efforts to reach agreement with the Orthodox churches themselves encountered growing difficulties, agreements were reached with the Armenian Apostolic Church, the Coptic Orthodox Church, and the Syrian Orthodox Church, none of them in communion with the ecumenical patriarch and the mainstream of Orthodoxy, stating that their faith in Christ, despite verbal differences in formulation, was the same as that of the Chalcedonian churches.

A promising start toward reconciliation with those mainstream Orthodox churches had resulted from Orthodox participation (as observers, not voting members) in the Second Vatican Council, and in the meetings, in Jerusalem and elsewhere, between Pope Paul VI and Ecumenical Patriarch Athenagoras. The pope's 1979 visit to Patriarch Demetrios at the Phanar had proven welcome and advanced the cause of union visibly.

19. Ronald G. Roberson, CSP, *The Eastern Christian Churches: A Brief Survey*, 6th ed. (Rome: Edizione Orientalia Christiana, 1999), 15–19.

Trouble came into these relations after the dissolution of the Soviet Union and the reemergent strength of the Greek Catholic Church in the now independent Ukraine.

Efforts for the reunion of East and West had gone on over many centuries. When the Fourth Crusade resulted in the capture and despoiling of Constantinople in 1204 and the installation of a Catholic bishop in the Hagia Sophia, relations were more deeply embittered rather than healed. A fifteenth-century declaration of restored unity signed by the Orthodox patriarch Joseph II in 1439 at the Council of Florence in the shadow of the threatened conquest of Constantinople by the Ottoman Turks was rejected when Patriarch Joseph returned home and was seen thereafter as a blackmail attempt by the Western Church, taking advantage of the Eastern Church's distress to force reunion as the price for military help that never came.

It became the policy of the Catholic Church in the seventeenth century to attempt piecemeal reunion of small breakaway units of the Eastern Churches with the Holy See. These new churches retained the Byzantine liturgy and style of government, though they were often pressured into Latinizing their practice.

The Russian Orthodox Church had especially resented this when a substantial Greek Catholic Church grew up in the Ukraine, labeled its members "Uniates," and saw them as a proselytizing salient of the Roman Catholic Church into historically Orthodox lands. The Soviet state, repressing all religion in its territories, had completely banned Ukrainian Catholicism, turned over its church buildings to the Orthodox, and regarded those who still practiced their Christian faith as Orthodox. In the resurgent Ukraine of the 1990s, now independent of Russia, these Catholics simply took back those buildings to conduct their own worship, to the great resentment of an Orthodox Church that was still suffering its own wounds from the Soviet period. The Orthodox once again saw this as proselytism, and it poisoned relations between the whole range of Orthodox churches and Rome.

In the meantime the pope appointed several bishops as apostolic administrators in Russia itself. Latin Catholic communities existed in various parts of Russia, largely as a result of forced movements of peoples during Stalin's time. The new bishops were to administer these local groups in Moscow, Novosibirsk, and Karaganda. This too was seen as proselytism by the Russian Orthodox Church. This church had suffered enormous losses—in property, in the authority of its bishops and pastors, in the training of its people in the faith—throughout the communist period, and it was in fact heavily afflicted with the proselytism of American Evangelical Christians who came with dazzling amounts of money to convert ill-instructed Orthodox Russians to their own churches. Catholics were the traditional proselytizers in Russian eyes, and with so much proselytism going on, the Russians concentrated their ire on the proselytizers they knew.

From June 17–24, 1993, a Joint International Commission for the Theological Dialogue between the Roman Catholic Church and the Orthodox Church met at Balamand University, an Antiochian Orthodox establishment in Lebanon. It attempted to lay out ground rules for the relation of Orthodox and Catholic Churches in Eastern Europe and elsewhere and to reignite the dialogue between them, a goal Pope John Paul hoped to realize before the millennial year 2000. Only a very modest outcome would result.

Uniate churches were the immediate topic of discussion, with the special problems of the Ukraine in the forefront. The resulting Balamand Document contained two fundamental recognitions. First was a Catholic recognition that the Uniate option would no longer be seen as an appropriate way to achieve the full reconciliation that was sought between "sister churches." On the other hand, the Orthodox acknowledged that the Eastern Catholic Churches had the right to exist and to meet the spiritual needs of their members. It was acknowledged that both shared the same faith and that neither should seek conversions. The Eastern Catholic Churches were encouraged to join the joint Catholic/Orthodox ecumenical dialogue.[20]

The Catholic participants returned home regarding this as all gain. But Ecumenical Patriarch Bartolomew, in his Phanar statement on the November 30th feast of St. Andrew, saw this only as the temporary toleration of an "abnormal" situation, until such time as "the Uniate churches finally realize where they belong."[21]

20. A full text of the Balamand Statement, posted by the Orthodox Christian Information Center on its official web site, with ample references, by link, to articles about the document, can be found at http://www.orthodoxinfo.com/ecumenism/balamand_txt.aspx.

21 Cited in Pontifical Council for Promoting Christian Unity, *Information Service* 84 (1993/III–IV): 38f.

In Greece, whose Orthodox Church had sent no delegation to Balamand, the agreement there was seen as facilitating and encouraging a "proselytism to the detriment of the Orthodox." A letter addressed to Patriarch Bartolomeus in December 1993 then denied that the Roman Catholic Church was a "sister church possessing means of salvation." It rejected Catholic sacraments and priesthood and refused to regard the pope as Bishop of Rome unless he would explicitly repudiate Rome's heresies. The primary influence here came from the monks of Mount Athos.

The Romanian Church formally accepted the Balamand Document, but when Metropolitan Nicholas of Banat issued a statement that the recognition of one another by Orthodox and Catholic Churches as "sister churches" meant that Eastern Catholics should also be regarded as "sister churches," many other Romanian Orthodox bishops demurred. A year before Balamand the patriarchate of Bucharest had published a ritual for the reception of "schismatic Roman Catholics and others" into the Orthodox Church, which included a prayer of expiation asking Christ to free these ex-Catholics "from the sleep of the deceit of heresy that leads to perdition." In that spirit, the Romanian bishops tended to see the Balamand Document as essentially a sellout.

The Greek Catholic leadership in Romania, too, remained unenthusiastic about Balamand. Bishop Georghe Gutin wrote of the Romanian Orthodox to the pope: "they have remained the oppressors, we the oppressed; they were collaborators with communism, while we were the victims of it; they were the attackers and we the defenders even up to this day."[22]

Repairing of the Breach

The pope would in fact visit Romania, May 7–9, 1999, and strike a positive relation with its bishops and the Patriarch Teoctist. Before that he went to great lengths to arrange a meeting with Russian Orthodox Patriarch Aleksy II. It was to have taken place not in Moscow, to which the pope would not be invited, but in Vienna, as John Paul would be on his

---

22. The whole of this Orthodox reaction to Balamand is discussed at length in appendix 1 to Roberson, *The Eastern Christian Churches.*

way to the Second European Ecumenical Assembly in Graz in June 1997. The meeting had been under discussion since Cardinal Cassidy had met Russian Orthodox officials in Moscow in December 1996. But the tension between the Russian Church and the Greek Catholics of the Ukraine was bound to make a meeting difficult. Rivalry between Aleksy, who headed the largest Orthodox Church, and Ecumenical Patriarch Bartolomew also played a role in frustrating the meeting, as Bartolomew insisted that if the pope were to meet Aleksy, he had to meet him also.

But the most dramatic meeting was with the Orthodox Church of Greece. It took place in 2001 as the pope made his pilgrimage in the footsteps of Paul from Greece to Syria to Malta. No pope had been in Greece for 1291 years. None of the Eastern Orthodox leaders came to greet him as he arrived. The monks of Athos were raging at his coming. In Athens he met Archbishop Christodoulos, head within the country itself of the Greek Orthodox Church. After a brief private meeting, the two spoke in public. Christodoulos first read out a list of thirteen offenses of the Roman Catholic Church against the Orthodox since the time of the Great Schism, prominent among them the sack of Constantinople in 1204. Since that time, he complained, "there has not been heard a single request for pardon" for what he called "the maniacal crusaders of the 13th century."[23]

John Paul answered in a manner that had become familiar for him by now, with neither excuse nor reproach. "For the occasions, past and present, when sons and daughters of the Catholic Church have sinned by action or omission against their orthodox brothers and sisters, may the Lord grant us forgiveness."[24] He spoke too of the sack of Constantinople as a matter of "deep regret" for Catholics.

Archbishop Christodoulos immediately applauded, and the demeanor of the pope won him great respect in Greece. He and Christodoulos met then on the Areopagus, where once Saint Paul had preached to the Athenians. Before the pope left they issued a "common declaration," saying: "We shall do everything in our power, so that the Christian roots of Europe

23. Luigi Sandri and Edmund Dooque, "In Greece and Syria, Pope John Paul II Tries to Heal Ancient Wounds," *Christianity Today* (May 2001).

24. Full text of the papal address on the Vatican web site, "Address of John Paul II to His Beatitude Christodoulos, Archbishop of Athens and Primate of Greece, Friday 4 May 2001," http://www.vatican.va/holy_father/john_paul_ii/speeches/2001/documents/hf_jp-ii_spe_20010504_archbishop-athens_en.html.

and its Christian soul may be preserved . . . We condemn all recourse to violence, proselytism and fanaticism, in the name of religion."[25] With that they recited together the Lord's Prayer, breaking a long-standing taboo that prohibited Orthodox from ever praying with Catholics.

But the pope was intent by now on quite radical measures to further the cause of unity among Christians. He had hoped from very early in his pontificate to see the millennial breach with the Eastern Church healed by the new millennium. That was not to be. He expected, too, to lead the church in Europe and the Americas, along with the rest of the world, in a great resurgence of faith and practice as he led the way into that millennium. For this he had become himself the preacher, traveling the world as no pope had ever done before and addressing vast audiences everywhere he went. The dwindling of Catholic and Christian practice toward the end of his pontificate had to have hugely disappointed him. Yet he discerned the causes in the power demands the church had made on the world, even in his own time, and addressed these directly, with astonishing humility, in the last years of his reign.

The encyclical *Ut Unum Sint,* signed March 25, 1995, took an enormous and daring step in this direction. We had become accustomed to John Paul stressing the irrevocable commitment of the Catholic Church to the ecumenical endeavor, as already proclaimed at Vatican II in *Lumen Gentium* (LG 8), yet never before had an encyclical been wholly devoted to this theme. Seeing how much the fervor of the council period had diminished, the pope tried to recall the professional members of the various commissions to the urgency of the task. He summoned Orthodox and Protestants alike, but he would make no assumptions on the part of his own Catholic Church, and went directly to the questions of authoritative jurisdiction that had been the core reasons for the ruptures both of 1054 and the sixteenth century.[26]

25. From the Vatican web site: "Common Declaration of Pope John Paul II and His Beatitude Christodoulos, Archbishop of Athens and All Greece, before the Bema of St. Paul, the Apostle to the Nations," May 4, 2001: http://www.vatican.va/holy_father/john_paul_ii/speeches/2001/documents/hf_jp-ii_spe_20010504_joint-declaration_en.html.

26. Full text of the encyclical, John Paul II, *Ut Unum Sint* (On Commitment to Ecumenism), May 25, 1995, (hereafter, UUS), on the Vatican web site: http://www.vatican.va/holy_father/john_paul_ii/encyclicals/documents/hf_jp-ii_enc_25051995_ut-unum-sint_en.html.

The office of Peter, the ministry of the Bishop of Rome, intended from the first to be a ministry of unity in the church, had become a sign of division. This had come about through history, human error, and sin, to the extent that for many Christians the memory of the papacy "is marked by certain painful recollections. To the extent that we are responsible for these, I join my predecessor Paul VI in asking forgiveness" (UUS 88).[27]

Thus far the theme of repentance had already become familiar. The pope noted how, in spite of such memories, the value of a unifying ministry at the service of the church was increasingly seen by other Christians, many of whom appeared ready to rethink the matter of "primacy." He wrote of his sense of "particular responsibility" to respond to this readiness "heeding the request made of me to find a way of exercising the primacy which, while in no way renouncing what is essential to its mission, is nonetheless open to a new situation" (UUS 95).[28]

Such an "immense task," he wrote, something Christians could not ignore, "I cannot carry out by myself." Hence, he asked:

> could not the real but imperfect communion existing between us persuade Church leaders and their theologians to engage with me in a patient and fraternal dialogue on this subject, a dialogue in which, leaving useless controversies behind, we could listen to one another, keeping before us only the will of Christ for his Church and allowing ourselves to be deeply moved by his plea "that they may all be one . . . so that the world may believe that you have sent me" (John 17:21)? (UUS 96)

Thus the Bishop of Rome, 941 years after the breach with Constantinople, nearly five centuries after the shattering of Western Christianity, appealed to all his brothers and sisters in Christian faith to help him redesign the papacy to serve as an office of unity for the whole church of Christ in the third millennium.

This encyclical *Ut Unum Sint* has yet to receive the response the pope requested. It constitutes an authoritative recognition that the exercise of

27. The pope refers here also to a previous statement he made on the important occasion of a visit to the World Council of Churches in Geneva on June 12, 1984.

28. The pope references here Vatican II, Decree on Ecumenism, *Unitatis Redintegratio* 14, and his own homily in the Vatican basilica in the presence of Demetrios I, archbishop of Constantinople and ecumenical patriarch. December 6, 1987, 3, to be found in *Acta Apostolicae Sedis* 80 (1988): 714.

the papal office, as it has developed historically, does not adequately serve the needs of the church. That remains the case even after the death of Pope John Paul and still deserves all the attention he asked from Christians of every tradition to whom the unity of the church is precious. When the retired archbishop of San Francisco, John Quinn, wrote a brave, helpful, and loyal response, suggesting new ways in which the papal office might be exercised, many Catholics were scandalized, thinking that only Christians other than Catholics should be making any such observations. But the invitation is serious, and it stands.

The pope continued on this course. In May of that same year, 1995, the planned canonization of Jan Sarkander, martyred during the religious wars of the early seventeenth century, drew an angry response from Czech Protestants, who saw Santander as having been involved in the forcible Catholicization of Protestant areas of Moravia in his time. John Paul replied, on the basis of scholarly research, that this new saint had never been guilty of violence against Protestants, and that his canonization honored simply Sarkander's fidelity to his priesthood at the cost of his life. Arriving on May 20th in the Czech Republic, he preached that the martyrdom of Sarkander "takes on an extraordinary ecumenical eloquence," reminding all Christians, however much separated, of their mutual "responsibility for the sin of division" and asking their prayers for the forgiveness of sin. "Indeed, we are all in debt to one another."[29]

Two months later, visiting Slovakia on July 2nd, John Paul added to his itinerary the monument at Košice, which honored Calvinists martyred in 1687 for their refusal to be forcibly converted to Catholicism.[30]

When, in 1997, Prague's Cardinal Miloslav Volk had come under heavy Catholic criticism for praising the Christian witness of the pre-Reformation reformer and Czech national hero Jan Hus, who had been burned at the stake in 1415, the pope visited the Czech Republic late in April, where he and Paul Czerny, who headed the Evangelical Church of the Brethren in twentieth-century succession to Hus, participated together in an ecumenical service at Prague's St. Vitus Cathedral to mark the millennium of the martyrdom of St. Adalbert, first evangelist

---

29. "Statements of the Pope in the Czech Republic, May 20–24, 1995," Pontifical Council for Promoting Christian Unity, *Information Service* 89 (1995/II–III): 69.

30. "Pope Pays Tribute to Calvinists," *The Independent*, July 3, 1995.

of Bohemia. In his sermon, John Paul praised the common witness to Christ of Protestants and Catholics during the communist persecution. In that witness they would find together the courage to forgive one another, breaking down "the barriers of mutual suspicion and mistrust . . . in order to build a new civilization of love."[31]

Such gestures became the commonplace of John Paul's ministry in the succeeding years, with words of acceptance and repentance directed to Protestants, Orthodox, and Jews, the latter culminating in his pilgrimage to Jerusalem in the millennial year 2000. The millennium was always in his sights, and if he could not celebrate accomplished union in that year, he would mark it with penitence for the many offenses of Christians that had marked their history throughout the two thousand years and brought about the divisions he so longed to heal.

On Sunday, March 12th, entering the penitential season of the millennial year 2000, the pope celebrated a "Day of Pardon," asking on behalf of the church forgiveness for past and present sins. He asked all Catholics to examine their consciences as they entered the new millennium. He did not single out specific periods in the history of the church but made his plea to God and man to forgive the use of violence even in intended service to the truth, with powerful recollection of the Crusades, the Inquisition, the persecution of Jews, and the violent responses to the Reformation. He referred to and endorsed the lengthy and explicit catalogue of these sins which he had caused to be published by the International Theological Commission shortly before.[32]

In his bull initiating the Holy Year, *Incarnationis Mysterium*, he had already invoked the "purification of memory" as one of the objectives of

---

31. Weigel, *Witness to Hope*, 765, describes the episode. For the text of the pope's homily at the April 27th service: John Paul II, "Forgive One Another's Wrongs," *L'Osservatore Romano* (April 30, 1997): 3.

32. The event caused a great sensation at the time. Cf. CNN, Sunday Morning News, "Pope John Paul II Makes Unprecedented Apology for Sins of Catholic Church," aired March 12, 2000, http://transcripts.cnn.com/TRANSCRIPTS/0003/12/sm.06.html. A fuller transcript of the pope's homily, including the intercessions by the cardinal prefects of Roman dicasteries, appears at the website of Boston College's Christian-Jewish Understanding Center, http://www.bc.edu/research/cjl/meta-elements/texts/cjrelations/resources/documents/catholic/johnpaulii/day_of_pardon_mass.htm. The Vatican's own website gives the procedure of this entire "Day of Pardon" at http://www.vatican.va/news_services/liturgy/documents/ns_lit_doc_20000312_presentation-day-pardon_en.html.

the millennial celebration. He spoke now of "infidelities to the Gospel committed . . . especially during the second millennium," of causative Christian responsibility "regarding atheism, religious indifference, secularism, ethical relativism, the violations of the right to life, disregard for the poor in many countries."[33] In asking forgiveness for such faults, he begged his hearers to forgive also the sins committed by others against them. The cardinal prefects of several dicasteries of the Holy See added their own prayers for the forgiveness of particular failings of the Christian community throughout its history. The Holy Year was thus marked with repentance as a means to healing the sins and divisions of the past.

Just after this, on August 6, 2000, the world read with consternation a document titled *Declaration, "Dominus Iesus," on the Unicity and Salvific Universality of Jesus Christ and the Church.*[34] This was the work of the CDF, but its publication had been authorized by the pope at an audience on June 16, 2000. The tone was utterly unlike any of the ecumenical statements we had been hearing from this pope for all those years. Doubtless, as a statement cataloguing all the restrictive measures taken to defend the specific claims of the Catholic Church over centuries, this document was accurate enough in summing up the traditional case for Catholic exclusiveness, and in that sense orthodox. But its outlook was narrow, searching for the reasons why an opening of hearts to other Christians could not be rather than seeking ways to uncover the common heritage of faith.

The document's strongest ecumenical outreach, a courtesy to the Orthodox Churches (which alone are accorded the title of "sister churches" by reason of their having the "genuine and integral substance of the Eucharist" and episcopacy in apostolic succession),[35] was to quote the Niceno-Constantinopolotan Creed at the beginning without the "Filioque."[36] Criteria for the legitimacy of Christian communities were

---

33. "Bull of Indiction of the Great Jubilee of the Year 2000," given at Rome November 29, 1999, on the Vatican web site: http://www.vatican.va/jubilee_2000/docs/documents/hf_jp-ii_doc_30111998_bolla-jubilee_en.html, 11, par. 3.

34. Full text on the Vatican web site at www.vatican.va/roman_curia/congregations/cfaith/documents/rc_con_cfaith_doc_20000806_dominus-iesus_en.html. Cf. also, chapter 14 of the present volume.

35. Ibid., 17.

36. Ibid., 1.

all defined by conformity to internal—and thus ultimately human—doctrinal decisions of the Roman Catholic Church, the ultimate criterion of which was submission to the jurisdiction of the Bishop of Rome. Faith had little to do with it.

How had this come about? One of John Paul's first acts after his election as pope had been to appoint Cardinal Joseph Ratzinger as prefect of the CDF. We have in more recent times come to know a different and more pastoral face of Joseph Ratzinger since he has become Pope Benedict XVI and recognized a different set of responsibilities than those he carried as head of the CDF. But so long as he worked in that latter capacity, he appears to have seen his duty as policing every doctrinal statement or trend to eliminate every innovation. Even where Vatican II had opened up new avenues that the pope avidly explored, the inclination of Cardinal Ratzinger was to interpret them in the narrowest possible way.

Pope John Paul placed vast trust in his colleague Joseph Ratzinger, met with him frequently and regularly, discussed all matters of concern to the church with him, and quite evidently valued his mentorship and monitoring over what was so clearly the pope's own thrust toward the creation of new relations of respect and peace among Christians and throughout the world. That Cardinal Ratzinger in turn valued and respected these aspirations in the Wojtyla pope was always clear as well, never more so than in his own subsequent actions and attitudes as pope and in the new restraint with which he now responds to creative initiative in the church.

So where is the legacy of Pope John Paul II with regard to the relations of the Catholic Church to other Christians? Surely we find it in his 1985 address to the Roman Curia, where he recognized the unity of the church as given once and for all by the Holy Spirit at Pentecost, in the generosity of his approach to Martin Luther and to the Orthodox Churches that so often reproached him and his church, in the masterly encyclical *Ut Unum Sint,* and in the spirit of repentance, admission of fault, and plea for forgiveness with which he celebrated the opening of the new millennium. These are enduring monuments to his custody of the church and his witness to his Master, Christ, for whom, as he remained conscious, he was merely vicar. The church, and the pope, he was more and more convinced as his papacy developed, must come with the modesty and humility of Christ.

14

John Paul II
and Interreligious Dialogue
Reality and Promise

Peter C. Phan

George W. Bush's preemptive Iraq War, as any war in the past, makes it abundantly clear that political problems cannot be solved by force but only by a process of peaceful dialogue and negotiation whereby the legitimate interests of all the parties-in-conflict are preserved and protected. Another lesson from the Iraq War is that religion can be harnessed both to foment violence and armed conflict, and to promote mutual understanding, peaceful coexistence, and reconciliation on national and international levels. With the looming threat of global conflicts and the "clash of civilizations," interreligious dialogue to achieve justice and peace has become one of the most urgent tasks for our time.[1] It comes as no surprise then that leaders of religious traditions as diverse as Buddhism, Christianity, Hinduism, Islam, and Judaism have issued insistent calls for interfaith dialogue as part of the quest for global reconciliation and peace. Among Christian leaders Pope John Paul II was unquestionably the foremost advocate, exponent, and practitioner of this dialogue in the last quarter of the twentieth century.[2]

1. As Hans Küng's dictum puts it trenchantly: "No peace among the nations without peace among the religions. No peace among the religions without dialogue between the religions. No dialogue between the religions without global ethical standards. No survival of our globe without a global ethic, a world ethic, supported by both the religious and the non-religious" (*Islam: Past, Present and Future*, trans. John Bowden [Oxford: OneWorld, 2007], 661–62).
2. By "interreligious dialogue" is meant the dialogue between Christianity (here, the Roman Catholic Church) and other religions, and not ecumenical dialogue, which seeks the

To appreciate John Paul's achievements in interreligious dialogue, it is necessary to consider both his activities to promote interreligious harmony and collaboration and his theology of interreligious dialogue. Methodologically, it would be helpful to study the latter in light of the former,[3] and both in light of the teaching of the Second Vatican Council.[4] I begin with a brief narrative of the pope's interreligious activities and highlight their theological significance. This is followed by an exposition of John Paul's theology of interreligious dialogue. I end by indicating areas where John Paul's theology of interreligious dialogue can be developed further with the view to elaborate a more adequate theology of interreligious dialogue.[5]

---

unity of various Christian denominations. Within the Roman Curia, ecumenical dialogue is under the jurisdiction of the Pontifical Council for Promoting Christian Unity, whereas interreligious dialogue is under the jurisdiction of the Pontifical Council for Interreligious Dialogue. However, dialogue with Judaism constitutes a special category, and the Commission for Religious Relations with the Jews is part of the Pontifical Council for Promoting Christian Unity. Recently, Pope Benedict XVI folded the Pontifical Council for Interreligious Dialogue within the Pontifical Council for Culture. In this essay, interreligious dialogue includes dialogue with Judaism as well as with other non-Christian religions.

3. The reason for this methodology, as will be made clear, is that in many important ways John Paul II's interreligious activities were "prophetic" or "symbolic" gestures that, to adopt Paul Ricoeur's celebrated phrase, "give rise to thought." They were not simply practical applications of the pope's theology of interreligious dialogue but outstrip it and hence open up new theological vistas, the significance of which was perhaps not fully appreciated by the pope himself.

4. A reference to Vatican II's teaching on Christianity's relationship to Judaism and other religions, especially in its decree *Nostra Aetate*, is necessary not only because John Paul II based his theology of interreligious dialogue on the council but also because he explicitly intended his pontificate (1978–2005) to be an implementation of Vatican II.

5. There are a huge number of studies of John Paul and interreligious dialogue. Primary and authoritative sources of John Paul's theology are his encyclicals. A convenient collection of these is Michael Miller, ed., *The Encyclicals of John Paul II* (Huntington, IN: Our Sunday Visitor, 1996). A helpful presentation and evaluation of John Paul's theology of interreligious dialogue is Byron L. Sherwin and Harold Kasimow, ed., *John Paul II and Interreligious Dialogue* (Maryknoll, NY: Orbis, 1999) and John Borelli, "John Paul II and Interreligious Dialogue," in *New Catholic Encyclopedia: Jubilee Volume, The Wojtyla Years* (Washington, DC: The Catholic University of America, 2001), 81–88. Other more recent helpful works include: Wayne Teasdale, *Catholicism in Dialogue: Conversations across Traditions* (Lanham, MD: Rowman and Littlefield, 2004) and Michael L. Fitzgerald and John Borelli, *Interfaith Dialogue: A Catholic View* (Maryknoll, NY: Orbis, 2006).

Iconic Figure and Symbolic Gestures

Absorbed by a passion for literature, especially dramatic literature, and for the theater, John Paul II, more than any other pope, had an acute sense of the power of symbolic gestures.[6] It is neither possible nor desirable to recount all of John Paul's activities large and small in the service of interreligious unity during his twenty-seven-year pontificate.[7] I will select only a few of the most significant events for consideration.

With regard to interfaith dialogue in general, at the top of the list stand no doubt the World Day of Prayer for Peace held in Assisi on October 27, 1986, and its sequel on January 24, 2002. Like his predecessor John XXIII, whose decision to call for an ecumenical council was greeted with vehement objections, John Paul startled some senior officials of the Roman Curia with his announcement on January 25, 1986, of his initiative to invite non-Christian leaders (in addition to non-Catholic Christians) to come to Assisi to pray for peace. The meeting was criticized as skirting dangerous syncretism. It was left to Bishop Jorge Mejía, then secretary of the Pontifical Council for Justice and Peace, to explain that the purpose of the Assisi meeting was not to have religious leaders "pray together"—which would be syncretism—but rather to "be together to pray." In fact, at the actual event, after John Paul's welcome of religious leaders at the Portiuncula, religious leaders went to separate places in Assisi to pray with their coreligionists for ninety minutes and afterward gathered in the piazza in front of the basilica. There, each religious representative offered a prayer for peace according to his or her own religious tradition.

---

6. There is a plethora of biographies of Karol Wojtyla. One, which borders on hagiography and is more a chronology than history, George Weigel's *Witness to Hope: The Biography of John Paul II* (New York: HarperCollins, 2005), offers in nearly a thousand pages detailed information on John Paul's life up to May 1999.

7. A useful collection of John Paul's writings on interreligious dialogue is Francesco Gioia, ed., *Interreligious Dialogue: The Official Teaching of the Catholic Church from the Second Vatican Council to John Paul II (1963–2005)* (Boston: Pauline Books and Media, 2006), (hereafter, ID). For convenience's sake, all citations from John Paul's writings are taken from this text, followed by the paragraph number (not page number) given on the margin of each page. Note that the English and the second edition of this work (2006) have two kinds of numbers, without the asterisk and with the asterisk. Those with asterisks are added to the original 1994 Italian edition.

In his address to the religious representatives in Assisi, John Paul clarified the purpose of the meeting:

> The fact that we have come here does not imply any intention of seeking a religious consensus among ourselves or negotiating our faith convictions. Neither does it mean that religions can be reconciled at the level of a common commitment in an earthly project which would surpass them all. Nor is it a concession to relativism in religious beliefs, because every human being must sincerely follow his or her upright conscience with the intention of seeking and obeying the truth.
>
> Our meeting attests only—and this is its real significance for the people of our time—that in the great battle for peace, humanity, in its very diversity, must draw from its deepest and most vivifying sources where its conscience is formed and upon which is founded the moral action of all people. (ID 535)

Despite this comprehensive explanation, the October Assisi meeting continued to rankle leading curial cardinals. To allay their fears the pope made a lengthy defense of it in an address to the Roman Curia on December 22nd of the same year.[8] But even such papal apologetics did not quell their opposition. John Paul had to fight against their resistance to further activities of this kind. Reportedly, he told Monsignor Vincenzo Paglia, chaplain of the Sant' Egidio Community,[9] to whom he had entrusted the organization of future meetings of prayer for peace: "Don Vincenzo, today I fought for you . . . and we won."[10]

Of non-Christian religions no doubt Judaism was closest to John Paul's heart. Personally, he had lifelong personal experiences with Jews.[11]

---

8. For the text of this address, see Gioia, *Interreligious Dialogue,* nos. 562–573.

9. Sant' Egidio Community, founded in Rome in 1968 at the initiative of Andrea Riccardi, is a "public Church lay association" headquartered at the Church of Sant' Egidio, Rome (hence its name), whose goals include prayer, evangelization, ecumenism, interreligious dialogue, and solidarity with the poor. Currently it has fifty thousand members in seventy countries.

10. Weigel, *Witness to Hope,* 522. Unfortunately we are not told who the opposing cardinals are, but it is not far-fetched to think of the then prefect of the Congregation for the Doctrine of the Faith, Cardinal Joseph Ratzinger, now Pope Benedict XVI.

11. For John Paul's own reflections on his experiences with Jews and Judaism, see his *Crossing the Threshold of Hope* (New York: Knopf, 1994), 95–100. He writes that Vatican II's teaching on the relationship between Christians and Jews in its decree *Nostra Aetate* reflects his personal experience: "The words of the Council's Declaration reflect the experience of

The house he was born in was rented from a Jewish family. One of his closest childhood friends was Jerzy Kluger, the son of the leader of the Jewish community in his native town of Wadowice, where the Jews made up about a quarter of the population. Also, despite its anti-Semitic history, John Paul's homeland was relatively hospitable to 3.5 million Jews, who in 1920 represented 10 percent of the total population; in no other European country did the Jews live in peace and security for so long as in Poland. Most important, John Paul's first-hand knowledge of the evils of Nazism and the Holocaust made him particularly sensitive to the plight of the Jews. Intellectually, he acknowledged his extensive indebtedness to Max Scheler (the subject of his *Habilitationsschrift*), Franz Rosenzweig, Martin Buber, and Emmanuel Levinas.[12] Theologically, John Paul was of course more informed about, and spiritually more at home with, Judaism than any other non-Christian religion.

Among John Paul's many symbolic gestures toward Judaism, several deserve notice. The first is his visit to the Roman Synagogue on April 13, 1986, the first pope ever to do so. He conceived the visit not just as a social or political gesture but as an explicitly religious act, the purpose of which was to pray together with Jews. Under John Paul, the "Fundamental Agreement: Israel-Holy See" was signed on December 30, 1993, providing for the recognition of the rights of the Catholic Church in Israel and negotiation toward full diplomatic relations between the two states.

During John Paul's pontificate, important Roman documents on Jews and Christians were issued, among which to be noted is *Notes on the Correct Way to Present the Jews and Judaism in Preaching and Catechesis in the Roman Catholic Church* (1985).[13] Throughout the 1990s, as John Paul prepared the church for the celebration of its third millennium, he urged Christians to repent of their past errors and sins. Among the many grievous sins was anti-Semitism. In 1993, John Paul intervened to have the Carmelite nuns who had moved in 1984 into a building on the border of the concentration camp in Auschwitz to close down their convent

---

many people, both Jews and Christians. They reflect *my personal experience* as well, from the very first years of my life in my hometown" (96, emphasis in original).

12. Cf. chapter 2 of the present volume.

13. This document must be read in relation with the 1974 document of the Commission for Religious Relations with Jews, *Guidelines and Suggestions for Implementing the Conciliar Declaration* Nostra Aetate.

and to transfer to another place out of respect for the Jewish victims of the Holocaust. In 1998, the Commission on Religious Relations with the Jews issued the document *We Remember: A Reflection on the Shoah*, which condemns Nazi ideology, describes the Shoah as an "unspeakable tragedy" and a "horrible genocide," acknowledges a "heavy burden of conscience" on Christians today, and calls for repentance.

Another grand gesture was John Paul's trip to the Holy Land in March 2000, where he prayed at the Western Wall and visited the *Yad Vashem*. In addition, throughout his long pontificate the pope held numerous meetings with various official Jewish organizations such as the American Jewish Committee and the International Jewish Committee on Interreligious Consultations, with Israeli politicians such as Simon Peres, and with diverse groups of local Jews on his many travels. Another powerful symbolic gesture was John Paul's appointment of Jean-Marie Lustiger, the son of Polish Jews who had migrated to France, as archbishop of Paris, to the consternation of the French Church.

These richly symbolic gestures of friendship and esteem toward the Jews on the part of John Paul should not gloss over other gestures of his that caused serious controversies. Among these was his 1987 meeting with Kurt Waldheim, former secretary-general of the United Nations and president of Austria, who had been an officer in the army of the Third Reich and had not expressed regret for his role in wartime human rights violations. Even though such a meeting was diplomatically inevitable, it created much dismay and concern, especially among Jewish leaders. Another controversial act was John Paul's 1998 canonization of Edith Stein, a convert from Judaism, a Carmelite nun (under the name of Sister Teresa Benedicta of the Cross), and a victim of the Nazi gas chambers at Auschwitz-Birkenau. Even though the pope spoke of Edith Stein as an "eminent daughter of Israel and faithful daughter of the Church," some Jews criticized her canonization as a covert attempt at "Christianizing" the Holocaust.

Next to Judaism in John Paul's areas of interreligious concern was Islam, the second largest religion after Christianity. With about 1.3 billion members, it is as large as the Catholic Church. Unlike the Christian-Jewish relation, where Christians generally dominate, that between Christians and Muslims has been a struggle between rivals of comparable political and military powers, despite the fact that the Qur'an contains positive statements about Jesus and Mary. There is no need to re-hearse here the Islamic conquest of North Africa, the home of Cyprian and Augustine, and of Southern Europe, and the Christian crusades against Muslims, whom Pope Urban II declared "an accursed race, a race utterly alienated from God."[14] Such long-standing hostile relation-ship between Islam and Christianity, both intensely mission-oriented religions, was exacerbated by the events of 9/11, and consequently, dia-logue between them has become an urgent and complex issue.

John Paul's relations with Muslims increased in frequency and im-portance during his long pontificate, often in response to political events. The first significant contact was his meeting with eighty thousand Mus-lim youths at a stadium in Casablanca, Morocco, on August 19, 1985, at the invitation of King Hassan II of Morocco. For the first time ever, a pope addressed a Muslim audience. During the Iran-Iraq War (1980–88), John Paul dispatched Cardinal Roger Etchegaray to Tehran and Baghdad to help ease the conflict. Again, following Saddam Hus-sein's invasion of Kuwait and prior to the 1990–91 Gulf War, the pope repeatedly called for a nonviolent solution to the problem in the Middle East. Finally, before the 2003 Iraq War, John Paul did everything he could to prevent it from happening. In all of these pro-peace activities, John Paul's concern was not only with the morality of war and its im-potence to resolve political issues but also with the enormous sufferings and destruction of Muslim communities.

Within the church, John Paul continued to foster friendly relations with Muslims through the Commission for Religious Relations with Muslims in the Pontifical Council for Interreligious Dialogue (which is parallel to the Commission for Religious Relations with Jews in the Pon-tifical Council for Promoting Christian Unity). At the 1995 special as-sembly for Lebanon of the synod of bishops, representatives of the Is-lamic community in Lebanon, one Sunni, one Shi'ite, and one Druze, were invited to take part in and address the assembly. They were also invited to share meals with the pope.

In all his addresses to Muslims, John Paul always highlighted the Christian and Muslim common belief in the one God and expressed his

14. Edward Peters, ed., *The First Crusade: The Chronicle of Fulcher of Chartres and Other Source Materials* (Philadelphia: University of Pennsylvania Press, 1971), 2.

admiration for the high ethical and religious demands Islam makes upon its followers, especially in terms of prayer, fasting, and almsgiving. At the same time, he also expressed his concern about restrictions on the religious and civil rights of Christians in Islamic countries and even violent persecutions against them, especially in Africa, the Middle East, and Southwest and Southeast Asia. He urged Christians and Muslims to work together for peace and justice, despite differences in their beliefs.

Finally, another religion with which John Paul had significant personal experiences is Buddhism. The pope's first public encounter with Buddhism was at the 1986 World Day of Prayer for Peace at Assisi already mentioned above. Among Buddhist participants was the Dalai Lama, with whom he met several other times subsequently. The pope also met with different groups of Buddhists, especially the Japanese (the Zen, Pure Land, Shingon, and Nichiren schools), Korean, Sri Lankan, and Thai Buddhists.

A rather unfortunate event in John Paul's otherwise friendly relations with Buddhists was the publication of his interview with Italian journalist Vittorio Messori in *Crossing the Threshold of Hope*, in which his characterization of Buddhism as an "a-theistic" religion caused strong protest by several groups of Buddhists, especially in Sri Lanka. During his visit to this country in January 1995, the pope went out of his way to affirm his admiration and respect for the teachings of the Buddha and the commitment of the Catholic Church to interreligious dialogue.[15]

John Paul II's Theology of Religion and Interreligious Dialogue

Undergirding John Paul's varied and numerous activities in interreligious dialogue is a theology of salvation and religion that is deeply rooted in Christology and ecclesiology. John Paul's understanding of Christ and the church is treated in other chapters in this volume; here the focus will be on his theology of interreligious dialogue. Such a theology bears the imprint of both Vatican II and John Paul's own theological vision.

---

15. Another religion which John Paul addressed to some extent is Hinduism. Addressing the followers of various religions in the United States in Los Angeles on September 16, 1987, he said: "To the Hindu community: I hold in esteem your concern for inner peace and for the peace of the world, based not on purely mechanistic or materialistic political considerations, but on self-purification, unselfishness, love and sympathy for all. May the minds of all people be imbued with such love and understanding," Gioia, *Interreligious Dialogue*, no. 596. See also no. 828*.

Vatican II: A Radical Turning Point in the Theology of Religion?

It is common knowledge that Vatican II marked a watershed event in the Catholic Church's attitude toward non-Christians and non-Christian religions. With regard to the former, the council affirms that they can, under certain conditions, obtain eternal salvation.[16] On the latter, Vatican II affirms that through the church's missionary activities "whatever good is found sown in people's hearts and minds, or in the rites and customs of peoples, is not only saved from destruction, but is purified, raised up, and perfected for the glory of God, the confusion of the devil, and the happiness of humanity" (LG 17, cf. AG 9).

Vatican II's fullest teaching on non-Christian religions is found in its declaration *Nostra Aetate*. The council begins by noting the unity of all humankind by virtue of its common origin and destiny, namely, God. It sees religions as diverse attempts at answering fundamental questions concerning the meaning of human existence. It goes on to expound briefly on different non-Christian religions, from the so-called primitive religions to world religions such as Hinduism, Buddhism, Islam, and Judaism. In this context, the council declares that "the Catholic Church rejects nothing of what is true and holy in these religions. It has a high regard for the manner of life and conduct, the precepts and doctrines which, although differing in many ways from its own teaching, nevertheless often reflect a ray of that truth which enlightens all men and women" (NA 2).[17]

It is important to note the difference between Vatican II's statements on individual non-Christians and those on non-Christian religions as such. Whereas the council's affirmation of the possibility of salvation for non-Christians marks an important advancement compared with the teaching of the Council of Florence (1442), it is its affirmation of the

16. *Lumen Gentium*, no. 16: "Those who, through no fault of their own, do not know the Gospel of Christ or his church, but who nevertheless seek God with a sincere heart, and, moved by grace, try in their actions to do his will as they know it through the dictates of their conscience—these too may attain eternal salvation." English translation of Vatican II documents is taken from *Vatican Council II: The Basic Sixteen Documents*, by Austin Flannery, OP (Northport, NY: Costello, 1996).

17. For a clear exposition of Vatican II's teaching on non-Christian religions, see Jacques Dupuis' two works, *Toward a Christian Theology of Religious Pluralism* (Maryknoll, NY: Orbis, 1997), 161–70, and *Christianity and the Religions: From Confrontation to Dialogue*, trans. Phillip Berryman (Maryknoll, NY: Orbis, 2002), 59–66.

presence of "elements of truth and grace"—a phrase borrowed from Karl Rahner—in non-Christian religions that is theologically significant for interreligious dialogue.

The question, however, is whether Vatican II has also taken the further step of affirming that non-Christian religions are themselves "ways of salvation," though ultimately dependent on Christ's saving action. In other words, are the "elements of truth and grace" present in non-Christian religions to be fulfilled in the church, through the church's mission, or do they act, in virtue of their autonomous and intrinsic truth and goodness, as "ways," "paths," or "means" of salvation for those who accept and live by them? The same question can be phrased differently in terms of interreligious dialogue: Is interreligious dialogue a one-way traffic in which the church only "purifies," "raises up," and "perfects" the elements of truth and grace present in other religions, since it already possesses these elements in their fullness and therefore in principle can do without other religions? Or is interreligious dialogue a two-way activity in which the church is genuinely enriched and complemented by these elements of truth and grace, since it may not possess them at all or may not possess them to the same degree as non-Christian religions?

While both alternatives can be defended by appealing selectively to various texts of Vatican II, it seems that neither the minimalist position (following the Jean Daniélou–Henri de Lubac "fulfillment theory," according to which non-Christian religions are superseded by Christianity) nor the maximalist one (following the John Hick–Paul Knitter "pluralist thesis," according to which Christianity and non-Christian religions are parallel ways of salvation) reflects Vatican II's position accurately.[18] On the contrary, Karl Rahner and Jacques Dupuis are correct in saying that while Vatican II does teach that there is a positive relationship between the church and non-Christian religions as such (and not only with non-Christian individuals), the council leaves the question of the positive role of non-Christian religions in salvation undefined and open for further theological debate. The council only asserts that the elements of truth

18. For a succinct and illuminating summary of Vatican II's teaching on non-Christian religions, with reflections on the two contrasting theological orientations present therein (Jean Daniélou vs. Karl Rahner), see James Fredericks, "The Catholic Church and the Other Religious Paths: Rejecting Nothing That Is True and Holy," *Theological Studies* 64, no. 2 (2003): 226–33.

and grace in non-Christian religions constitute "as it were, a secret presence of God" (AG 9) and "the seeds of the Word" (AG 11) and are to be considered as "a preparation for the Gospel," given to them by Christ himself (LG 16).

Similarly, with regard to the goal of interreligious dialogue, while Vatican II urges Catholics "to enter with prudence and charity into discussion and collaboration with members of other religions" and "while witnessing to their own faith and way of life, acknowledge, preserve and encourage the spiritual and moral truths found among non-Christians, together with their social life and culture" (NA 2), the council does not say whether through this dialogue the church itself is enriched by the elements of truth and goodness present in non-Christian religions, either because the church does not possess these elements of truth and goodness or possesses them less perfectly than other religions.[19]

The above brief overview of Vatican II's teaching on non-Christian religions and interreligious dialogue serves as an indispensable background to John Paul's theology of the same realities. In fact, John Paul's theology of religion and interreligious dialogue is deeply indebted to Vatican II, as his repeated and numerous quotations from conciliar texts make abundantly clear. As a result, his theology bears the notable theological openness of Vatican II. By the same token, it also inherits some of the ambiguities inherent in the council's teaching.

On the one hand, John Paul restricted himself to reaffirming Vatican II's teaching on the possibility of salvation of non-Christians and on the presence of elements of truth and grace in non-Christian religions. On the other hand, some of the pope's statements, and in particular his symbolic gestures, do open up new horizons in which to think further on some of the issues left open by Vatican II. I will begin with a

---

19. James Fredericks correctly summarizes Vatican II's position on non-Christian religions: "Nowhere in its documents does the council unambiguously recognize the other religions as actual mediations of the saving grace of Jesus Christ as Rahner argues in his theology" ("The Catholic Church and the Other Religious Paths," 233). The operative word here is "unambiguously," since Fredericks himself acknowledges that there are passages in Vatican II's documents (e.g., *Gaudium et Spes* 20 and *Ad Gentes* 3) that seem to lean toward Rahner's position.

succinct exposition of John Paul's understanding of the relationship between Christianity and non-Christian religions and of the nature and modality of interreligious dialogue. Next, I will consider in some detail those teachings of his that seem to hold out promising trails to move beyond the theological tensions in Vatican II.

1. At the basis of John Paul's theology of religion is his bedrock and oft-repeated faith conviction that Jesus is the unique and universal savior. This is the *cantus firmus* of the pope's innumerable encyclicals and speeches on mission and interreligious dialogue, whether addressed to his fellow Christians or to the followers of other religions. Any theology of religion or any interfaith dialogue that jeopardizes this Christological truth of faith in the least is thereby roundly rejected.[20]

2. Affirmed with equal firmness and frequency is John Paul's conviction about the mission of the church to proclaim Christ as the only and universal savior for all humanity. John Paul saw no conflict between evangelization and interreligious dialogue; on the contrary, he maintained that the latter is an intrinsic part of the former: "Interreligious dialogue is part of the Church's evangelizing mission. Understood as a method and means of mutual knowledge and enrichment, dialogue is not in opposition to the mission *ad gentes*; indeed, it has special links with that mission and is one of its expressions . . . Salvation comes from Christ and . . . dialogue does not dispense from evangelization."[21]

3. With regard to the possibility of salvation of non-Christians and the famous formula *extra ecclesiam nulla salus* (outside the church, there is no salvation), John Paul offered an extensive commentary. The pope reaffirmed Vatican II's teaching that salvation is possible outside the

20. There is no need to cite from John Paul II's voluminous writings to confirm this fundamental teaching. To avoid cluttering the text with citations, I refer readers to the volume edited by Francesco Gioia already cited above for a selection of important texts from John Paul's writings. Among these, the following should be noted in connection with interreligious dialogue: (1) Encyclicals: *Redemptor Hominis* (1979), *Dives in Misericordia* (1980), *Dominum et Vivificantem* (1986), *Redemptoris Missio* (1990), and *Fides et Ratio* (1998); (2) Apostolic Exhortations: *Ecclesia in Africa* (1995), *Ecclesia in Asia* (1999), *Novo Millenio Ineunte* (2001), and *Ecclesia in Europa* (2003); (3) Apostolic Letters: *Redemptionis Anno* (1984) and *Tertio Millennio Adveniente* (1994).

21. Gioia, *Interreligious Dialogue*, no. 178, cf. also, no. 685, and 713. The relationship between evangelization and dialogue is expounded at great length in the Joint Document of the Pontifical Council for Interreligious Dialogue and the Congregation for the Evangelization of Peoples entitled *Dialogue and Proclamation* (1991). See ibid., nos. 926–1013.

visible confines of the church. He noted, however, that this possibility "does not justify the relativistic position of those who maintain that a way of salvation can be found in any religion, even independently of faith in Christ the Redeemer . . . Rather, we must maintain that the way of salvation always passes through Christ, and therefore the church and her missionaries have the task of making him known and loved in every time, place and culture. Apart from Christ 'there is no salvation'" (ID 931*).

Concerning the *extra ecclesiam nulla salus* formula, John Paul observed that, correctly understood, this principle does not exclude the possibility of salvation outside the church. Rather, it means that "for those who are not ignorant of the fact that the Church has been established as necessary by God through Jesus Christ, there is an obligation to enter the Church and remain in her in order to attain salvation" (ID 832*). Furthermore, it means that even though it is possible to obtain salvation outside the church, such salvation is "in mysterious ways" related to the church: "In order to take effect, saving grace requires acceptance, cooperation, a yes to the divine gift; and this acceptance is, at least implicitly, oriented to Christ and the Church. Thus it can be said that *sine Ecclesia nulla salus*—'without the Church there is no salvation': belonging to the Church, the Mystical Body of Christ, however implicitly and indeed mysteriously, is an essential condition of salvation" (ID 832*). Hence, "dialogue should be conducted and implemented with the conviction that the Church is the ordinary means of salvation and that she alone possesses the fullness of the means of salvation" (ID 178).

4. John Paul was deeply convinced that true dialogue, especially interreligious dialogue, is a spiritual discipline with its requisite virtues, without which it degenerates into a monologue in search of domination. Because dialogue "presupposes the search for what is true, good and just for every person, for every group and every society," it demands first of all that there be "openness and welcome"; that "each party should accept the difference and the specific nature of the other party"; that one search for "what is and what remains common to people, even in the midst of tensions, opposition and conflicts" and for "what is good by peaceful means" (ID 412).

5. Of the many and various modalities or forms of interreligious dialogue, John Paul highlighted four throughout his pronouncements.

These are described by a joint document of the Pontifical Council for Interreligious Dialogue and the Congregation for Evangelization of Peoples as follows:

a) The dialogue of life, where people strive to live in an open and neighborly spirit, sharing their joys and sorrows, their human problems and preoccupations.

b) The dialogue of action, in which Christians and others collaborate for the integral development and liberation of people.

c) The dialogue of theological exchange, where specialists seek to deepen their understanding of their respective heritages, and to appreciate each other's spiritual values.

d) The dialogue of religious experience, where persons, rooted in their own religious traditions, share their spiritual riches, for instance with regard to prayer and contemplation, faith and ways of searching for God or for the Absolute.[22]

Of these four forms of dialogue, John Paul put the premium on religious experience, and more precisely, on being together to pray (including fasting and pilgrimage), which he considered the most effective means to achieve interreligious harmony and world peace. No wonder he made dialogue through prayer the central focus of the historic Assisi World Day of Prayer for Peace meetings. John Paul was careful to avoid the appearance of syncretism in this dialogue through prayer and made a clear distinction between "being together to pray" and "praying together." He explained:

> What will take place in Assisi will certainly not be religious syncretism but a sincere attitude of prayer to God in an atmosphere of mutual respect. For this reason the formula chosen for the gathering at Assisi is: being together in order to pray. Certainly we cannot "pray together," namely, make a common prayer, but we can be present while others pray. In this way we manifest our respect for the prayers of others and for the attitude of others before the divinity; at the same time, we offer

22. Gioia, *Interreligious Dialogue*, no. 966. See also, nos. 421 and 659, where John Paul mentions many forms of dialogue, including the doctrinal field, the field of daily relationships, working together for a more just society, comparing spiritual experiences and sharing forms of prayer as ways of meeting with God, and intermonastic dialogue.

them the humble and sincere witness of our faith in Christ, Lord of the universe. (ID 531)

Even with this careful caveat, John Paul's insistence on prayer and spirituality in general as the soil in which interreligious dialogue can grow is perhaps one of his most distinctive and long-lasting contributions to interreligious dialogue. For him prayer was the most powerful link uniting all believers: "What seems to bring together and unite, in a particular way, Christians and believers of other religions is an acknowledgment of the need of prayer as an expression of man's spirituality directed toward the Absolute" (ID 371). Addressing the 1995 Plenary Assembly of the Pontifical Council for Interreligious Dialogue, the pope, referring to the assembly's theme, "The Dialogue of Spirituality and the Spirituality of Dialogue," said: "The theme of spirituality constitutes a natural meeting point for followers of different religious traditions and a fruitful subject for interreligious dialogue" (ID 844*). Indeed, of the four forms of dialogue—of life, action, theological exchange, and religious experience—it is the last that is, according to John Paul, the most important, and one that gives "a depth and quality which will preserve these from the danger of mere activism" (ID 844*).

6. Why did John Paul think that sharing religious experiences among the followers of different religions would be the best way to bring about interreligious harmony and world peace? The answer to this question broaches an aspect of the pope's theology of religion that seems to represent a step beyond Vatican II. It is this theology that undergirds his initiative of inviting representatives of various religions to come to Assisi to pray for peace, a project that, as has been mentioned above, caused much opposition among some officials of the Roman Curia. In his lengthy address to the Roman Curia on December 22, 1986, John Paul appealed to the teaching of Vatican II, especially as contained in the texts of *Lumen Gentium* and *Nostra Aetate* cited above, to argue for the necessity of all people, not only Catholic and non-Catholic Christians, to pray for peace. The reason for the acceptability of prayer of all people, he goes on to say, is that

every authentic prayer is under the influence of the Spirit "who intercedes insistently for us . . . because we do not even know how to pray as we ought," but he prays in us "with unutterable groaning" and "the one who searches hearts knows what are the desires of the Spirit" (Rom 8:26-27). We can indeed maintain that every authentic prayer is called forth by the Holy Spirit, who is mysteriously present in the heart of every person. (ID 572)[23]

So far, John Paul's affirmation of the presence of the Holy Spirit in the heart of every praying human being was a rather uncontroversial extension of Vatican II's teaching on the possibility of salvation for non-Christians. In a later authoritative writing, i.e., his encyclical on mission *Redemptoris Missio* (December 7, 1990), John Paul took a step further in affirming this presence of the Holy Spirit not only in individuals but also in religions:

> The Spirit, therefore, is at the very source of man's existential and religious questioning, a questioning which is occasioned not only by contingent situations but by the very structure of his being. (DV 54)

> The Spirit's presence and activity affect not only individuals but also society and history, peoples, cultures and religions. Indeed, the Spirit is at the origins of noble ideals and undertakings which benefit humanity on its journey through history . . . It is the Spirit who sows the "seeds of the Word" present in various customs and cultures, preparing them for full maturity in Christ (LG 17; cf. AG 3, 15).

> Thus, the Spirit, who "blows where he wills" (cf. John 3:8), who "was already at work in the world before Christ was glorified" (*Ad Gentes* 4), and who "has filled the world . . . holds all things together (and) knows what is said" (Wis 1:7), leads us to broaden our vision in order to ponder his activity in every time and place (cf. *Dominum et Vivificantem*, 53). I have repeatedly called this fact to mind, and it has guided me in my meetings with a wide variety with peoples. (ID 176–77)

While affirming the presence of the Spirit in all peoples' cultures and religions, John Paul insisted strongly and repeatedly on the fact that this

23. In his encyclical *Dominum et Vivificantem* on the Holy Spirit promulgated earlier (May 18, 1986), John Paul points to the presence of the Spirit before the Incarnation: "We cannot limit ourselves to the two thousand years which have passed since the birth of Christ. *We need to go further back*, to embrace the whole of the action of the Holy Spirit even before Christ— *from the beginning*, throughout the world, and especially in the economy of the Old Covenant. For this action has been exercised, in every place and every time, indeed in every individual, according to the eternal plan of salvation . . . Grace, therefore, bears within itself both a Christological aspect and a pneumatological one" (169–70).

Spirit is the same Spirit who was at work in the Incarnation and in the life, death, and resurrection of Jesus:

> He [the Spirit] is therefore not an alternative to Christ, nor does he fill a sort of void which is sometimes suggested as existing between Christ and the Logos. Whatever the Spirit brings about in human hearts and in the history of peoples, in cultures and religions serves as a preparation for the Gospel (*Lumen Gentium* 16) and can only be understood in reference to Christ, the Word who took flesh by the power of the Spirit. (ID 177)

However the relationship between Christ and the Spirit and between their respective activities in history is conceived, it is undeniable that John Paul's pneumatology offers a theological basis for an affirmation of the positive role of non-Christian religions that does not contradict Vatican II but represents an—albeit small but nonetheless significant—step beyond the council. Whereas Vatican II does affirm that "the unique mediation of the Redeemer does not exclude but rather gives rise to a manifold cooperation which is but a sharing in this one source" (LG 62), the "manifold cooperation" referred to is the role of Mary in the history of redemption. Taking a step beyond Vatican II, John Paul extended this notion of participation or sharing to non-Christian religions and recognized in them "participated forms of mediation of different kinds and degrees," though "they acquire meaning and value only from Christ's own mediation, and they cannot be understood as parallel or complementary to his" (RM 5).

Because of this presence of the Holy Spirit in all religions, in John Paul's view, there are in all religions "the so-called *semina verbi* (seeds of the Word)." Citing *Lumen Gentium* 13, the pope said that, according to the council, "the Holy Spirit works effectively even outside the visible structure of the Church, making use of these very *semina verbi*, that constitute a kind of common soteriological root present in all religions."[24] Again, while it is true that Vatican II affirms the presence of the *semina verbi* in non-Christian religions, it does not affirm, as John Paul does, that "all religions"—including Hinduism, Buddhism, Islam, and the so-called primitive religions, and not only Judaism with which Christianity is intrinsically connected—possess a "common soteriological root." The

---

24. John Paul II, *Crossing the Threshold*, 81.

question naturally arises: in virtue of this "common soteriological root," can it be said that non-Christian religions are "ways of salvation"?

A Step Further?

There is no doubt that of all popes John Paul contributed most to inter-religious dialogue through his richly symbolic actions and his theology of religion, especially his pneumatology. This he could achieve thanks to his unique life experiences and the teaching of Vatican II which he fully appropriates. Yet, in spite of the fact that he regarded non-Christian religions as "participated forms of mediation of different kinds and degrees" in the mediation of Christ and that he saw a "common soteriological root" in all religions, John Paul never asserted that non-Christian religions are salvific or function as ways or means of salvation for their adherents, either in connection with Christ and the church or independently of them. Yet, in contemporary Catholic theology of interreligious dialogue, the question of whether non-Christian religions possess a salvific efficacy of their own, either independently of Christ and the church or in dependence on them, is unavoidable. How this question is answered may have significant ramifications for the future of interreligious dialogue.

A recent declaration of the CDF, *Dominus Iesus* (DI 2000), asserts unequivocally that "it would be contrary to the faith to consider the Church as *one* way of salvation alongside those constituted by the other religions, seen as complementary to the Church or substantially equivalent to her, even if these are said to be converging with the Church toward the eschatological kingdom of God" (DI 21).[25] One of the basic reasons for this assertion is the declaration's stark distinction between "belief" and "faith," the former the result of non-Christian religions and the latter the exclusive preserve of Christianity: "The distinction between theological faith and belief in the other religions must be firmly held. If faith is the acceptance in grace of revealed truth . . . then belief, in the other religions, is that sum of experience and thought that constitutes the human treasury of wisdom and religious aspiration,

---

25. For the text of *Dominus Iesus* and critical reflections on it, see *Sic et Non: Encountering Dominus Iesus*, eds. Stephen Pope and Charles Helfling (Maryknoll, NY: Orbis, 2002).

which man in his search for truth has conceived and acted upon in his relationship to God and the Absolute" (DI 7).[26] Since, according to *Dominus Iesus*, non-Christian religions are *only* human endeavors, more or less successful, to reach out to God, they cannot be said to have any salvific significance, even for their adherents, perhaps not even in dependence on Christ and the church.

We have seen above that John Paul affirmed that the Holy Spirit (and hence, not mere human religiousness) is "at the very source of man's existential and religious questioning," especially in prayer, and that "the Spirit's presence and activity affect not only individuals but also society and history, peoples, cultures and *religions*" (RM 28, emphasis added). Of course, the pope hastened to add that the Holy Spirit is "not an alternative to Christ, nor does he fill a sort of void which is sometimes suggested as existing between Christ and the Logos" (RM 29). Furthermore, the Spirit's activity, the pope insisted, is "not to be separated from his particular activity within the Body of Christ, which is the Church" (RM 29).

In light of this teaching, it does not seem contrary to the faith to suggest that non-Christian religions can function as "ways of salvation" to their adherents, if one adds that this function is exercised in dependence on the mediation of Christ and on the church in its role as sacrament of salvation. To put it differently, non-Christians, the possibility of whose salvation is affirmed by Vatican II, if they are saved, are saved *through* their religions, not *in spite of* them.

This theologoumenon has been suggested, somewhat indirectly, by a 1991 joint document of the Pontifical Council for Interreligious Dialogue and the Congregation for Evangelization of People, *Dialogue and Proclamation*: "Concretely, it will be in the sincere practice of what is good in their own religious traditions and by following the dictates of their conscience that the members of other religions respond positively to God's invitation and receive salvation in Jesus Christ, even while they do not recognize or acknowledge him as their Savior" (ID 953). The salvific value of non-Christian religions is affirmed, more clearly albeit

---

26. Clearly, *Dominus Iesus*'s absolute contrast between "belief" in non-Christian religions and "faith" in Christianity reflects John Daniélou's "fulfillment theology" and contradicts John Paul's pneumatological theology of religion.

elliptically, by a 1997 statement of the International Theological Commission entitled *Christianity and the World Religions*. Appealing to John Paul's pneumatological theology of religion, it says:

> Given this explicit recognition of the presence of the Spirit of Christ in the religions, one cannot exclude the possibility that they exercise as such a certain salvific function, that is, despite their ambiguity, they help men achieve their ultimate end. In the religions is explicitly thematized the relationship of man with the Absolute, his transcendental dimension. It would be difficult to think that what the Holy Spirit works in the hearts of men taken as individuals would have salvific value and not think that what the Holy Spirit works in the religions and cultures would not have such value. The recent magisterium does not seem to authorize such a drastic distinction.[27]

Speaking from its concrete experiences and existential context, the Catholic Bishops' Conference of India leaves no doubt as to the salvific role of non-Christian religions:

> In the light of the universal salvific will and design of God, so emphatically affirmed in the New Testament witness, the Indian Christological approach seeks to avoid negative and exclusivistic expressions. Christ is the sacrament, the definitive symbol of God's salvation for all humanity. This is what the salvific uniqueness and universality of Christ means in the Indian context. That, however, does not mean there cannot be other symbols, *valid in their own ways*, which the Christian sees as related to the definitive symbol, Jesus Christ. The implication of all this is that for hundreds of millions of our fellow human beings, salvation is seen as being channeled to them not in spite of but *through and in* their various sociocultural and *religious* traditions. (emphasis added)[28]

Both the International Theological Commission and the Catholic Bishops' Conference of India are careful to emphasize not only the dependence of non-Christian religions on Christ but also their connection with the church. *Dominus Iesus* rejects any view that holds that the action of the Holy Spirit in non-Christian religions is "outside or parallel to

---

27. International Theological Commission, *Christianity and the World Religions*, see *Origins* 27 (August 14, 1997): 149–66, at no. 64.

28. *The Asian Synod: Texts and Commentaries*, ed. Peter C. Phan (Maryknoll, NY: Orbis, 2002), 22.

the action of Christ" (DI 12) and that non-Christian religions are "complementary to the Church or substantially equivalent to her" (DI 21). Regarding the dependence of the salvific role of non-Christian religions on Christ and on their "connection" with the church, official magisterium contents itself with affirming their fact. As to *how* non-Christian religions fulfill their saving function in dependence on Christ, Vatican II simply says that the Holy Spirit makes the salvation brought about by Christ available to non-Christians in ways known to God (AG 7).

John Paul went a step further and spoke of "participated mediations" of non-Christian religions in the unique mediation of Christ. While acknowledging these positive contributions of Vatican II and John Paul II, it seems necessary to note that even in these explanations there lurks the danger of subordinating the Spirit and his activity in history to Christ and his work. While no separate and autonomous "economy" of the Spirit must be thought of apart from that of Christ, by the same token the Spirit and his work must not be made dependent upon or subordinate to Christ and his work. To use a metaphor of Saint Irenaeus's, the Son and the Spirit are the "two hands" of God operating in the world. While there is only one economy of salvation of God the Father, the two divine hands, i.e., the Son and the Spirit, who carry it out—in *perichoresis* with each other and with the Father—do not do so in the same place, at the same time, in the same manner, on the same persons.[29] Just as the Spirit is not an alternative to or replacement of Christ, so Christ is not an alternative to or replacement of the Spirit. Thinking of the Spirit functioning salvifically in non-Christian religions allows us to attribute to them a positive and intrinsic value and refer to them as "ways of salvation" in a manner that detracts neither from the uniqueness and universality of Christ nor from the role of the church as the universal sacrament of salvation.

---

29. Perhaps a remark about the "order" of the Trinitarian processions is helpful. Very often we use the expression "Father, Son, and Spirit" and unconsciously we think that there is a hierarchical or worse, temporal, "order" (*taxis*), from the first (unoriginated origin) to the second (generated source) to the third (spirated by both the first and second persons). In this scheme, the Spirit cannot "do" anything "before" or "apart from" the Son but only "after" and "in dependence on" the Son because the Spirit comes "after" and "from" the Son. Needless to say, such a view is heretical. On the contrary, because of the eternal circumincession (*perichoresis*), no one divine person can be and act without, "before" or "after" or "independently" of the other two.

Again, with regard to the *how* of the "connection" of non-Christian religions with the church, Vatican II affirmed (and John Paul repeated) that they are "oriented" (*ordinantur*) to the church. But what does this "orientation" mean? To answer this question, the theology of the reign of God must be introduced here. It is well known that prior to Vatican II, there was a double identification: the church is identified simply with the reign of God, and the Roman Catholic Church is identified with the church. Vatican II modifies the second identification by declaring that the church of Christ "subsists in the Catholic Church," thereby recognizing that "many elements of sanctification and of truth are found outside its visible confines" (LG 8). On the first identification, the council teaches that the church is here and now "the seed and the beginning" of the kingdom and that it is its mission to proclaim and establish it among all peoples (LG 5), thereby affirming an intrinsic connection, both in nature and in historical development, between the church and the kingdom, perhaps even an identity between them.[30]

John Paul II was the first to clearly affirm a distinction between the church and the kingdom of God: "It is true that the inchoate reality of the Kingdom can also be found beyond the confines of the Church among peoples everywhere, to the extent that they live 'Gospel values' and are open to the working of the Spirit who breathes when and where he wills" (RM 20). Of course, the locus par excellence of this kingdom of God among non-Christians is their religious traditions.

In this sense, non-Christian believers are members of the kingdom of God and actively build it up when they live the "Gospel values" and are open to the action of the Holy Spirit. In no sense, however, can this membership in the kingdom of God be construed to mean that non-Christians "belong" to the church, as implicit members, as the document *Christianity and the World Religions* of the International Theological Commission, already cited above, does (no. 7). Similarly, their "orientation" or "ordination" to the church cannot be taken to mean that they are members of or belong to the church by means of a desire, explicit or implicit.

30. Jacques Dupuis maintains that Vatican II still identifies the church with the kingdom of God. See his *Toward a Christian Theology of Religious Pluralism* (Maryknoll, NY: Orbis, 1997), 334–36 and *Christianity and the Religions: From Confrontation to Dialogue* (Maryknoll, NY: Orbis, 2002), 198. I believe that the identification, if there is one, is very weak insofar as the church is said to be only "the seed and the beginning" and not the whole reality of the kingdom of God.

John Paul taught that there is in non-Christians who are saved a "mysterious relationship with the church" (RM 10), and that there is a "specific and necessary role" of the church in their salvation (RM 18). In light of the theology of the kingdom of God and the membership of non-Christians within it, it can now be said that their "orientation" to the church does not mean that the church exercises a "mediation" by way of an efficient causality for their salvation (as it does for Christians), but rather that insofar as the church is a sacrament of the kingdom of God, and insofar as non-Christians are also members of the same kingdom of God, there is a "mysterious relationship" between them. And, insofar as the church is the "ordinary" sign and instrument, willed by God, of the kingdom of God, it has a "specific and necessary role" in the salvation of non-Christians, even though these are not its members. They remain members of their own religious traditions, which therefore exercise a positive role in their salvation as their "paths" or "ways." Jacques Dupuis puts it succinctly: "While the church is the 'universal sacrament' of the Reign of God in the world, the other traditions too exercise a certain sacramental mediation of the Reign, different, no doubt, but no less real."[31]

Only an interreligious dialogue that respects and affirms the salvific function of each religion (though, of course, Christians may want to affirm the function of their own religion in a special way, just as Jews, Muslims, Hindus, Buddhists, etc., do the same for theirs) can be an effective vehicle for bringing about justice and peace in a world threatened by ever-increasing conflicts, and in this way contribute, each religion in its own way, to the coming of the kingdom of God.

31. Dupuis, *Christianity and the Religions*, 117.

Time Line*

1920	May 18: Karol Józef Wojtyla is born to Karol Wojtyla and Emilia Kaczorowska in Wadowice, Poland
1929	April 13: Death of his mother, Emilia
1932	December 5: Death of his brother, Edmund
1934–38	Keenly involved in theatrical productions
1938	June 22: Begins studies in language and literature (Polish Philology) at Jagiellonian University in Krakow
1940	Begins working as a quarry worker following outbreak of World War II
	Participant in underground theatre
1941	February 18: Death of Karol Sr., his father
1942	Embarks on studies for priesthood at "underground" seminary in Krakow, Poland
1946	October 20: Ordination to the diaconate
	November 1: Ordination to the priesthood
	November 26: Begins doctoral research at the Angelicum, Rome; from December resides at Pontifical Belgian College
1947	July 3: Awarded his licentiate in theology
	Summer: Spends time in France, Belgium, and the Netherlands, including pastoral work to Polish workers in Belgium

* Two very full and detailed chronologies of the significant events in the life and papacy of John Paul II can also be found at the Online Archives of the Holy See. Where sources have conflicted, in most cases the dates provided by these "official" chronologies have been followed. I am indebted to these chronologies, also, for clarification concerning a number of further issues with regard to particular events during the life of John Paul II.

Pre-Pontificate:
http://www.vatican.va/news_services/press/documentazione/documents/santopadre_biografie/giovanni_paolo_ii_biografia_prepontificato_en.html#1969

From Pope John Paul II's Election to His Death:
http://www.vatican.va/news_services/press/documentazione/documents/santopadre_biografie/giovanni_paolo_ii_biografia_pontificato_en.html

1948   June 14–19: Successfully defends doctoral thesis on *The Problem of Faith According to Saint John of the Cross* (doctor of philosophy)

July 8: First pastoral posting to Niegowić, near Gdów

December 16: Awarded master's degree in theology from the Jagiellonian University (1942–46) and doctorate in sacred theology

1949   August: Moved to St. Florian's Parish, Krakow

1954   Begins teaching at University of Lublin

Habilitation thesis successfully completed (December 1953 defense) for his thesis, *An Evaluation of the Possibility of Constructing a Christian Ethic on the Basis of the System of Max Scheler*

1956   December 1: Appointed chair of ethics at KU Lublin

1958   September 29: Installed as titular bishop of Ombi and auxiliary bishop of Krakow

1960   January: Publishes thesis on Scheler

Publishes *Love and Responsibility*

1962–65   Attends Second Vatican Council in Rome

1962   April 15: Becomes member of the Polish Episcopal Commission for Education

1963   December 5–15: Pilgrimage to Holy Land with fellow bishops attending Vatican II

1964   Installed as archbishop of Krakow (nominated by Paul VI on December 3, 1963)

1966   December 29: Made first president of Episcopal Commission for the Apostolate of the Laity

1967   April 13–20: First meeting of Council for the Laity

June 28: Appointed to College of Cardinals by Pope Paul VI (to titular church of Saint Cesareo in Palatio)

Declines to attend first general synod of bishops as Cardinal Wyszyñski is refused a passport

1969   February 28: Visits Jewish community and the synagogue in Kazimierz, Krakow

Visits Canada and the United States for the first time

October 11–28: Takes part in first extraordinary synod of bishops

December: Publishes *The Acting Person*

1971   September 30–November 6: Participates in and addresses second general synod of bishops (elected to Council of the Secretary General of Synod)

1972   May 8: Synod of Krakow begins (and runs until June 1979)

Publishes *Sources of Renewal*

1973   March 2–9: Attends Eucharistic Congress in Australia; also visits Philippines and New Guinea

November: Visits France

1974   September 27–October 26: Serves as relator to doctrine section of the third general synod of bishops on evangelization

1976   March 7–13: Delivers Lenten retreat to papal household

July 23–September 5: Visits United States of America once again (to attend the eucharistic congress)

November 22: Leads Polish delegation to Rome for conference to begin preparatory work on new Apostolic Constitution for Ecclesiastical Studies

1977   September 30–October 29: Fourth general assembly of synod of bishops; again elected to Council of Secretary General of Synod

1978   October 16: Elected supreme pontiff—the 263rd to follow Peter—and chooses the name of his predecessor who died after only thirty-three days in office (who in turn had combined the names of his two predecessors); the first non-Italian pope in over four-and-a-half centuries and the first pope from a Slavic country

October 22: Mass to celebrate his installation as pope

1979   Begins the first of his 104 pastoral visits beyond Italy. In this year alone visits the Dominican Republic, Mexico (where he addresses third general conference of CELAM at Puebla), the Bahamas (January–February), Poland (June), Ireland, and the United States (September–October, including his visit to the UN where he addresses United Nations General Assembly), and Turkey (November)

March 4: First encyclical, *Redemptor Hominis*, is circulated throughout the church

April 16: Releases apostolic constitution, *Sapientia Christiana*

1980   Visits several Africa nations—Zaire, Congo, Kenya, Ghana, Burkina Faso, and The Ivory Coast (May); then visits France (May–June), Brazil (June–July), and Germany (November)

September 26–October 25: Fifth ordinary general assembly of the synod of bishops on "The Role of the Christian Family in the Modern World"

November 30: Second encyclical, *Dives in Misericordia*, is circulated

December 31: In apostolic letter, *Egregiae virtutis*, names Saint Cyril and Saint Methodius as joint patrons of Europe

1981   Visits Pakistan, the Philippines, Japan, and United States (February).

January 15: Receives delegation from Polish free trade union, *Solidarność*, including its leader, Lech Walesa

May 13: Survives assassination attempt by Mehmet Ali Ağça in St. Peter's Square though seriously wounded and endures five-hour operation and ten weeks in hospital

July 3: Establishes papal commission to reinvestigate the "Galileo Affair"

September 14: Encyclical, *Laborem Exercens*, distributed

November 14:– Post-synodal apostolic exhortation, *Familiaris Consortio*, released

November 25: Appoints Cardinal Joseph Ratzinger as prefect of the Congregation for the Doctrine of the Faith

1982   Visits Nigeria, Benin, Gabon, Equatorial Guinea (February); Portugal (May, where he prays and gives thanks before the Shrine of Our Lady of Fatima for his life being spared one year earlier); Britain (England, Scotland, and Wales, May–June, including a joint statement following an ecumenical service with Robert Runcie, archbishop of Canterbury on May 29); and Brazil and Argentina (June, the UK and latter visits taking place in the year of the conflict between those nations over the Falkland Islands/Islas Malvinas—prior to visiting either country he celebrated a mass for peace between the countries at St. Peter's on May 22); and, also in June, Switzerland and San Marion; in November he visits Spain

September 15: Receives Yasser Arafat, head of the Palestinian Liberation Organization, at the Vatican

1983   January 25: Promulgation of new Code of Canon Law

March: Visits Portugal then several countries in Central America and the Caribbean (Costa Rica, Honduras, Panama, El Salvador, Guatemala, Belize, Haiti, and Nicaragua, where he admonishes priests involved in socialist politics there); visits Poland again (June); then a pilgrimage to Lourdes, France (August); and then visits Austria (September)

September 29–October 29: Sixth ordinary general assembly of the synod of bishops on "Penance and Reconciliation in the Mission of the Church"

November 5: Issues letter on 500th anniversary of birth of Martin Luther (meets with Lutheran community in Rome on December 11)

December 27: Visits his would-be assassin in prison and forgives him in person

1984 Visits United States (May); South Korea, Papua New Guinea, the Solomon Islands, and Thailand (May); Switzerland (June); Canada (September); Spain, the Dominican Republic, and Puerto Rico (October)

September 3: CDF issues *Libertatis Nuntius* (Instruction on Certain Aspects of the Theology of Liberation)

December 11: Post-synodal apostolic exhortation, *Reconciliatio and Poenitentia* (On Reconciliation and Penance in the Mission of the Church Today)

1985 Visits Peru, Venezuela, Trinidad and Tobago (January–February); the Netherlands, Luxembourg, and Belgium (May); Togo, the Ivory Coast, Cameroon, Central African Republic, Zaire, Kenya, and Morocco (August); Switzerland and Liechtenstein (September)

February 19: Receives Israeli prime minister, Simon Peres

February 27–February 19: Receives USSR foreign minister, Andrei Gromyko

March 30–31: World Youth Day in Rome

Addresses gathering of 80,000 Muslim youths at Casablanca, Morocco

June 2: Encyclical, *Slavorum Apostoli*

November 25–December 8: Extraordinary synod of bishops on twentieth anniversary of the close of Vatican II

1986 January 31–February 11: Visits India, including exchanges with Buddhists, Hindus, Jains, and Muslims; also visits St. Lucia, Colombia (July); Bangladesh, Singapore, Fiji, New Zealand, Australia, and the Seychelles (November–December)

April 5: CDF issues *Libertatis Conscientia* (Instruction on Christian Freedom and Liberation)

April 13: Visits the synagogue of Rome

May 18: Encyclical, *Dominum et Vivificantem*

October 27: Gathers sixty-three leaders and two hundred representatives of twelve world religions in Assisi for World Prayer for Peace

1987 Visits Chile, Uruguay, and Argentina (March–April); Germany (April–May); Poland (June); United States and Canada (September)

March 2: CDF issues *Donum Vitae* (Instruction on Respect for Human Life in its Origin and on the Dignity of Procreation)

March 25: Encyclical, *Redemptoris Mater*

March 31–April 13: Second World Youth Day held in Buenos Aires

October 1–30: Seventh ordinary general assembly of the synod of bishops on "The Vocation and Mission of the Lay Faithful in the Church and in the World"

December 3: Visit of Demetrios, Ecumenical Patriarch of Constantinople; joint declaration signed

December 30: Encyclical, *Sollicitudo Rei Socialis*

1988   Visits Uruguay, Bolivia, Peru, Paraguay, Curaçao (May); Austria (June); Zimbabwe, Botswana, Lesotho, Swaziland, Mozambique (September); and France (October)

August 15: Releases apostolic letter, *Mulieris Dignitatem* (On the Dignity and Vocation of Women)

October 8: Visits and addresses European parliament in Strasbourg

1989   Visits Madagascar, La Réunion, Zambia, Malawi (April–May); Norway, Iceland, Finland, Denmark, Sweden (June); Spain (August); and South Korea, Indonesia, and Mauritius (October)

January 30: Releases post-synodal apostolic exhortation, *Christifideles Laici* (On the Vocation and the Mission of the Lay Faithful in the Church and in the World)

August 19–21: World Youth Day in Santiago de Compostela

September 29–October 2: Receives visit from Robert Runcie, archbishop of Canterbury

December 1: Mikhail Gorbachev becomes first leader of the USSR to visit the Vatican

1990   Visits Cape Verde, Guinea-Bissau, Mali, Burkina Faso, Chad (January–February); Czechoslovakia (April); Mexico, Curaçao, and Malta (May); Malta again, Luqa, Tanzania, Burundi, Rwanda, and the Ivory Coast (September)

September 30–October 28: Eighth ordinary general assembly of the synod of bishops on the "The Formation of Priests in Circumstances of the Present Day"

October 18: Promulgation of *Code of Canon Law for the Eastern Churches*

December 7: Encyclical, *Redemptoris Missio*

1991   Visits Portugal (May); Poland (June and August); Hungary (August); and Brazil (October)

January 15: Sends letters to presidents of United States and Iraq trying to help avoid the escalation of the crisis in the Gulf (following earlier appeal on December 25, 1990, and followed by meeting of bishops from all countries involved in the war in March)

February 5: Lech Walesa returns to Vatican, this time as president of Poland

August 13: Attends sixth World Youth Day in Częstochowa, Poland

May 1: Encyclical, *Centesimus Annus*

November 29–December 14: Special assembly for Europe of the synod of bishops on "So that we might be witnesses of Christ who has set us free"

1992   Visits Senegal, Gambia, Guinea (February); Angola, São Tomé, and Príncipe (June); and the Dominican Republic (October, where he attends the fourth general conference of CELAM)

April 7: Releases Post-synodal apostolic exhortation, *Pastores Dabo Vobis* (On the Formation of Priests in the Circumstances of the Present Day)

October 11: *Catechism of the Catholic Church* released (revised in 1998)

October 31: Report of the papal commission to reinvestigate the "Galileo Affair" admits error in the church's position regarding the scientist's findings

1993   Visits Benin, Uganda, Sudan (February); Albania (April); Spain (June); Jamaica, Mexico, United States (August); Lithuania, Latvia, Estonia (September)

January 9: Prayers for Peace in Assisi, with particular focus on the Balkans conflict

August 6: Encyclical, *Veritatis Splendor*

August: Eighth World Youth Day in Denver, USA

December 30: Signing of agreement between Holy See and State of Israel, with the Vatican officially recognizing the latter for the first time

1994   Visits Croatia (September)

January 1: *Motu Proprio, Socialium Scientiarum* marks the official foundation of the Pontifical Academy of Social Sciences

February 2: *Gratissimam Sane* (Letter to Families) to mark the International Year of the Family

February 11: *Motu Proprio, Vitae Mysterium* marks the foundation of the Pontifical Academy for Life

March 17: Visit of prime minister of Israel, Yitzhak Rabin

April 7: Concert to commemorate remembrance of the Shoah staged at the Vatican; attended by Pope John Paul II and Elio Toaff, the chief rabbi of Rome

May 22: Release of apostolic letter, *Ordinatio Sacerdotalis* (On Preserving Priestly Ordination to Men Alone)

June 15: Formalization of diplomatic ties between Holy See and State of Israel

September 5–13: International Conference on Population and Development, held in Cairo; delegation from Holy See attends

October 9–20 Ninth general ordinary assembly of the synod of bishops on "The Consecrated Life and Its Role in the Church and in the World"

October 20: Publishes *Crossing the Threshold of Hope*

October 25: Initiation of official and permanent working contacts between Holy See and the Palestine Liberation Organization

November 10: Apostolic letter, *Tertio Millennio Adveniente*, released

1995   Visits Philippines (with largest ever estimated gathering of people flocking to see him in Manila, which hosts the tenth World Youth Day), Papua New Guinea, Australia, and Sri Lanka (January); Czech republic, Poland (May); Belgium (June); Slovakia (June–July); Cameroon, South Africa, and Kenya (September); United States, including another visit to the United Nations, where he addresses the General Assembly once again (October)

March 6–12: UN World Summit of Social Development in Copenhagen, Denmark; delegation from Holy See attends

March 25: Encyclical, *Evangelium Vitae*

May 25: Encyclical, *Ut Unum Sint*

June 27–29: Visit of Ecumenical Patriarch of Constantinople, Bartholomew I, including signing of joint declaration

September 4–15: Fourth UN Conference on Women in Beijing, first occasion at which an official Vatican delegation is led by a woman, Mary Ann Glendon

September 14–20: Special assembly for Africa of the synod of bishops

September 14: Post-synodal apostolic exhortation, *Ecclesia in Africa* (On the Church in Africa and its Evangelizing Mission towards the Year 2000)

December 25: *Urbi et Orbi* Christmas message released on the internet for the first time

1996   Visits Guatemala, Nicaragua, El Salvador, Venezuela (February); Tunisia (April); Slovenia (May); Germany (June); Hungary and France (September)

March 25: Post-synodal apostolic exhortation, *Vita Consecrata* (On the Consecrated Life and Its Mission in the Church and in the World)

November 1: Commemorates 50th anniversary of ordination to the priesthood

November 13: Addresses opening of UN World Food Summit, Rome

November 15: Publishes *Gift and Mystery: On the Fiftieth Anniversary of My Priestly Ordination*

December 3–6: Visit of George Carey, archbishop of Canterbury, and signing of joint declaration

December 19: Yasser Arafat visits the Vatican a second time

1997   Visits Bosnia and Herzegovina, Czech Republic (April); Lebanon (May); Poland (May–June); France (August); Brazil (October)

January 23–26: Visit of Aram I Keshishian, Catholicos of Cilicia of the Armenians, including signing of joint declaration

February 3: Visit of prime minister of Israel, Benjamin Netanyahu

May 10–11: Special assembly for Lebanon of the synod of bishops (with issuing of post-synodal apostolic exhortation, *A New Hope for Lebanon*)

June 16: Writes letters to Israeli prime minister and Palestinian Liberation Organization president with relation to the peace process in the Middle East

August 21–24: Twelfth World Youth Day in Paris

October 19: Saint Thérèse of Lisieux proclaimed a Doctor of the church

1998   Visits Cuba (January); Nigeria (March); Austria (June); Croatia (October)

March 12: Release of *We Remember: A Reflection on the Shoah* by the Pontifical Commission for Religious Relations with the Jews

April 19–May 14: Special assembly for Asia of the synod of bishops on "Jesus Christ the Savior and his Mission of Love and Service in Asia: '. . . that they may have life and have it abundantly'"

May 18: *Motu Proprio, Ad Tuendam Fidem* released

May 21: *Motu Proprio, Apostolos Suos* released

268 The Vision of John Paul II

May 30: Meeting with members of new ecclesial movements and communities, Rome

June 12: Yasser Arafat received at the Vatican once more

June 18: Nelson Mandela received at the Vatican

September 14: Encyclical, *Fides et Ratio*

November 22–December 12: Special assembly for Oceania of the synod of bishops on "Jesus Christ and the Peoples of Oceania: Walking His Way, Telling His Truth, Living His Life"

November 29: Release of papal bull to announce the jubilee year of 2000, *Incarnationis mysterium*

1999   Visits United States and Mexico (January, where he signs the post-synodal apostolic exhortation *Ecclesia in America*); Romania (May); Poland (June); Slovenia (September); India (where in New Delhi he signs the post-synodal apostolic exhortation *Ecclesia in Asia*); Georgia (October)

March 11: Visit to Vatican of Seyyed Mohammad Khatami, the president of Iran

April 26: Israeli foreign minister, Ariel Sharon, received at Vatican

October 1–23: Second special assembly for Europe of the synod of bishops, on "Jesus Christ Alive in His Church: The Source of Hope for Europe"

October 1: *Motu Proprio, Spes Aedificandi* declares Saints Bridget of Sweden, Catherine of Siena, and Teresa Benedicta of the Cross co-patronesses of Europe

October 28: Interreligious assembly held in Rome

October 31: Signing in Augsburg of Catholic Church and World Lutheran Federation *Joint Declaration on the Doctrine of Justification*

November 5–9: Special assembly for Asia of the synod of bishops

December 24: Begins the jubilee year by opening the holy door of St. Peter's, Rome

2000   Visits Egypt, Mount Sinai (February); Jordan (March); also in March, fulfills ambition to visit the Holy Land; prays at the Wailing Wall in Jerusalem for forgiveness from Jews for the wrongs perpetrated against them by Christians in the past; visits Portugal, the shrine to Our Lady of Fatima

January 18: Ecumenical service to commemorate the opening of the holy door of St. Paul's Outside-the-Walls and commencement of Week of Prayer for Christian Unity

February 15: Yasser Arafat visits Vatican again and joint "Basic Agreement" between Holy See and Palestinian Liberation Organization signed

February 22: Commemorative ceremony on "Abraham, Our Father in Faith" as part of jubilee celebrations and prior to John Paul II's jubilee pilgrimage travels

March 12: Day of Pardon, where forgiveness is requested for the sins of those acting on behalf of the church (held at St. Peter's); release of International Theological Commission document *Memory and Reconciliation: The Church and the Faults of the Past*

May 1: Celebrates "Jubilee of Workers" in Rome

May 7: Ecumenical service for Twentieth-Century Witnesses to the Faith (Colosseum, Rome)

June 5: Visit of Vladimir Putin, president of the Russian Federation

August 15–20: Fifteenth World Youth Day in Rome

June 18–25: International eucharistic congress held in Rome

September 5: CDF releases *Dominus Iesus* (On the Unicity and Salvific Universality of Jesus Christ and the Church)

November 8–11: Visit of His Holiness Karekin II, Catholicos of All Armenians, with ecumenical celebration and signing of joint communiqué

2001   Following in the "footsteps of St Paul," visits Greece, Syria, Malta (May), Kazakhstan, and Armenia (September). In Athens, he apologizes for sins by Catholics against Orthodox Christians. In Damascus, Syria, he becomes the first pope to visit and pray at a mosque. Also visits Ukraine, including visit to Babi Yar Holocaust Memorial in Kiev (June)

January 6: Holy door of St. Peter's is closed, marking the end of the jubilee year; releases apostolic letter, *Novo millennio ineunte*

January 25: Ecumenical service held in St. Paul's Outside-the-Walls to conclude Week of Prayer for Christian Unity

February 18: Seventeen-hundredth anniversary of the Baptism of the Armenian People celebrated with Armenian Rite Liturgy in St. Peter's

September 30–October 27: Tenth ordinary general assembly of the synod of bishops on the "The Bishop: Servant of the Gospel of Jesus Christ for the Hope of the World"

November 18: Asks Catholics to spend a day of fasting for peace in the light of 9/11 and its aftermath in Afghanistan

November 22: Post-synodal apostolic exhortation, *Ecclesia in Oceania*

December 13: Meets with bishops of the Holy Land

2002   Visits Azerbaijan and Bulgaria (May); Canada, Guatemala, and Mexico (July–August), and then, also in August, a final visit to Poland

January 24: World Day of Prayer for Peace, Assisi, gathering of leaders of many churches and religions

March 11: Metropolitan Panteleimon of Attiki leads Greek Orthodox delegation in visit to Vatican

April 7: Day of Prayer for Peace in the Holy Land

July 23: Attends seventeenth World Youth Day in Toronto

October 7: His Beatitude Teoctist, Orthodox Patriarch of Romania, visits Vatican and joint declaration is signed

October 16: Releases apostolic letter, *Rosarium Virginis Mariae*, which adds the Luminous Mysteries to the rosary and inaugurates the Year of the Rosary

2003   Visits Croatia (June), marking the 100th official pastoral visit abroad of his pontificate, then Bosnia and Herzegovina (June); Slovakia (September)

March 5: Day of Fasting for World Peace

March 6: Publishes collection of poetry, *Roman Triptych: Meditations*

April 17: Encyclical, *Ecclesia de Eucharistia*

June 28: Post-synodal apostolic exhortation, *Ecclesia in Europa*

October 2: Visit of Rowan Williams, archbishop of Canterbury

2004   Visits Switzerland (June) and then makes his final and 104th pastoral visit, poignantly, to Lourdes, France (August), where he speaks to fellow "sufferers" hoping for an end to their suffering, and commemorates 150th anniversary of the dogma of the immaculate conception

May 14: Publishes *Rise, Let Us Be On Our Way*

June 29: Visit of His Holiness Bartholomew I, Ecumenical Patriarch of Constantinople, with a joint declaration being signed

August 28: Patriarch Aleksy II receives from the pope the Icon of the Kazan Mother of God as a gift to Russian Orthodox Church and Russian peoples

October 17: Opens Year of the Eucharist

November 27: Ecumenical Patriarch of Constantinople, Bartholomew I is given the relics of Saint John Chrysostom and Saint Gregory Nazianzen

2005   February 23: Publishes *Memory and Identity*

March: Becomes seriously ill

April 2: Dies in the evening after reportedly speaking his final words to aides earlier that afternoon: "Let me go to the house of the Lord"

April 8: Cardinal Joseph Ratzinger (as prefect of College of Cardinals) presides over the funeral mass of the man he would soon succeed as pope

June 28: First phase of the cause for the beatification of John Paul II begins

Contributors

Mario I. Aguilar holds a chair in divinity and is professor of religion and politics at the University of St. Andrews, Scotland. He is the author of numerous books including *The History and Politics of Latin American Theology*, 3 volumes.

Charles E. Curran is the Elizabeth Scurlock University Professor of Human Values at Southern Methodist University. He has served as president of three national professional societies—the American Theological Society, the Catholic Theological Society of America, and the Society of Christian Ethics. He was the first recipient of the John Courtney Murray Award for Distinguished Achievement in Theology given by the Catholic Theological Society of America. The College Theology Society presented him with their Presidential Award for a Lifetime of Scholarly Achievements in Moral Theology. His most recent publications include: *Catholic Moral Theology in the United States: A History*; *Loyal Dissent: Memoir of a Catholic Theologian*; and *The Moral Theology of Pope John Paul II*.

Raymond G. Helmick, SJ, is a priest of the New England Jesuit Province. Educated at Weston College (Jesuit Province of New England), Hochschule St. Georgen (Frankfurt), and Union Theological Seminary (New York). He has worked since 1972 in conflict resolution and mediation in Northern Ireland, Lebanon, the countries of former Yugoslavia, East Timor, and Southern Africa, as well as with Israelis and Palestinians and with Kurds of Iraq and Turkey. He has served as associate director of the Centre for Human Rights and Responsibilities in London (1973–81), is cofounder of the Centre of Concern for Human Dignity (a joint project of the English and Irish Jesuit Provinces, 1979–81), co-founder and senior associate in the Conflict Analysis Center, Washington, DC (from 1983), and has been professor of conflict resolution in the department of theology, Boston College, since 1984. His numerous publications include: *Forgiveness and Reconciliation: Religion, Public Policy and Conflict Transformation* (coeditor with Rodney Petersen); *A Social Option: A Social Planning Approach to the Conflict in Northern Ireland* (coauthored with Richard Hauser); *La question libanaise selon Raymond Eddé: Correspondance et mémoires*; and *Negotiating Outside the Law: Why Camp David Failed.*

Paul Lakeland is the Aloysius P. Kelley, SJ, Professor of Catholic Studies at Fairfield University in Connecticut. His most recent books are *Postmodernity: Christian Identity in a Fragmented Age; The Liberation of the Laity: In Search of an Accountable Church*, which received the 2004 U.S. Catholic Press Association Award for the best book in theology; and *Catholicism at the Crossroads: How the Laity Can Save the Church.* He is a member of the American Academy of Religion, where he recently completed a six-year term as chair of the Theology and Religious Reflection Section, and the Catholic Theological Society of America. He is chair of the editorial board of *Religious Studies Review* and co-convener of the Nashville, Tennessee–based independent ecumenical association of systematic and constructive theologians, the Workgroup for Constructive Theology. He is currently at work on an edition of the selected writings of Yves Congar.

Gerard Mannion serves as chair of the Ecclesiological Investigations Research Network and is presently a senior fellow of the faculty of theology, Katholieke Universiteit Leuven. Educated at the universities of Cambridge and Oxford, he has lectured at church-linked colleges of the universities of Oxford and Leeds and as associate professor of ecclesiology and ethics at Liverpool Hope University. Founding director of the *Centre for the Study of Contemporary Ecclesiology*, he has published widely in the fields of ecclesiology and ethics, as well as in other aspects of systematics and philosophy. Recent books include *The Routledge Companion to the Christian Church* (coedited with Lewis Mudge); *Ecclesiology and Postmodernity: Questions for the Church in Our Time*; and *Church and Religious Other: Questions of Truth, Unity and Diversity* (editor).

Paul McPartlan is a priest of the Archdiocese of Westminster and Carl J. Peter Professor of Systematic Theology and Ecumenism at The Catholic University of America, Washington DC. He is a member of the International Theological Commission, and also a member of the international commissions for theological dialogue between the Roman Catholic Church and the Orthodox Church, and the Roman Catholic Church and the World Methodist Council. He is the author of *The Eucharist Makes the Church: Henri de Lubac and John Zizioulas in Dialogue*, *Sacrament of Salvation: An Introduction to Eucharistic Ecclesiology*, and numerous articles on ecclesiology and ecumenism. He also edited John Zizioulas' book, *Communion and Otherness*.

Judith Merkle is professor of religious studies at Niagara University, New York. She lectures and writes in the area of social ethics, Catholic social thought, church and culture, moral theology, and religious life in contemporary society. She is the author of *From the Heart of the Church: The Catholic Social Tradition* and other articles and chapters in books. Dr. Merkle is currently writing *Being Faithful: Moral Responsibility in Modern Society*. She is a member of the Sisters of Notre Dame de Namur.

Ronald Modras is professor of theological studies at Saint Louis University, where he has taught since 1979. He received his doctorate at the University of Tübingen (Germany), where he studied under professors Hans Küng and Joseph Ratzinger. He has written extensively in scholarly journals on the philosophy of Pope John Paul II. His most recent book is *Ignatian Humanism: A Dynamic Spirituality for the 21ˢᵗ Century*, a topic he has lectured on widely in both the United States and Europe.

Peter C. Phan currently holds the Ignacio Ellacuria Chair of Catholic Social Thought at Georgetown University. He has earned three doctorates, one from the Salesian Pontifical University, and the other two from the University of London. He has written and edited some twenty books and three hundred essays on various aspects of theology. His latest books include *Christianity with an Asian Face*, *In Our Own Tongues*, and *Being Religious Interreligiously*. His current theological interests include interreligious dialogue, Asian Christology, Asian liberation theology, and mission.

Susan Rakoczy, IHM, is a lecturer in spirituality at St. Joseph's Theological Institute, Cedara, and honorary professor in the School of Religion and Theology of the University of KwaZulu-Natal in South Africa. Her most recent book is *Great Mystics and Social Justice: Walking on the Two Feet of Love*. She is working on a book on discernment and another on the interface of psychology and spirituality with a colleague from the School of Psychology of the University of KwaZulu-Natal.

Gemma Simmonds, CJ, is a sister of the Congregation of Jesus. She has degrees in modern languages and systematic theology from Cambridge and London Universities and a doctorate in theology from Cambridge. She lectures in pastoral theology and spirituality at Heythrop College, University of London, and works in religious formation, lecturing worldwide on the theology of religious life. She translated Henri de Lubac's *Corpus Mysticum* and has published chapters and articles in the *SCM Dictionary of Spirituality*; *Dancing on the Edge: Church, Chaplaincy & Higher Education*; *Routledge Companion to the Christian Church*; and *Cambridge Companion to the Jesuits*.

James Voiss, SJ, teaches systematic theology at Saint Louis University. He received his PhD from the University of Notre Dame in 2000. His dissertation research focused on the underpinnings of disagreement between Karl Rahner and Hans Urs von Balthasar on questions of structural change in the postconciliar church. He has published essays on the thought of both theologians as well as on issues in ecclesiology.

Michael Walsh spent most of his working life as a librarian of Heythrop College, University of London, though in addition to his role as librarian he was for a long time review editor, then editor, of *The Heythrop Journal*. He has since been a visiting professor at Liverpool Hope University. He has written, edited, or translated some twenty-five books, including: *The Secret World of Opus Dei*; *John Paul II, A Biography*; and *Catholicism: The Basics*. He is currently revising J. N. D. Kelly's *The Oxford Dictionary of Popes*.

Index

social structures, 145–47
socialism, 23, 110, 148
socialization, 48, 124
Society of Jesus (Jesuit Order), 93,
    202, 206–9
sociology, 155, 157
solidarity, 114, 130, 211
episcopal, 192
Solidarity (*Solidarność*), 22
Soviet Union (*see* USSR)
spirituality, 4, 42, 76, 111, 212,
    248–49
Stagaman, David, 103–4
Stalin, Joseph, 225
Stein, Edith, Saint, 16, 240
Suenens, Leon Joseph, 184, 187, 191
Sullivan, Francis A., 90, 101
syncretism, religious, 237
Synod of Bishops, 53–56, 70, 89,
    153, 171, 173, 184–99, 200–201,
    211
Synoptic Gospels, 132
Syrian Orthodox Church, 224
    of India, 219

teaching authority (*see* magisterium)
Teresa of Avila, Saint, 176, 212
theologians, Catholic, 2, 41, 69, 72,
    78–106, 125, 130–31, 137–39,
    144–58, 148–58, 210–12, 216
theology, 11, 78–106, 107, 130–31,
    141, 148–51, 164, 177, 210–12,
    220–21, 226, 236, 254
theonomy, 141
Thérèse of Lisieux, Saint, 213
Thomas Aquinas, Saint, 30–31, 34,
    36, 40, 50–51, 56, 140–42, 160
Thomism, 16, 30–31, 34–36, 38, 41,
    43, 73
    "Lublin Thomism," 33–36
    transcendental, 122
tradition, 29, 34, 131, 134–41, 138,
    158, 161, 181

transcendence, 121
Trent, Council of, 222, 224
trinitarian theology, 54–55, 64–66
Trinity, doctrine of, 48–49, 54–55,
    118, 120, 129, 138, 169, 219, 221,
    255
truth, 43–45, 52, 74, 75, 98–99, 113,
    116, 221, 128–43, 232, 243–46,
    256
Tudjman, Franjo, 25

Ukeritis, Miriam, 213
Ukraine, 24, 225–26
Uniate churches, 60, 225–26,
Union of International Superiors
    General, 200, 214
Unitatis Redintegratio, 54, 59, 216
United Nations, 11, 161, 240
United States Conference of
    Catholic Bishops, 96, 178
United States of America, 23, 94, 96,
    109, 180, 213
Uruguay, 148, 152
USSR, 22, 148, 213, 225

values, 113
Vatican I (First Vatican Council), 57,
    79, 102, 185–86, 197
Vatican II (Second Vatican
    Council—for conciliar documents
    see individual entries), 5, 8, 15,
    17, 43, 45–61, 62–64, 66, 72, 75,
    79–80, 85–86, 89, 91–92, 96,
    98–99, 102, 105, 107, 111–12,
    125, 135, 139, 144–47, 151, 160,
    185–92, 195–97, 201, 203–4,
    209–10, 212–14, 215–17, 224,
    234, 236, 242–46, 249–56
Volk, Miloslav, 231

Wadowice, 13, 26, 52
Walesa, Lech, 22
war, 121, 241
Ward, Mary, 176